The

Blue Chip Investment Strategy

The Blue Chip Investment Strategy

QUALITY, VALUE, AND TIMING FOR INCOME AND APPRECIATION

C. Colburn Hardy

A GROLIER COMPANY

1987 Franklin Watts
New York Toronto

Library of Congress Cataloging-in-Publication Data

Hardy, C. Colburn.
The blue chip investment strategy.

Includes index.
1. Stocks—United States. 2. Investments—United States, I. Title.
HG4963.H37 1987 332.63'22 87-14726
ISBN 0-531-15525-0

Printed in the United States of America
6 5 4 3 2 1

Contents

The Blue Chip Investment Strategy

Part 1

BASIC TABLES AND STOCK MARKET DATA

Listing financial tables in the front of the book places first things first and provides the data needed to make financial projections, improve selections, and judge investment results. Investors can get an idea of not only where they are going but what they can expect when they get there. With Blue Chip stocks, they can be sure of enhancing their wealth.

To manage money successfully, there are some key concepts you must understand:

- While working
  The importance of regular savings
  The Magic of Compounding
  The benefits of pension plans
  The need for clearly defined financial goals
- After retirement
  The importance of preserving (but not freezing) capital; that is, you must know how much capital you can safely withdraw each year and how long your savings will last

TABLE I-1
The Magic of Annual Compounding

SINGLE INVESTMENT	Rate of Return				
End of Year	6%	8%	10%	12%	15%
5	1.34	1.47	1.61	1.76	2.01
10	1.79	2.16	2.59	3.11	4.05
15	2.40	3.17	4.18	5.47	8.14
20	3.21	4.66	6.73	9.65	16.37
25	4.29	6.85	10.83	17.00	32.92
30	5.74	10.06	17.45	29.96	66.21

$1,000 invested at 10%, with annual compounding, after 20 years will grow to $6,730 ($1,000 X 6.73); after thirty years to $17,450.

ANNUAL CONTRIBUTIONS					
5	5.64	5.87	6.11	6.35	6.74
10	13.18	14.49	15.94	17.55	20.30
15	23.28	27.15	31.77	37.28	47.58
20	36.79	45.76	57.27	72.05	102.44
25	54.86	73.11	98.35	133.33	212.79
30	79.06	113.28	164.49	241.33	434.75

$1,000 invested annually for twenty-five years ($25,000) at a 12% yield will compound to $133,330 ($1,000 X 133.33).

Source: David Thorndike, ed. *Thorndike Encyclopedia of Banking and Financial Tables,* (Boston: Warren, Gorham & Lamont).

- At all times
  The importance of quality in investments
  The need to cast an over-the-shoulder glance at inflation

For convenience, these exhibits assume investments in pension plans where income and appreciation are tax-deferred until withdrawal. The same sums, if invested in taxable portfolios, will bring reduced returns so that the available-to-compound capital will be less and the ultimate assets smaller.

For investors, Table I-1 is most important. It illustrates the powerful force of compounding: earning income on income by reinvesting, promptly, all profits (from dividends, interest, and capital gains). This shows that a single investment that continues to earn a 10% annual rate of return will grow 1.61 times in five years ($1,000 to $1,611), 2.59 times in ten years, and 6.73 times in twenty years. This assumes that all income is reinvested annually. With monthly compounding, the growth is slightly faster at the same 10% yield: 1.65 times in five years; 2.71 in ten years and 7.33 in twenty years.

With annual contributions, the impact is, roughly, about ten times as valuable: at 10% over thirty years, the factor is 164.49 versus 17.45 for the static sum. That's why it pays to save regularly and to keep all assets working.

Or to put it another way, note:

The importance of time. At a 10% rate of return, in the first five years, the multiplier for a single investment is 1.61; in the five years between years 20 and 25, it's 10.83, about six times as rewarding because there's more income earning income.

With annual contributions, time is even more valuable. The investment value triples in twenty years—$1,000 annually ($20,000) to $57,270—and more than quintuples in thirty years—$30,000 to $164,490.

The impact of an extra 2% rate of return. A single sum of $1,000, at 10%, grows to $6,730 in twenty years but, at 12%, compounds to $9,650. Regular annual contributions of $1,000 at 12% over thirty years grow to $241,330 versus $98,350 with a 10% average annual yield.

Targets

If you are like most folks, you will set specific time/dollar goals for your savings. The most convenient date is at retirement when you plan to stop regular work, begin receiving your pension

TABLE I-2
ANNUAL CONTRIBUTIONS NEEDED TO
BUILD A $50,000 PENSION FUND

Average Yield	20 years	30 years	40 years
6%	$13,590	$ 6,324	$ 3,231
8	10,926	4,414	1,930
10	8,730	3,040	1,130
12	6,940	2,072	652
15	4,880	1,150	281

benefits and, probably, Social Security. Usually, this will mark the end of saving systematically and the start of enjoying the assets built up over the years.

Table I-2 shows the annual contributions needed to accumulate a $500,000 pension fund. This will assure $50,000 to $75,000 a year for as long as most people can expect to live. Add Social Security of $15,000 to $20,000 (more in the future), and most people will have ample funds for a financially secure retirement plus a safety net from personal investments.

That goal can be difficult if the investment yields are low and the time span limited; at a 6% rate of return, over 20 years, the annual contributions to a Keogh or Professional Corporation plan must be $13,590. With a 12% yield (probable when you concentrate on Blue Chips), you will need only about half as much: $6,940 a year. And if the savings are continued for thirty years (starting at age forty with retirement at seventy), they will have to be less than $100 per month below the maximum allowed with an Individual Retirement Account.

That does not mean that, because you are young and struggling financially, you should lower these annual savings and hope to catch up later. The less you save and the longer you delay, the tougher it will be to reach your goals.

Example: if you start contributions to a pension plan at age twenty-five and continue these for forty years, with a 10% average annual yield, to reach $500,000, all you need is $1,130

TABLE I-3
Annual Withdrawals When Pension Plan Assets Continue to Be Invested: $100,000 Base

Years	8%	10%	11%	12%	13%	15%
10	$ 8,242	$ 7,567	$ 7,260	$6,970	$6,697	$6,198
15	10,464	9,306	8,798	8,332	7,904	7,145
20	11,955	10,362	9,688	9,082	8,536	7,594
25	12,956	11,005	10,203	9,495	8,867	7,807

Assume that you've saved $100,000, expect a 10% average annual yield, and plan to make withdrawals for twenty years. The two columns cross at $10,362. Your fund is 9.65 times larger ($100,000 divided by $10,362) so you can make withdrawals of $965 per month, or $11,580 a year,

The chart can also be used to figure how much capital you'll need to yield $100 a month: i.e., you want $1,000 a month for twenty years and think you can earn 12% on the starting capital. The columns intersect at $9,082. You'll need ten times that sum, or $90,820.

annually. But if you delay the program until age thirty-five, you will have to set aside almost three times as much: $3,040.

Whether your savings are to be invested through a pension plan or personal portfolio, make the first check every month to your bank, broker, or mutual fund. The amount is not as important as the discipline. You can always add more money in the future or, if you run into trouble, reduce the amount. At the outset this allocation may be difficult, but in a few months you will learn to live without these saved dollars.

Conversely, when you reach that $500,000 goal, review the situation. Do not save too much. It is foolish to stint yourself and family to accumulate wealth that realistically can provide more income than you can spend in retirement.

Because so many people are skeptical of these projections, let's look at another view of what will happen with withdrawals. Table I-3 shows the dollar benefits of a $100,000 pension

TABLE I-4
How Many Years Your Money Will Last

With Annual Withdrawals of	When the Assets Are Growing at This Rate 6%	8%	10%	12%
10%	15	20		
12	11	14	18	
14	9	11	13	17
15	8	9	11	14

Source: C. Colburn Hardy, *Funk & Wagnalls Personal Money Management* (New York: Thomas Y. Crowell).

portfolio. The income will be taxable at your then current rate but can be less if the assets are withdrawn in a lump sum under five year averaging (unless the rules are changed).

With personal pension plans, the minimum payments are set by IRS tables based on the ages of the participant and spouse. When both are age seventy, the amounts allowed are 1/18 in the first year, 1/17 in the second year, etc. This would be $5,555 annually, considerably less than the amounts shown on the table. But your total payouts would be greater because the remaining assets continue to compound tax-free.

Table I-4 shows how long your money will last at various rates of withdrawal and yields. Assets invested at a 10% yield with an annual withdrawal of 10% will last forever; at a 12% return, you can take out 15% for fourteen years.

Inflation

A final factor that must be considered with long-term investments is the erosion of capital by inflation. At this time, a 3% average annual rate appears likely for the near future, but this can be higher.

TABLE I-5
Calculating the Impact of Inflation

	Annual Rate			
Years	3%	4%	5%	6%
5	1.16	1.22	1.28	1.34
10	1.34	1.48	1.63	1.79
15	1.56	1.80	2.08	2.40
20	1.81	2.19	2.65	3.21
25	2.09	2.67	3.39	4.29

To determine how many future dollars will be needed to buy the same goods and services, multiply the current dollars by the appropriate factor. Thus, with a 3% inflation rate, in twenty years you will need $18,100 for every $10,000 in income now ($10,000 x 1.81).

Source: David Thorndike, ed., *Thorndike Encyclopedia of Banking and Financial Tables* (Boston: Warren, Gorham & Lamont).

With inflation your savings will buy fewer goods and services so, for you to stay even, your assets will have to be greater. As shown by Table I-5, with 3% inflation over twenty years you will need $18,100 for every $10,000 now. Actually, for most older folks, inflation is not overly onerous because they eat less, drive less, and, except for medical costs, make fewer major expenditures. Still, if you plan to retire early or expect that you and/or your spouse will live unusually long, move up your investment goal.

How the Stock Market Changes

Everyone knows that the stock market fluctuates (that's the price you pay for liquidity), but how many understand what this means? And how can you take advantage of this knowledge?

To achieve the most rewarding returns, it is important to manage your money in relation to basic changes in the stock market as shown by Table I-6, covering the three major groups of securities over some forty years. This means:

1. Shifting part of your holdings when economic and financial conditions change, from equity to debt when there's a business downturn and back again when the trend is reversed.
2. Reorganizing the types of common stocks, getting out of electronics when there is overproduction and price-cutting (and thus prospects of lower profits) and into oil stocks when petroleum prices appear likely to rise. These decisions are discussed in Chapter 3.

Most of these switches should be limited to about 30% of your portfolio, depending on your personal risk levels and should be temporary, seldom over a couple of years. The majority of investments, both personal and fiduciary, should continue to be in common stocks because these are growing, profitable holdings that will increase your wealth. Table I-6 shows why.

The index price for the three categories—Dow Jones Industrial Average stocks, the Dow Jones Corporate Bond Average, and U.S. Treasury bills—was 100 in 1946. Forty years later, the indices were 6,750, 856, and 652, respectively. These are total investment returns: price appreciation plus reinvested income (that Magic of Compounding). If someone had invested $1,000 in the thirty stocks that made up the Dow Jones Industrials in 1946 and reinvested all income as these component companies changed, that investor would have $67,506. With the same sum, the bond total sould be $8,556 and the T-bill portfolio $6,524—assuming regular rollovers at maturity.

These figures are the strongest argument for investing in common stocks. With quality corporations, the results of the stock investments would be even greater because half, or fewer, of the Dow companies have had, or now deserve, a quality rating.

TABLE I-6

Comparative Investment Performance: Stocks Versus Bonds: 1946–mid-86

Total Investment Returns: Price Appreciation plus Income Reinvested

	Dow Jones Industrial Stocks			Dow Jones Corporate Bonds			U.S. Treasury Bills		
	Index	Per Cent Return		Index	Per Cent Return		Index	Per Cent Return	
Year	Price	Year	Cumulative	Price	Year	Cumulative	Price	Year	Cumulative
1946	100.00	. . .	. . .	100.00	. . .	. . .	100.00	. . .	. . .
1950	171.49	+26.4	+14.4	110.27	+ 4.25	+2.47	104.03	+ 1.23	+0.99
1955	467.38	+26.6	+18.7	123.00	+ 0.47	+2.33	112.60	+ 1.75	+1.33
1960	718.87	− 6.1	+15.1	129.00	+ 9.07	+1.84	129.54	+ 2.96	+1.87
1965	1340.27	+14.4	+14.6	157.58	+ 1.46	+2.42	151.55	+ 3.99	+2.21
1970	1398.68	+ 9.2	+11.6	199.05	+16.92	+2.91	199.13	+ 6.54	+2.91
1975	1746.02	+44.7	+10.4	284.24	+14.53	+3.67	265.34	+ 5.92	+3.42
1980	2594.32	+22.2	+10.0	340.23	− 5.04	+3.67	388.61	+11.74	+4.07
1981	2501.76	− 3.6	+ 9.6	344.13	+ 1.15	+3.57	443.52	+14.13	+4.35
1982	3179.88	+27.1	+10.1	476.52	+38.47	+4.43	491.59	+10.84	+4.52
1983	4005.56	+26.0	+10.5	517.88	+ 8.68	+4.55	534.89	+ 8.81	+4.64
1984	4057.86	+ 1.3	+10.2	598.33	+15.53	+4.82	587.07	+ 9.76	+4.77
1985	5419.15	+33.5	+10.8	759.54	+26.94	+5.34	631.81	+ 7.62	+4.84
1986 (mid)	6750.66	+47.5	+11.2	855.66	+24.23	+5.59	652.41	+ 6.95	+4.86

Source: Wright Investors' Service

There have been periods when fixed income securities were more rewarding: in 1960, when stocks fell 6% and bonds rose 9%; in 1981, when stocks fell and bonds started to climb withever-higher yields (except for a modest gain in 1983). People who bought bonds made a lot of money with minimal risks. Many are still doing so in 1987.

Those switching decisions are not easy. In 1984, stocks barely moved; in 1985, they roared up and were still soaring in 1987. These figures don't show it, but the biggest stock gains were early in 1986, while those of bonds remained fairly high and stable.

Liquid assets, such as Treasury bills, were wise investments only for short periods in 1980, 1981, and 1982 when yields were at record peaks. Fortunately, with these short-term holdings, there's daily compounding and, with no commissions, the costs of entry and exit are minimal.

Note the terrific impact of cumulative returns: for stocks, in the almost forty years the annual rates of total return were below 10% only once, in 1981, and in strong markets were over +40%. The fixed income rewards rose slowly and steadily and since 1982 have been more or less steady arond 5% a year.

These changes sound simple and, in hindsight, logical, but honestly now, how many of you recognized the wisdom of such action in the past? Cutting down on stocks in late 1980 and loading up on T-bills? Or, in 1984, moving part of your savings out of equities into bonds?

As you will learn throughout this book, common stocks have been the most rewarding investments. In the last nineteen years (which, I assume is the experience span of most readers), as measured by the Standard & Poor's 500 Composite, stocks have risen from about 80 to over 250, the AA Corporate Bond Average has fallen from 81 to 52, and interest rates (the yield of money market funds and CDs) are at almost the same 5% to 6% despite some startling swings in between.

Quality stocks (shares of Blue Chip corporations) have been even more profitable. They will continue to be steady winners. To learn why and how to buy and sell them, read on.

Part 2

INTRODUCTION TO PROFITABLE INVESTING

This book is about fundamental investing: the kind that every intelligent individual **knows** is best for savings in both personal and pension plan portfolios. It is designed for those who read *The Wall Street Journal, Forbes, Barron's, Financial World,* and, to a limited degree, *Money* and personal finance magazines. These are concerned investors who want to preserve their capital, to receive ample income, and, most important, to make their money grow. They recognize the folly of *How to Make a Million Dollars in Fifteen Minutes.*

From writing and teaching, I am persuaded that there is an increasing number of these men and women who want to learn how to invest conservatively, how to select securities and mutual funds, and how to structure and manage their personal and pension plan portfolios successfully. They have, or anticipate having, $50,000 or more in savings. At times, some are willing to take fliers with new issues, packaged deals, and special "opportunities," but most are smart enough to understand the importance of quality and value as preached by almost every responsible financial publication and by all really successful money managers.

Basically, this means investing in Blue Chips: securities of corporations that are financially strong, have long and fairly consistent records of high profitability, and whose managements have the skill and capacity to continue better-than-average growth. These corporations make money so you make money.

The purpose of this book is to provide information that can help investors at all levels to make more money with their savings. Anyone who follows these principles will avoid the disastrous consequences that have resulted from following a specific system/technique so vigorously espoused by some self-styled professionals in their books, market letters, lectures, seminars, and TV shows. Usually, these "experts" make more money from their promotions than from their investments. And their readers/listeners lose money.

In this book, there is no single, simple formula which can be used but there is a great deal about investment criteria, research, and the importance of systematic procedures and personal discipline. Some of the concepts may be difficult for some individuals to utilize effectively because they lack information, but all of the principles/practices are sound and can be adapted by anyone willing to do his/her homework, follow proven-profitable policies, and use common sense.

The information and comments reflect my close association with John Winthrop Wright, president of Wright Investors' Service (WIS), as a public relations adviser and currently as a director of the corporation. This firm now manages some $4.5 billion in fiduciary funds and, for a quarter of a century, has had an audited record of total returns, after commissions, averaging almost 12% annually, far above the stock market averages. Individuals who are not restricted, as I am, by client criteria and the need for liquid assets for pension fund payouts, should do better when they follow the same basics.

N.B. (1) In case this appears to be a plug for business, please note that Wright rarely accepts accounts under $500,000 and prefers to service institutional investors such as pension funds, banks, and foundations. (2) The Wright organization has been most helpful with information, charts, and tables, but the conclusions are *mine,* do not necessarily reflect those of John Wright and his staff, and in some cases may result in different interpretations. Similarly, the explanations of investment analysis represent my interpretations of the methodology. *I am a writer, not a professional investment adviser.*

To help the reader make wise decisions, many chapters contain checklists and examples. At all times, the text tries to explain the risks of speculation and warns against the siren songs of stock market hype. The safest, surest way to make money with investments is by buying common stocks of Blue Chip corporations. Since there will be periods when debt issues can be more rewarding, there are chapters on fixed income holdings.

There are also sections on special securities/contracts such as options and, of course, a detailed explanation on how to judge and choose mutual funds. There are no chapters on new issues, tax shelters, futures, commodities, etc., because for individuals these are almost always speculations, not investments.

Everyone—novice, sophisticate or professional—who follows the principles outlined, pays attention to proven profitable concepts and procedures, and acts logically can expect to achieve consistently superior performance. The results may not always be as high as those trumpeted by some professionals but, over the time of a true investment program, they will be above average because the most profitable companies make the most money for their shareholders.

This is not a how-to book in the usual sense. It is intended to be interesting, informative, educational and to enable the reader to understand the strategy and tactics of fundamental investing, how to apply them effectively, and how to recognize personal and financial limits. The emphasis is positive but, recognizing the realities of the stock market and its sponsors/promoters and agents, it also lists negatives and warnings.

In a sense, the theme is the same as that of the fable of the race between the hare and the tortoise. The hare's actions were more exciting, more volatile, and more visible than those of the slow-moving, deliberate rival, but the tortoise did win the race!

No one can predict the course of the stock market over the

short term but, by concentrating on investments in Blue Chips, the intelligent investor can make logical projections of the future prospects of these quality corporations. Not all of the methods outlined will work all of the time, but, over more than twenty-five years, the stocks on the Wright Investors' Service Recommended List have outperformed the averages every year except one!

Background

To give you an idea of what's ahead and where I am coming from, here are some points to consider and, usually, to remember in investing:

- Money in a savings account is not working productively toward the primary investment goal of total returns: income plus appreciation. With a 6% yield, taxed at the soon-to-be maximum 28% tax rate, the net is 4.32%. This will be further eroded by inflation. At a 3% rate, the real reward will be a tiny 1.32%.

  By investing in Blue Chip stocks, the average annual rate of total returns should be a minimum of 15%: 3% dividends plus 12% capital gains. After that 28% tax bite, the net will be 10.8%, and with growth the impact of inflation will be less. That 15% annual return is 66% better than that of the overall stock market over more than sixty years.
- All investments should be prudent: "[to] observe how men of prudence, discretion and intelligence manage their affairs, considering the probable income as well as the probable safety of the capital to be invested."
- Over the short term, the stock market is inefficient; over the long term, it sets reasonable values.
- In Wall Street, the crowd thinks with emotions; the wise investor thinks with brains, relies on research, and considers the logical rewards against the possible risks.

- Invest only when you understand the company, its business, its financial statements and can realistically project why its shares should be worth more. Heed the counsel of Benjamin Graham, dean of Wall Street commentators: "In forty-four years of Wall Street experience and study, I have never seen dependable calculations made about common stock values or related investment policies that went beyond simple arithmetic or the most elementary algebra. When there are complex equations, take this as a warning signal that the operator was trying to substitute theory for experience and usually to give speculation the guise of investment."
- In planning investments, look for fertile fields and companies that are well managed and highly profitable.
- Buy only stocks of companies that make you (and your spouse) feel good.
- Always think of the purchase of any security as if you were buying the whole company. Only rarely would you plan to sell in six months.
- When you buy any stock, write down your objective. Before selling, refer to that original goal.
- When you buy stocks of quality companies when they are unpopular (and thus at bargain prices), most of the risks have been wrung out. Any purchase will be profitable eventually, but if you delay buying until corporate prospects are improving, you will make money faster.
- Be sensible, not euphoric. Buy low and sell high is a Wall Street rainbow that many chase and few catch.
- Fall in love with a company, but never with its stock.
- Always remember that the stock market does not care about you, your hopes, ambitions, or needs.
- Do not look back. You cannot reverse the effects of that judgment, and worrying about a mistake won't make the price of the stock go up.
- Most Wall Street theories are little more than excuses to justify the purchase of overvalued securities.
- Too many analysts are seduced by their own projections and forget, or minimize, values.

- Do not be disturbed by losses on individual risks but keep an eye on the gain or loss of the total portfolio. Insurance companies go on the theory that losses are inevitable and should be distributed over an entire group of insured. They estimate aggregate losses, charge the entire group enough to cover loss plus reasonable expenses/profit. Always expect losses, prepare for them, and minimize their effect by good management elsewhere.
- Be patient. Common stock profits take time. Investing is like planting a flower garden, where you sow the seeds, fertilize, water, spray, and nurture. Not all the flowers will come up and even fewer will blossom, but the better the quality of the seeds/plants and the more tender their care, the more profuse and beautiful the flowers will be.
- As an amateur investor, you are competing in a professional's market. You can win only if you stick to selected areas which you have learned to understand and can afford. Futures, indexes, options, and similar contracts are vehicles used for hedging by major investors. When you take the other side of such speculations, you are usually playing out of your league.
- The best investment profits are always made with the stocks of companies that make the most money.
- The American free enterprise system is highly competitive and only a few well-run corporations continue to be major leaders and thus their stocks profitable investments over many years.

Note these changes in the most profitable corporations in fifteen years:

1961	1986
Avon Products	American Home Products
Eastman Kodak	Dow Jones & Co.
Heublein, Inc.	James River Corp.
Motorola, Inc.	Limited, Inc.
Polaroid Corp.	Tandy Corp.
Schlumberger. Ltd.	Wal-Mart Stores
Sperry & Hutchinson	Wang Laboratories

Of the 1961 most profitables, Avon, Kodak, Polaroid, and Schlumberger have been struggling for several years, Heublein and S&H have been absorbed, and Motorola is just beginning to move back to a high return in equity.

Many Blue Chips do retain a quality rating, but their profitability declines so that their shares are no longer worthwhile investments. When you buy Blue Chips, do not lock them away for your grandchildren; keep abreast of their progress (or lack thereof) and sell when they become fully valued. That's what this book is all about.

Chapter 1

QUALITY IS THE KEY

To understand the meaning of "quality" (in this book, the term is synonymous with Blue Chips), let's go back to the basic concept of equity investing: that each share of common stock represents ownership of a portion of the assets, profits, and dividends of the corporation. The principles are the same whether you use your savings to become a partner in your brother-in-law's incorporated filling station or to buy shares of IBM. The more successful the business, the less your risk and the greater your eventual reward. In one sentence: the higher the quality of the enterprise, the safer and more profitable your investment.

In the stock market, quality is the record of corporate investment acceptance, financial strength, profitability, and growth. These are the marks of Blue Chip corporations, as shown by the proven ability of management to increase revenues and earnings year after year—with few, temporary interruptions—and to compound these profits at average rates above those of other publicly owned firms. The higher the rate and the greater the consistency of profitable growth, the better the quality of the corporation and, thus, of its securities. As will be repeated throughout this book: **more profits can be made, consistently, with less risk, with investments in quality stocks than with any other type of security!**

Yet, it is amazing how easily so many people exchange their hard-earned savings for securities/deals on the basis of hope, not facts; of promises, not performance; of tips, not research.

Most individuals who make such mistakes are speculators, whether they admit it or not. They buy stocks with a "story." They prefer the make-believe of something for nothing, are influenced by day-to-day news and usually acquire stocks when they are popular (and, by definition, overpriced) and sell them near their lows. Such tactics are illogical, foolish, and expensive, but they are typical and frequent. At times, these pseudoinvestors may make quick profits with a few holdings but, except in a strong bull market, they will lose money with the majority of such commitments!

True investors buy quality stocks, preferably when undervalued, and sell them when they become fully priced. They know that over the long term they will make money from modest and growing dividends and substantial price appreciation. With the exception of some stable utilities, quality corporations boost their sales and earnings by 10% annually. They pay out 25% to 50% of their profits and invest the balance in new products, new markets, new plants, more modern equipment, and research and development for continued growth. With an ever-larger base and the same rate of profitability, the companies will earn more dollars and pay higher dividends. Such outstanding results attract more investors, and the increased demand raises the prices of their stocks. On average, a quality corporation will double its assets, earnings, and dividends every seven years. And best of all, the dollars retained for growth are not immediately taxable to the shareholder.

Added plus: such records of consistent performance make it possible to predict with considerable confidence the future of

TABLE 1-1
Projecting Prices of Quality Stocks With Earnings and Dividends +10% Annually

Year	Per Share		Price/Earnings Ratio		
	Earnings	Dividends	16	14	18
1976	$1.75	$1.00	28	24	31
1977	1.92	1.10	31	27	35
1978	2.11	1.21	34	30	38
1979	2.32	1.33	37	32	42
1980	2.55	1.46	41	36	46
1981	2.80	1.61	45	39	50
1982	3.08	1.77	49	43	55
1983	3.39	1.95	54	47	61
1984	3.73	2.14	60	52	67
1985	4.10	2.35	66	57	74

corporate earnings, and thus to a large degree the price movements of their common stocks.

Example: In 1976, Investor Ike, looking for a good long-term investment, checked American Home Products (AHP). The company was rated AAA by Standard & Poor's, had boosted earnings an average of 12% annually, and paid out about 60% of profits in dividends. Growth plus income equals good total returns.

The stock was trading at 28, a price/earnings ratio of about 16, which was above that of the overall stock market but not out of line with other drug stocks. To be conservative, Ike assumed that future earnings would rise 10% a year and made these projections: the same multiple in normal markets, 14 in recessive periods, and 18 in buoyant years (Table 1-1).

Thus, Ike felt that under almost all conditions his investment in this quality stock would double in price and, plus dividends, would bring his total returns well over +12% annually. He bought 100 shares of AHP for his son's college trust fund and projected that this $2,800 investment would grow to $7,592: 39 points capital gains plus $1,592 dividends.

Here's what happened (digested to save space):

Year	Earnings	Dividends	Stock Price
1976	$1.75	$1.00	28
1979	2.51	1.50	30
1981	3.18	1.90	37
1983	4.00	2.40	54
1985	4.70	2.90	67

The dividends were higher, $1,867, and the stock one point above target. The $2,800 grew to $8,570: appreciation of $3,900 plus payouts of $1,867 = +$5,767, an annualized rate of return of over 12%.

The point is that with quality stocks you can manage your savings, make realistic projections and look for higher values in the future. That's what investing is all about!

Standards of Investment Quality

Fundamental investing starts with a disciplined, systematic methodology to determine what stocks are eligible for serious investment consideration.

To be eligible for inclusion in the Approved Wright Investment List (AWIL), a corporation must meet thirty-two specific major standards of quality (see Table 1-2). The basic criteria have not been changed since they were initially established in 1965, but there have been frequent refinements in their measurements as made possible with improved computer technology.

This list is not developed by random selection nor by a group of people who decide what stocks of what companies they "like" at a specific time. AWIL is a carefully culled group of major corporations which meet the four basic standards which go into the measurement of quality: investment acceptance, financial strength, profitability, and growth. No matter how attractive the price of the stock nor how enticing their current investment

TABLE I-2 Wright Standards of Quality

WRIGHT QUALITY RATING	**NORMAL MINIMUM STANDARDS FOR LISTING ON *THE APPROVED WRIGHT INVESTMENT LIST* AND EXPLANATORY PARAGRAPH (¶) REFERENCE NUMBERS ARE INDEXED BELOW.**							
INVESTMENT ACCEPTANCE	MARKET VALUE 3 Year Average		TRADING VOLUME 3 Year Average	TURNOVER RATE 3 Year Average	EXCHANGE MARKETS	INSTITUTIONAL INVESTORS Number of Funds, Insurance Cos., etc.	SHARE-HOLDERS	CLOSELY HELD SHARES % of Total
A: Outstanding B: Excellent C: Good { Minimum Acceptable Rating	TOTAL All Shares Outstanding	PUBLIC Excluding Closely Held						
	¶103.1	¶103.11	¶103.2	¶103.3	¶103.4	¶103.5	¶103.6	¶103.7
¶103-103.01	*AWIL Minimum:* $100 mil	*AWIL Minimum:* $100 mil	*AWIL Preference Minimum:* $50 mil	*AWIL Preference:* less than 50%	*AWIL Preference:* NYSE	*AWIL Preference Minimum:* 20	*AWIL Preference Minimum:* 3,000	*AWIL Preference Maximum:* 35%
FINANCIAL STRENGTH	SHAREHOLDERS' EQUITY		PREFERRED STOCK % of Capital Equity, Pfd Stk & L.T. Debt	LONG TERM DEBT % of Capital Equity, Pfd Stk & L.T. Debt	FIXED CHARGE COVERAGE RATIO Ratio of Pretax Income to Interest & Preferred Divs	WORKING CAPITAL Current Ratio Current Assets/ Current Liabilities	CONVERTIBLE SECURITIES	
A: Outstanding B: Excellent C: Good { Minimum Acceptable Rating	TOTAL Capital & Surplus	% OF CAPITAL Equity, Pfd Stk & L.T. Debt					TOTAL OUTSTANDING % of Common Shares	POTENTIAL DILUTION % Reduction in Earnings
	¶104.1	¶104.11 ¶104.12	¶104.2 ¶104.21	¶104.2 ¶104.31 ¶104.32	¶104.4 ¶104.71	¶104.5 ¶104.74	¶104.6	¶104.61
[illegible]	*AWIL Preference Minimum:* $50 mil	*AWIL Minimum:* 50%	*AWIL Maximum:* Depends on	*AWIL Maximum:* 40%	*AWIL Preference Minimum:* 3.5:1;	*AWIL Preference Minimum:* 2:1;	*AWIL Preference Maximum:* 30%	*AWIL Preference Maximum:* 15%

& STABILITY	AVERAGE 10 Years Unadjusted	TIME-WEIGHTED NORMAL Adjusted Rate†	BASIC TREND Adjusted Annual Rate†	STABILITY INDEX	% PAYOUT OF EARNINGS TIME-WEIGHTED NORMAL Adjusted Average†	% RETURN ON EQUITY TIME-WEIGHTED NORMAL Adjusted Average†	% RETURN ON EQUITY BASIC TREND Adjusted Annual Rate†	INCOME % Of Total Capital Adjusted Rate†
A: Outstanding B: Excellent C: Good { Minimum Acceptable Rating ¶105-105.02	¶105.1 *AWIL Preference Minimum:* 11%	¶105.11 ¶105.31 *AWIL Minimum:* 11%	¶105.12 *AWIL Minimum:* No Significant Decline	¶105.13 ¶105.14 *AWIL Minimum:* 60%	¶105.2 *AWIL Preference Minimum:* 10% *Maximum:* 75%	¶105.21 *AWIL Preference Minimum:* 5%	¶105.22 *AWIL Preference:* No Significant Decline	¶105.3 ¶105.31 *AWIL Preference Minimum:* 15%
GROWTH**	AVERAGE* 10 Years Unadjusted Annual Rate Per Share	EARNINGS GROWTH TIME-WEIGHTED NORMAL Adjusted Annual Rate Per Share†	EARNINGS GROWTH BASIC TREND Adjusted Annual Rate Per Share†	STABILITY INDEX	EQUITY GROWTH TOTAL TIME-WEIGHTED NORMAL Annual Rate Per Share††	EQUITY GROWTH EARNED TIME-WEIGHTED NORMAL Adjusted Annual Rate Per Share†	DIVIDEND GROWTH TIME-WEIGHTED NORMAL Annual Rate Per Share††	SALES OR REVENUES GROWTH TIME-WEIGHTED NORMAL Annual Total Amount††
Normal Minimum: 6% Normal Annual Compound Rate Adjusted For Stability ¶106-106.02	¶106.1 *AWIL Preference Minimum:* +4%	¶106.11 *AWIL Minimum:* +4%	¶106.12 *AWIL Minimum:* No Significant Decline	¶106.13 *AWIL Minimum:* 60%	¶106.2 *AWIL Preference Minimum:* +4%	¶106.21 *AWIL Minimum:* +4%	¶106.3 *AWIL Preference Minimum:* +4%	¶106.4 *AWIL Preference Minimum:* +4%

All profitability and growth records are time-weighted annual rates per common share (except sales growth and operating income). NOTES: (†): Adjusted for trends, cyclical variations, strikes and nonrecurring charges and credits; (††): Adjusted for trends only; (*): Compound Annual Rate based on earnings reported for last 12 months vs 10 years ago; (**): The composite growth rating is derived after adjusting the time-weighted "normal" growth by stability and profitability.

Reprinted by permission of Wright Investors' Service.

"story," Wright does not invest in any corporation which fails to meet these quality standards.

Since these ratings were first published in 1964, the average total investment return of appreciation and dividend income of all stocks which have met these standards has been over +11% average annual compound rate. By comparison, similar results for the Dow Jones Industrial Average (DJIA) were +7.8% and for the Standard & Poor's (S&P) 500 Stock Composite, +8.9%.

To give you an idea of the superiority of these approved corporations:

- The average return on equity is about 17.2%, compared to 9% for the DJIA stocks and 13% for those of the S&P 500.
- The growth rate has averaged about 14% a year in earnings versus 6% for the S&P 500. These high rates of profitable growth make it possible for these quality investments to return far more than needed to offset inflation, which erodes the rewards of fixed income holdings.
- The dividends averaged 3.6% versus 4.9% for the S&P 500.
- Losses over the years have been few and small. Of 198 recommended stocks, thirteen were sold for less than their purchase price, and with four of these the dividend income was greater than the loss.

N.B. There can be no guarantee that the results will be comparable in the future but twenty-five years is a long time span in the investment business.

Determination and Measuring Quality

Under the Wright system, the objective is to identify those corporations which: (1) are substantial, well established, and favorably known in the securities market and to institutional investors, (2) have ample financial reserves and working capital, (3) consistently make a high return on stockholders' equity, and (4) report ever-greater growth. These stocks will become more attractive to investors over time.

The four prime criteria are investment acceptance, financial strength, profitability, and growth. All of these apply to business corporations, but the first two can also be used with governments and governmental agencies whose bonds may be considered as investments under certain conditions.

The records of all NYSE-listed corporations and an increasing number of those on the AMEX or traded over the counter are analyzed over twenty years (when possible), reviewed periodically, and rated in each of the four categories by a composite of a weighted average that takes into account specific subcomponents, ratios, and trends. Such details are possible only with computers.

The results are shown by letters: A, outstanding; B, excellent; C, good or minimum acceptability. To be eligible for inclusion in the AWIL, a company must score well in every one of the thirty-two subdivisions. These standards are strict but still flexible enough to permit revisions due to unusual circumstances which may temporarily adversely affect the quality of the corporation.

The numeral is a composite of eight individual standards, and measures the annual corporate growth rate. Thus, the ratings are for mighty IBM, AAA11; for much smaller Ames Department Stores, BBA20.

Quality Components

The quality rating is the result of two factors:

Earned (E) component. This is directly related to corporate fundamentals and comes from dividend income plus price appre-

TABLE 1-3
A Sampling of Some Wright Stock Buy Recommendations
Last 5½ Years 1/1/81–6/30/86

Stock	Selected		Date & Price Sold	Price	Investment Return			Months
	Date	Price	Or Current Status	6/30/86	Price	Dividends	Total	Held
Albertson's, Inc	1/ 9/85	26¾	Active List	46¾	74.8%	4.3%	79.0	17.6
Alco Standard	1/ 9/85	31¼	Active List	42½	36.0%	5.9%	41.9%	17.6
American Brands	12/15/82	45½	10/12/83 56¼	93¼	23.6%	5.8%	29.5%	9.72
American Brands	1/ 9/85	62⅛	11/20/85 59¾	93¼	−3.8%	6.3%	2.5%	10.3
American Standard	7/27/83	34¾	4/16/86 44¼	42½	27.3%	12.7%	40.0%	32.66
Ametek Inc.	3/12/86	29¾	Active List	29⅞	0.4%	0.8%	1.3%	3.6
Amoco	11/ 4 81	54⅞	3/12/86 60⅜	60¼	10.0%	23.2%	33.2%	52.21
Angelica Corp.	3/27/85	19½	Active List	29½	51.3%	3.8%	55.1%	15.1
Archer Daniels	6/11/81	10	Active List	18¼	82.6%	4.2%	86.8%	60.62
Arkla, Inc.	6/13/84	20⅛	Active List	18⅜	−8.7%	10.7%	2.0%	24.54
Atlantic Richfield	11/11/81	46	4 /2/86	52	15.8%	27.3%	43.0%	52.67
Auto Data Processing	10/13/82	28¾	2/ 1/84 35⅝	35⅜	23.9%	2.3%	26.2%	15.64

Stock	Selected Date	Selected Price	Date & Price Sold Or Current Status	Price 6/30/86	Investment Return Price	Investment Return Dividends	Investment Return Total	Months Held
Avnet, Inc.	6/13/84	32¾	11/14/84 31⅛	28⅞	−5.0%	0.4%	−4.6%	5.1
Avnet, Inc.	1/22/86	34¼	Active List	28⅞	−15.7%	0.7%	−15.0%	5.2
Bandag	10/13/82	33½	7/13/83 53⅜	80⅛	59.3%	2.2%	61.5%	9.01
Barry Wright Corp.	2/12/86	19⅝	Active List	20⅞	6.4%	0.8%	7.1%	4.5
Bausch & Lomb	12/14/83	25¾	Active List	39	51.5%	7.62%	59.0%	30.52
Bellsouth Corp.	1/16/85	33½	Active List	62¾	87.3%	10.6%	97.9%	17.4
Blue Bell	10/05/83	35½	11/23/84 47⅝	z	34.2%	5.5%	39.7%	13.63
Borden	3/ 3/82	15⅞	8/17/83 26⅝	49⅜	68.8%	10.9%	79.6%	17.47
Borg Warner	6/ 6/84	19⅛	Active List	35⅛	83.7%	9.7%	93.3%	24.77
Briggs & Stratton	5/ 9/84	30⅛	5/29/85 28½	37⅜	−5.4%	7.2%	1.8%	12.65
Brown Group, Inc.	2/1/84	30¼	Active List	38⅛	26.0%	11.2%	37.3%	28.91
Burndy Corp.	11/16/83	20⅜	6/19/85 11¼	12¾	−44.8%	6.2%	−38.6%	19.09
CBI	5/19/82	33⅞	5/15/85 25¼	24⅞	−25.5%	13.7%	−11.7%	35.88
CPC International	12/21/84	39¾	4/24/85 42⅛	73	6.0%	2.8%	8.7%	4.07

FIGURE I-1 The Securities Markets and the Economy

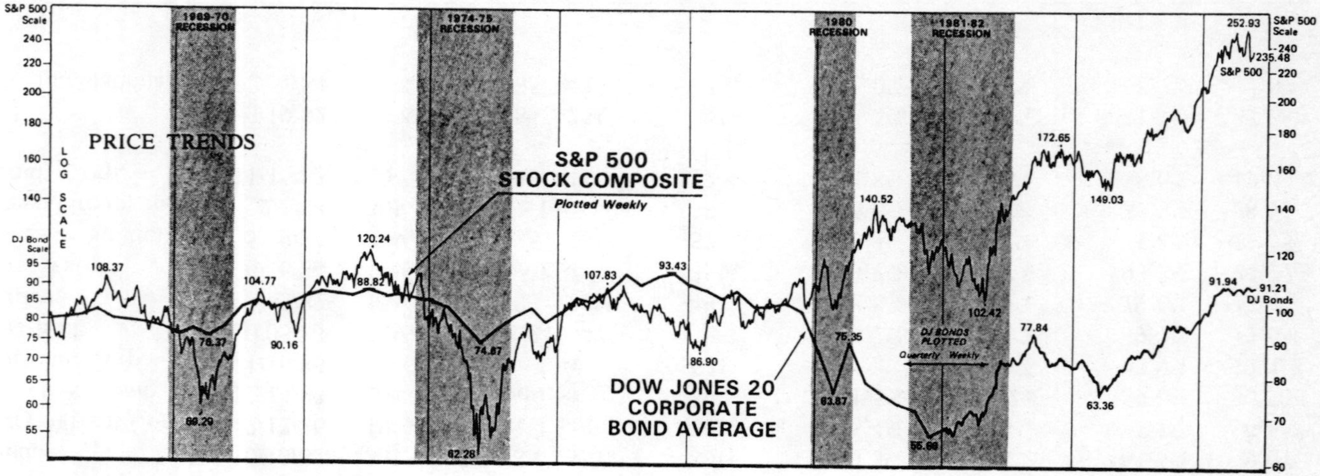

Source: Wright Investors' Service

ciation which parallels the company's normal rate of growth in sales, earnings, equity capital, and payouts. These are the marks of profitable growth.

Unearned (U) component. This is investor-related in that it is derived from the changes in the price/earnings ratios which reflect investors' revised estimates of the company's potential for future growth as well as shifts in the outlook for common stocks generally and rates of returns from other investments.

The U component is inherently speculative because it depends on investor attitudes and outside factors which can only be "guesstimated." Its impact is primarily on short- and intermediate-term price movements. Speculators, impressed by deviations from the long-term E trend, enter the market in over- or undervalued situations to achieve quick gains and often cause stocks to move from under- to overvalued prices. In the late 1960s, enthusiasm for the U component was responsible for the rapid rise in the price of new stock issues; in the mid-1970s, the reaction from the two-tiered market's overvaluation of so-called one-decision stocks sent many quality shares plummeting; in the mid-1980s, bull market euphoria pushed almost all stocks to record highs.

For investors, the important thing to realize is that the E component can be projected with confidence based on the stable records of many high-quality corporations; the U factor is only a guess at what other investors may decide to favor or disfavor. Speculators may be lucky once or twice but there's no way they can avoid losses, and the ultimate results will at best reflect how little they lose rather than how much they make.

Growth Rating

"Growth" is a magic word in the stock market and especially with Wall Street brokers and analysts. But growth is in the eye of the holder, so always beware of the use of this word.

TABLE 1-4
Growth of a Quality Company
Melville Corp., Rated AAA18 by Wright Investors' Service

	1975	1979	1983	1985
Revenues (in $ millions)	$908	$2,023	$3,923	$4,775
Earned growth rate	19.6%	18.6%	16.9%	14.6%
Earnings per share	0.90	2.02	3.36	4.07
Dividends per share	0.24	0.70	1.09	1.44
Book value per share	3.37	7.10	13.46	18.06
Stock price range	10–3	16–13	48–30	53–35

Earnings/dividends/book value adjusted for three-for-one stock split in 1983.

EARNED GROWTH

Usually, growth describes the increase in corporate sales and earnings, but what really counts is the *Earned Growth,* the increase in equity capital through reinvestment of retained earnings after the payment of dividends. This is tax-free money that is plowed back into the company to speed its growth in all meaningful areas.

To determine the earned growth rate, use this formula:

$$EGR = \frac{E - D}{BV}$$

EGR = earned growth rate
E = earnings per share
D = dividends per share
BV = book values per share

In Table 1-4, for Melville Corp. (MES), the calculations for 1979 would be

$$EGR = \frac{2.02 - 0.70}{7.10} = \frac{1.32}{7.10} = 18.59\%$$

The true value of each share of common stock increased by 18.6% in 1979. That's a high rate because, on the average, the EGR of the S&P 500 has been about 8%.

Note that in the four years between 1975 and 1979, the earnings and book value about doubled, from $0.90 to $2.02 and from $3.37 to $7.10, and the dividends almost tripled. In the next four years, the growth of profits and payouts rose more slowly, but the value of the shareholders' investment doubled. As the revenues grew in percentages, gains in other areas slowed.

Note, too, that investors were slow to recognize such profitable progress. The stock moved up in the first four years, took off to triple in price in the next time frame, then bounced in the erratic market but hit a new high, in the 70's, in 1986.

EGR is the most reliable measure of investment growth because, over the long term, the rise of earnings and dividends usually depends on a corresponding growth of the capital invested in the business. EGR is always useful because it is applicable to all types of businesses, whether drug firms or fast-food chains, and thus permits meaningful comparisons. For inclusion on the AWIL, the minimum EGR is 4%, but over the years the average has been substantially higher.

By WIS standards, the EGR must be maintained for two consecutive five-year periods. Consistency is the true jewel of corporate performance. Many small companies start out with a spectacular record of growth but falter as they move into more competitive markets. Quality must be earned and maintained.

TOTAL EQUITY GROWTH

The annual rate of growth of book value over ten years is known as *total equity growth.* It provides a second checkpoint for the true growth of a corporation. An acceptable minimum is 4%.

Again, there should be exceptions with both of these standards when there are extenuating circumstances, such as a nonrecurring loss, an unavoidable profit reduction due to events beyond management's control, or a temporary by-product of an acquisition.

EARNINGS GROWTH

It's also important to analyze *earnings growth,* which is measured in four ways:

Average annual rate, the point-to-point of the annual rate of growth, usually calculated over ten years. For AWIL the minimum is 4%, but for all approved stocks this has been more than double.

Time-weighted normal growth of earnings. This is the same figure adjusted for cyclical variations, corporate trends, or situations beyond the control of management, including fluctuations in the tax rate and nonrecurring charges. Standard: 6%.

Basic trend earnings growth. This is another computer calculation which is expressed graphically to show the relation of actual corporate profits to a projections based on past performance. Basically, there should be no significant decline, but exceptions are made.

Stability of the company's earnings growth compared to the average of the S&P 500: 75% normal minimum but as low as 60% under some circumstances.

DIVIDEND GROWTH

Because investors are interested in returns on their money, dividend growth is important, too. This is checked in two ways:

Dividend growth is a straight mathematical calculation of the annual rate of increase in payments to common shareholders. This should average 4% over ten years but may be modified if corporate management chooses to reduce or eliminate the payouts to increase growth of retained earnings; e.g., Crown Cork & Seal's profit rate and earned growth rate have averaged over 13% for the past decade, but it pays no dividends.

Sales/revenues growth. This is more interesting than significant. Generally, higher income results in greater growth but not when management opts for profits over volume. On the average, this total should keep moving up at about 4% a year.

Summary

In making money with securities, there is no substitute for quality. This can be established only on the basis of its past performance. There is no way to determine the quality of a new company. That's why no new issues can be considered investments.

Nor are name and fame marks of excellence. That the company is big and well known does not by itself qualify its stock as a worthwhile holding. Only six of the thirty companies that make up the Dow Jones Industrial Average meet Wright standards of quality!

Investment Acceptance

This reflects the acceptability of a security and the distribution of its shares among investors, primarily the institutions that account for some two-thirds of all NYSE transactions. This criterion also measures the adequacy of the floating supply of the company's common stock and, to a large degree, the liquidity of the investment. Without adequate investment acceptance, no widely held stock will move up in price.

Keep in mind that the activity of quality stocks is dominated by, and in some cases almost controlled by, institutional investors. These professional money managers look for corporations that:

- Have a large floating supply of stock with enough market value and trading volume to support orderly accumulation or liquidation of block positions. They want to be able to trade thousands of shares without unduly upsetting the market: to buy steadily at relatively stable prices, to sell quickly without triggering sharp price declines.
- Have a publicly owned equity investment large enough to warrant the degree, and cost, of analysis and evaluation necessary for sound investing of large sums.

To the individual who buys and sells a few hundred shares, such liquidity may seem unimportant. Not so. When the supply of stock is limited, unusual volume can cause sharp gyrations in the marketplace. This is rewarding when the move is up but can be disastrous when it's down. Without sufficient liquidity, there will not be enough major investors ready to support the stock when an unjustified decline starts. *Proof:* the erratic movement of preferred stocks, with few shares and limited liquidity, with shifts of two or three points from one trade to the next.

In the determination of investment acceptance, there are subcategories:

MARKET VALUE

This is what investors believe the company is worth. It is calculated on two bases:

1. *Total market value.* The number of outstanding shares multiplied by the average annual price of the stock over the past three years.

2. *Public market value.* The same multiplication after the deduction of all shares known to be closely held. *Example:* XYZ Corporation has 25,000,000 shares of common stock outstanding, with 3% (750,000 shares) closely held. The average market price for the stock, 1983–85, was 80.6.

Thus, the total market value was $2,015,000,000: 25,000,000 × 80.6. The public market value was $1,954,550,000.

These values must extend over three years. In the 1960s and to some degree in 1986, when shares of many marginal firms were selling at superprices, their market values were temporarily over $100 million but, in reality, they will still be $25 million corporations.

For quality investments, the minimum market value of all outstanding shares should total $100 million for industrial corporations, and $50 million for banks and insurance firms. Generally, however, these standards are flexible. With Kellogg Company, where 35% of the common stock is held by a foundation, the public market value has been as low as $91 million, but, as the value of its shares rose, Kellogg met all quality standards.

A corollary consideration is the maximum, safe, manageable investment level. On the basis of experience, WIS sets this at 2.5% of the readily available outstanding common shares. Above that percentage, it becomes difficult to accumulate or to sell shares without substantially affecting the stock price.

With the mythical XYZ Corporation, this would be 606,250 shares or a total investment, for all funds under WIS control, of $488,637.

In effect, this standard limits WIS holdings primarily to shares of corporations listed on the NYSE. However, it also permits investments in a handful of small companies traded on the AMEX and an even smaller number on the Over-The-Counter market when there are a number of brokers making a market for the stock so that prices are competitive, with narrow spreads between bid and asked quotations.

TRADING VOLUME

What is required here is a minimum average total of shares traded annually, expressed in dollars. To be specific, the security must trade an average of at least $50 million per year over three years. For XYZ, this means 4,752,000 shares traded overall, averaging 1,168,000 shares a year or about 600 shares per trading day. This requirement may be reduced for stocks whose market values are well above minimum standards.

Corollary to this is a moderate turnover rate: less than 50% of outstanding shares annually during the last three years.

OWNERSHIP

Three thousand shareholders of 100 shares or more, including institutional investors (mutual funds, insurance companies, bank trust funds, pension and profit-sharing plans, and foundations) as shown in Table 1-2. *N.B.* With the proliferation of mutual funds (one a day recently), these figures should probably be higher.

The investment standards of some of these professional organizations may not be as high nor as strict as those of Wright Investors' Service, but they all set criteria for stocks to be eligible for their approved lists, buy and sell thousands of shares at a clip, and, because of their fiduciary responsibilities, tend to concentrate on stocks of companies with good management records. But, of course, there are exceptions, primarily those professionals who try tricky tactics or become involved in self-serving situations. *Caveat emptor.*

CLOSELY HELD SHARES

Generally, the maximum ownership by one investor or group should be 35%. It's a plus when a fair amount of stock, say 15% to 20%, is held by officers and directors. You know then that management has a positive stake in the performance of the company.

TURNOVER RATE

This is the percentage of outstanding shares which are exchanged during a year based on a three-year average. Use this formula:

$$TR = \frac{TV}{N}$$

TR = the turnover rate

TV = the trading volume per year

N = the number of shares outstanding

Example: Upjohn Company, the drug firm, reported a three-year trading average of 27,978,000 shares or an annual volume of about 9.3 million. Since the outstanding shares totaled 31 million, the TR was 30%.

The acceptable range for annual turnover should be between 25% and 35%. When it's much higher, the stock is becoming a speculation, not an investment.

Unusual stock market activity in a stock is a warning signal, especially when it's a continuing trend. Something—good or bad—is happening. Very light trading volume in one stock when most others are active may mean a change in the direction of the price movement.

In any case, wait for confirmation. With rumors of takeovers or corporate restructuring, almost anything is possible these days.

STOCK EXCHANGE LISTING

Preferably, a quality stock should be listed on the New York Stock Exchange. There are, however, many excellent corporations, notably banks, bank holding companies, and insurance firms, whose stocks are actively traded on regional stock exchanges or OTC (Over The Counter).

For investors, there are definite advantages with NYSE-listed stocks:

- A ready market is available in that an experienced, well-financed specialist stands ready to buy or sell the stock at all times.
- Full data on prices and volume are published after each trading day.
- All corporations must meet and maintain rigid stock exchange standards of financial soundness and broad public ownership and adhere to full reporting rules.
- Complete, accurate information is readily available: on the company, through regular financial reports; on insider transactions, from corporate officers, directors, and major shareholders.

- Stockholders' rights are protected through the rules of membership on the exchange.

Listing on the Big Board is no guarantee of quality, but it's a good place to start looking for investment opportunities.

At this time, the minimum requirements for NYSE listing are:

- Demonstrated earning power of either $2.5 million before federal income taxes for the most recent year and $2 million pretax for each of the preceding two years, or an aggregate, for the last three fiscal years, of $6.5 million together with a minimum of $4.5 million for the most recent fiscal year.
- Market value of publicly owned shares between a minimum of $9 million and a maximum of $10 million, depending on market conditions.
- A total of 1.1 million common shares publicly held.
- Either 2,000 holders of 100 shares or more or 2,200 stockholders plus average monthly trading volume, for the most recent six months, of 100,000 shares.

If a member company fails to continue to meet basic conditions, it is subject to delisting.

On the other hand, when a high percentage of shares is closely held (and this applies primarily to smaller corporations), it's wise to be cautious. Decisions may not always be in the best interests of public shareholders. The controlling family may include a number of older people who want high dividends, thus limiting funds for corporate reinvestment for growth. Or the individuals may be in such high tax brackets that they prefer to hold down dividend payouts.

With all companies with closely held shares, there is:

- The chance that a large block of stock may be brought to market and thus depress the stock price.
- The probability that the shares will sell at multiples lower than those of competitors with wide public ownership.

- The possibility of a takeover so that there may be a quick run-up of the stock price.

These days, with so many takeovers by Wall Street promoters, who shoot only for fast gains and use costly junk bonds that almost mandate divestitures, it's difficult to be sure that stocks of some companies are worthwhile, long-term investments. The solace is that usually the shares will command a probably unwarranted (but welcome) premium.

Financial Strength

A quality corporation must be financially strong. That means a sound, uncomplicated capital structure not subject to substantial dilution, no excessive debt, and adequate working funds to permit management to make investments and acquisitions.

These criteria rule out many small firms whose prospects may be bright but which have limited resources and whose financing has been primarily by debt, either directly or through convertible securities. In the financial world, quality has to be earned.

Specifically, financial strength represents the amount and availability of the corporation's resources in relation to the current and potential requirements as measured by the following criteria.

$$\frac{\text{COMMON SHAREHOLDERS' EQUITY}}{\text{CAPITAL INVESTMENT AT CORPORATE BOOK VALUE}}$$

This translates in dollars to a minimum of $50 million; in percentages—as a ratio to total capital (the total of the value of the common and preferred stock plus long-term debt)—for most corporations, 50%; for utilities, 30%; for financial firms, 25%; and for transportation companies, 45% to 60%.

These varying percentages reflect the type of industry. They are lower for utilities because they require huge investments in plant and equipment; and for transportation companies, such as railroads and airlines, because their equipment is usually leased or acquired under mortgage agreements.

LONG-TERM DEBT TO TOTAL CAPITAL

For industrials, this should not exceed 40%; for utilities, 60%; for financial companies, 70%; and for transportation firms, 35% to 50%. Or to put these ratios in another form: quality corporations should have no more than $4 debt for each $6 equity and for each $10 total capital.

Both of these figures are reference points and will vary widely between types of corporations. They are low for drug firms, high for utilities, and may be modified for companies that require large facilities, are highly profitable, and/or have strong working capital.

A substantial portion of the money available to management should be furnished by the owners of the business, not by lenders.

By definition, quality corporations have limited debt so that there is no doubt as to the ability of the organization to fulfill financial obligations. But it is important to watch the direction of that debt ratio. Usually, this will decline over the years, but if it rises, it's time to recheck and, probably, lower the quality rating. It is also important to view debt in relation to corporate liquidity and profitability.

Example: Dow Chemical Co. has been on and off the Approved Wright Investment List over the years. The problem has been management's policy of financing expansion and acquisitions with debt. Dow is a highly profitable company but that alone is not, and never should be, the dominant factor in determining quality.

Low debt, with minimal interest payments, affects earnings more than financial strength. A company with a 40% debt ratio and a current ratio (current assets to current liabilities) of 2:1 is on the edge of acceptability. But a long-term debt ratio of 41% with a current ratio of 5:1 is OK.

Examples: Barry Wright, Inc., a manufacturer of supplies for computers and information media, has a low current ratio of 3:1 and a 1.5% debt to equity ratio: $1.6 million debt versus $107.9 million common equity. Very favorable.

Duke Power Co., a profitable utility in an industry where current ratio is not significant, has a 43% ratio of debt to equity: long-term debt of $2,721 million and preferred stock of $696.6 million with common equity of $2,932.4 million.

N.B. If you want to speculate with nonquality stocks, watch out when the company's long-term debt is over 75% of equity. A small stumble in profits can mean a serious drop in earnings and will leave little money to pay interest and amortization and probably nothing for stockholders. In the 1980s when soaring interest rates created a credit crunch and liquidity crisis, many debt-laden corporations got into dire trouble. The values of both their bonds and common stocks fell sharply.

On the other hand, in prosperous times, heavy debt can provide leverage. After mandated payments, most of the remaining income goes directly to shareholders. Securities of such corporations are *always* speculations, not investments.

Be especially wary when convertible securities are involved. As a guideline, stay away from any stocks of any company where, if a conversion should be made, the reduction in profits will be greater than 15%. Such situations must be examined carefully because, when the debt becomes equity, interest is no longer paid so that the overall corporate financial strength may be improved.

SPECIAL RATIOS FOR SPECIAL INDUSTRIES

With financially oriented corporations, there are different ratios reflecting their methods of financing and the fact that their operations are influenced or controlled by government. Banks and bank holding companies have ready access to additional funds from Federal Reserve banks and their capital includes the following deposits: *short-term,* such as demand deposits and certificates of deposit; *medium-term,* that is, time certificates for up to eight years; *long-term,* that is, debentures maturing in ten or twenty years. These make it possible for the bank to conduct its business of transferring money.

Here are standards for banks and bank holding companies:

- Common stockholders' equity: a minimum of 65% of total capital and 3.5% of total assets
- Total capital, at least 6% of total deposits
- Cash and securities including amounts due from other banks, 40% of total deposits
- Loan losses, net of recoveries, no more than 0.35% of total loans outstanding in the most recent fiscal year or the average of the last three or five years.

Fixed charge coverage ratio. This indicates how adequately the profits cover the payments for debt obligations. It is computed as a ratio of pretax income to the total of all interest, amortization, and dividends on the preferred stock. Minimum ratios: 3.5:1 for industrial/service corporations, 2:1 for utilities, and 2.5:1 for transportation companies.

Now do you see why some of the best-known companies—most airlines, almost all steel firms, and conglomerates that rely on junk bonds—do not qualify for a quality rating?

With most professionals, these standards are flexible in that when a quality company makes an acquisition that boosts its debt too high, they sell the shares and remove it from their recommended list but keep reviewing its progress. If the expansion works well and the cash flow is sufficient to lower the loans, the company may regain its rating and eventually become a buy recommendation.

In making calculations, WIS pays attention to the effects of possible dilution from the exercise of options and warrants and the conversion of securities. By and large, quality companies do not have to resort to such kickers but there are notable exceptions: K-Mart and IBM, for example. The maximum expansion of outstanding common shares is 30%, and the dilution of earnings

15% per common share. *Exceptions:* (1) when the company consistently reports results on a fully converted basis; (2) when the potential earnings increase, made possible by the additional paid-in capital, computed at no more than the current profit rate, will be sufficient to offset dilution resulting from more shares.

With utilities, a broader standard is used because of their heavy reliance on debt financing. The ratio of annual dividends paid to shareholders to total corporate cash flow, before payment of common dividends, should be at least 2.5:1. This measures the coverage of annual dividends by cash flow: the sum of after-tax income available to the common stocks plus depreciation, net deferred taxes, and other miscellaneous cash income. The higher this ratio, the greater the ability of the company to fund new capital expenditures internally. A utility that distributes 50% of its earnings will have a lot more money for new plants than one that pays out over 70%.

Working capital is the money the company has to conduct and expand its business. This is expressed as a ratio of current assets to current liabilities and should be 2:1. That means that, if all bills are paid, the shareholders will own half of the current assets.

Realistically, the ratio varies according to the type of business. Corporations dealing in large, expensive products such as automobiles or heavy machinery have a high ratio: for Sunstrand Corporation, 2.6:1. Distribution companies, such as Albertson's, the supermarket chain, with a cash, fast turnover business, have low ratio, 1.6:1. Defense firms have receivables almost equivalent to cash as they can count on progress payments under their government contracts. And, of course, the ratios are not important for financial institutions which are in the money business. To be rated quality, a company must have ample ready dollar resources.

Summary

Financial strength is a key factor in quality investments. In many cases, the best common stocks are those of companies which have little or no debt. Then, the shareholders own everything and almost always can count on a substantial share of all profits.

Still, lack of debt may not be a mark of quality if management is overly conservative and not willing to expand as rapidly as it could with borrowed funds. Smart managers maintain a judicious balance between debt and equity capital.

Profitability and Stability

Of the four basic criteria for quality, profitability and stability are "first among equals." Profitability is the objective of corporate organizers. They invest money—their own and that of friends and associates—in anticipation of ever-higher returns from increased dividends and rising values of the securities of the enterprise.

PROFITABILITY

Profitability measures the record of corporate management: (1) the rate and consistency of net return on shareholders' equity capital investment at corporate book value; (2) the profits/losses of the company during generally advancing economic periods and thus the ability to withstand adverse financial developments.

Without continuing profits, there can be no sustained growth, financial strength, or investment acceptance. *The single most important factor in successful investing is* ***profitability***.

STABILITY

Stability is essential for long-term investments. Investors will always pay more for shares of a corporation with a history of steady, sustained earnings growth than for stocks of one with the same average rate of growth but with year-to-year profits subject to cyclical variations.

There will be temporary lapses when overenthusiasm due to actual or anticipated earnings will send the price of a stock to a record high or an unrealistic low. Over the years, however, the shares of a corporation with a consistent upward trend of profits will always command a higher multiple than those of erratic moneymakers. *The best stocks are those of companies that make the most money year after year.*

Profitability can be determined and checked easily by the amateur investor. Stability is more difficult to calculate and judge, but the broad outlines will become evident from a review of the corporate results over a period of time.

Calculating the Profit Rate

The profit rate (PR) is also known as the return on equity (ROE). It measures the ability of corporate management in terms of the rate of return on shareholders' equity capital investment at corporate book value: the assets back of each share of common stock. The figure can be found in most annual reports and usually is shown over several years in the summary at the back.

Think of it this way: each January, you and other stockholders give the directors and officers of the corporation X number of dollars. At year's end, the profits per share are Y dollars. The measure of profitability is the percentage of return on the initial investment.

To calculate the PR, divide the earnings per share of common stock by the per share book value of that common stock at the beginning of the year. The result is expressed:

$$PR = \frac{P}{BV}$$

PR = Profit Rate

P = Profit per common share for the last reported year

BV = Net value of the total assets of the company, i.e., what is left after all liabilities, including bonds and preferred stock, are subtracted

Example: in 1985, American Home Products, a diversified drug/food manufacturer, started the year with a per share book value of $13.70. It earned $4.70 per share. The PR was 34.3%.

$$PR = \frac{4.70}{13.70} = 34.3\%$$

This was a very high rate of return in equity as the same figures for the S&P 500 Stock Composite were: profit per share, $14.93; book value, $115, for a PR of 13%.

A high PR is a starting point for a high quality rating but it must be maintained fairly well during both prosperous and recessive periods. By measuring the trend and consistency of the corporation's PR, the investor can avoid unacceptable risks with shares of corporations with marginally competent or ineffectual management which thus are vulnerable to economic downturns and adverse developments.

Under WIS standards, the unadjusted PR should average, over ten years, at least 11%, i.e, net after-tax earnings of 11¢ on each $1 of equity. This figure is flexible. It may be reduced (but not below 8%) for companies in regulated industries such as utilities, for finance companies, and insurance firms, and then only (1) when the company's average PR has been at least equal to that of similar corporations in the same industry, or (2) when there have been temporary situations beyond the control of management, or (3) as part of reorganization.

Example: PepsiCo, Inc., was retained on the Wright Approved Investment List in 1982–83–84 when the company's PR dropped from 20.7% in 1981 to 13.8%, 16.7%, and 11.2%, respectively, due to a major corporate restructuring that involved a new distribution system and sale of several subsidiaries. The important investment considerations were confidence in management and the long-term trend. Patience paid off as the stock, adjusted for a split, moved from around 15 to over 35 in 1986.

For most investors, the straight PR is a valuable guideline, but for greater accuracy and reliability, Wright calculates the corporate PR on a time-weighted basis and makes adjustments for cyclical variations and trends. The PR target is still 11% annually, but this is modified by computer calculations to take into account the effects of economic downturns, temporary industry depressions, and other factors that inhibited management's moneymaking ability.

To repeat: always watch the trend of the profit rate. This should show no significant decline in any one year unless there has been an equal or greater decline for comparable companies in the same industry. An ever-lowering return on equity is a warning signal: for two years, it flashes yellow and for three consecutive years, red, after which it usually will no longer be a worthwhile investment (at which time a professional money manager like Wright would remove it from the A List).

Here again, there's flexibility when the company continues to earn a high rate of return. With Dun & Bradstreet, the PR fell from 30.5% in 1984 to 24.1% in 1985. But such profitability was still so rewarding that most shares were held, although no new purchases were made.

Similarly, when there are two companies with the same average profitability for the past decade and one has been improving over the last three years while the other has been declining, the uptrending corporation would be favored over the downtrender regardless of other factors such as price/earnings ratios:

	Profit Rate		
Company	1983	1984	1985
Winn-Dixie	20.8%	19.4%	17.3%
Kroger Co.	11.7	14.6	16.0

Curiously, these trends must have been missed by many investors because the price of WIN rose 56% (from 25 to 39) while that of KR went up only 41% (from 34 to 48). But, for my money, KR was a far wiser investment.

STABILITY INDEX

This shows the stability of the PR in relation to that of the overall stock market, that is, whether the profitability of the corporation is more or less volatile than that of other NYSE securities. The minimum percentage, for Wright standards, is 60% for approved companies, 76% for the S&P 500.

That means that to qualify as or to be retained for a quality stock, the company's earnings must not decline more than 40% below the overall average. This stability index is calculated on an inverse basis.

Example: in 1985, corporate profits, after taxes, fell about 10%—from $16.64 billion to $14.93 billion. Any corporation whose earnings fell by more than 14% (40% more than the average) was no longer classified as a quality investment.

Here again, you must be realistic. Wright makes exceptions for circumstances beyond management's direct control.

In calculating the stability index, Wright uses complex formulas that involve deviation of earnings over ten years and conversion of the percentage of depreciation to reach a number from 0 to 100. Obviously, the higher the stability index, the more stable and thus the more attractive, for investment, is the corporation. This refers to profit stability, not stock market stability (or its converse, volatility).

Here are ratings of typical companies:

	Stability Index	
Company	Earnings	Market Price
AMP, Inc.	71%	75%
Dayton-Hudson Corp.	91	69
Hilton Hotels	75	74
K-Mart Corporation	74	75
Merck & Company	95	82
Wal-Mart Stores	92	53

NORMAL CASH DIVIDEND PAYOUT

This is the percentage of profits distributed to common shareholders. Generally, this should be at least 10% but not more than 75%. The minimum may be waived when: (1) the omission of significant cash dividends is a deliberate corporate policy designed to finance corporate growth rather than an action forced by the necessity of conserving working capital; (2) the high dividend payout: (a) does not indicate any reduction in financial strength such as if the company continued to pay out more than its current profits per share, (b) does not indicate any weakness in management's objectives and ability to achieve continuing corporate growth—if the company used bookkeeping changes to boost reported earnings, (c) appears justified in view of future corporate prospects despite a temporary decline in profits during cyclical periods or when there were strikes or disastrous events.

Example: Schlumberger, Ltd., the oil supply/electronics firm, raised its dividend from $1.12 to $1.20 per share in 1985 even though its earnings plummeted from $4.10 to $1.17 per share.

OPERATING INCOME AS PERCENTAGE OF TOTAL CAPITAL

This shows the pretax dollars earned on total invested capital. It's a variation of the profit rate designed to take into account the differing rates of federal taxation. This should average at least 15% but may be reduced to not less than 10%: (1) when the corporate tax rate is significantly less than 50% because of continuing tax benefits (as distinguished from tax-loss carry forwards); (2) when both the rate and stability of earnings growth have been clearly superior to those of similar companies in its industry.

N.B. This will probably become more significant under the Tax Reform Act because the corporate tax rate will be uniform and less subject to special credits. These revisions will impact especially on low- and nonquality corporations.

Summary

These detailed criteria may appear overwhelming to amateur investors but they are important tools for professionals. You may not be able to make all of these calculations, but you can understand trends and recognize the type of information which is so important in determining investment quality.

Successful money management requires far more than a glib report on corporate prospects which are usually more enthusiastic than factual. The time to pick winners and spot losers is long before Wall Street starts to spread its prejudiced word.

In investing, you are competing with professionals who often have access to inside information long before it becomes available to the general public. For most amateurs, this disadvantage can be offset by careful investigation of the trends of corporate performance and policy as shown by profitability and stability. To a large extent, the collection and interpretation of such data is the mark of a successful money manager. Most of the facts are available in corporate reports if you take the time to look for them and relate them to past performances and future prospects.

Watch Out for Significant Changes

Quality cannot be taken for granted. It must be monitored constantly to catch new trends, to judge how the nature of the company may be affected by internal events such as managerial changes, especially when there are interruptions in the regular process of succession of management such as the hiring of a new chief executive.

This subject doesn't come under any specific quality category, but it is very important. When you invest, you are buying management. IBM is a marvelous example of executive succession. There are always a dozen competent, experienced executives ready for every top position. The passage of power is made smoothly and quietly without upsetting the market price of the stock.

By contrast, Wang Labs and Burroughs Corp. (not a quality

company) have never built such administrative strength. The first is controlled by one man with no heir apparent other than family members; the second had to go outside to find a new CEO.

Whenever any major corporation does not promote one of its own people to the top executive post, it's a sign of managerial weakness, a shift in underlying control, or dissatisfaction on the part of controlling stockholders.

There are, of course, times when outsiders can be beneficial, but when this occurs, go slow and do not buy the stock until the new executive has proven him/herself.

Moving into New Fields

Another time to be wary is when the company goes outside the scope of its established business: a steel corporation buying an oil firm, a utility taking over a drug chain, and so on. Such action will alter the character of the corporation and be a real test for management.

No matter how successful a company has been in one area, it will take four or five years for the top executives to learn the new business. There are situations where the old management will be retained and may even become dominant in the acquiring firm but, generally, ventures into unfamiliar areas are not successful . . . at least, not for a while. That's why only a handful of conglomerates, all well-established firms with a long record of proven profitability and growth, ever become top-quality companies.

That doesn't mean that there have not been exceptions. Emhart Corp. was a medium-size hardware manufacturer which moved up to the billion-dollar class by acquisitions in specialty machinery, fasteners, and electronics. Initially, the results were good: from 1975 to 1977, a sharp rise in profitability, from 12.9% to 18% to 22%. Then came trouble. In 1979, the ROE dropped to 13.9%, edged up to 16.5% in 1980, and for the next three years held at about 17%. The investor made a few points with EMH stock, but it took four years for worthwhile appreciation.

A major acquisition or shake-up of officers does not guarantee future corporate success. That your broker waxes enthusiastic or the news stories are glowing is not a sound reason to hurry to spend your money. Make 'em prove their ability!

Turnarounds

Turnarounds are always more difficult and take longer than anticipated. It's easy for newcomers to sell off losing divisions and make news headlines with their predictions, but the only true measure of corporate management is *performance*—the bottom-line results for at least two and preferably more years.

With major corporations, it takes months for outsiders to learn the business, to judge personnel, and to take actions that will reverse the downtrend in sales and profits. Never expect miracles in business. They do happen—Chrysler and International Harvester—but not often. And the amateur has no way of judging what is really taking place. Add luck and such speculations may be profitable.

Insider Transactions

These are better for speculations than investments. Under SEC rules, stock purchases or sales by corporate officers, directors, and individuals or groups holding substantial blocks of stock, must be reported. This information, available some weeks after the transactions, is published in the financial press and, in greater detail, in several advisory reports.

With investments, the number of insider deals is more important than the volume of shares involved. When the number of insiders buying continues to be greater than the number selling, chances are that there's good news ahead: an acquisition, unusually high profits, or a shift in corporate control. Vice versa when the majority of insiders are selling.

Either way, insider action is a signal that something is happening and should be investigated further when you are interested in the company. There may be legitimate reasons for such activity: the pressure of taxes, the need for estate planning, etc.

When the dollars involved are small and the transactions are made by second-tier executives, be cautious. Very few corporate officers make money *trading* in their company's stock. They may know the business, but predicting what will happen to the stock depends on the attitude of other investors, which may have little to do with corporate performance or prospects over the short term.

About the best one can say about insider transactions is that they add excitement to speculating. They are seldom significant with investments, which by definition are long-term holdings.

Quality Corporations in Trouble

Even the best companies have problems now and then. Some are due to management mistakes (the lethargy of Xerox in failing to meet Japanese competition), new methods of marketing (Great Atlantic & Pacific Tea Co.), and governmental policies (deregulations of airlines and trucking). And in a few cases they are the result of pressures beyond management's control: hurricanes that down utility lines, floods that halt production, international crises such as the terrorist attacks that crimped European air travel.

Most corporate declines, however, are due to management's mistakes or at least to their lack of prescience: the failure to establish proper financial controls, to react quickly, and to act firmly.

With major corporations whose revenues and profits can be

checked, trouble will be signaled well before there's a drop in the price of the stock. With some companies, the alert investor should spot the trend from personal observation: the auto industry, with its oversize, overpriced cars losing out to foreign competition; the cigarette companies, faced with strong public concern about smoking causing cancer; oil companies when the price of gasoline plummeted.

Financial troubles are more difficult to spot but usually are signaled well before there's a decline in the price of the stock. The earnings will be erratic, the financial strength will be diminished, or the industry prospects clouded.

The first signs will probably involve accounting: shifting the method of reporting to boost current income; i.e., a utility reporting a 27¢ per share rise in net profits, with 14¢ of that gain the result of a new billing policy whereby management included income from services billed but not yet rendered; and an industrial corporation accelerating depreciation to improve cash flow, etc. Time to be cautious and, probably, to consider selling the stock.

Next, there will probably be a corporate restructuring—getting rid of a subsidiary, selling and leasing back the headquarters buildings—or defeasance: discharging debts without actually paying them off prior to maturity. For example, the company arranges for a broker to buy a portion of the outstanding bond issue at the lower-than-par market price. The broker then exchanges the bonds for a new issue of corporate stock with a market value equal to that of the bonds and sells the shares at a profit. The corporate balance sheet is improved without harming operations or prospects. Finally, the company reports an after-tax gain because the debt was paid off at less than face value.

Another popular tactic is to shift excess assets from the corporate pension fund to the company. This is possible because, with the recent high investment yields and reduced work forces, many pension funds have more than ample reserves. The transfer provides the company with welcome cash and adds substantially to "reported" earnings.

These actions may be beneficial to the corporation, but they should always be viewed with skepticism and considered in relation to the total financial analysis. A one-shot deal will probably be a smart management decision, but when similar revisions occur among subsidiaries, watch out. The best companies make their money by operations, not manipulations.

Summary

This has been a long and detailed chapter. Some of the material/methods are beyond the scope of the amateur investor, but they are included to stress the complexity of truly professional security analysis and as a warning against the glib commentaries from the research departments of many brokerage firms and the majority of market letters. Quality is relatively rare, applicable to only 400 to 500 corporations, about 10% of widely traded stocks.

Note, too, that the fact that a company deserved a quality rating at one point is no guarantee that this superior appellation will be continued. Here are some companies that were highly rated in 1978 but are no longer on the Approved Wright Investment List (or similar compilations of successful professional money managers): AT&T, Black & Decker, General Motors, Gulf Oil, Johns Manville, Long Island Lighting, Petrolane, Revlon, Safeway Stores, Texaco, and Union Carbide.

On the other hand, some corporations have continued their profitable growth: AMP, Inc., Coca Cola, Emerson Electric, Lilly (Eli), Lubrizol, Merck & Co., and Raytheon, to name a few.

At times, these stocks should have been sold, but soon they became buy candidates, as shown by examples throughout the text. For successful investing, the key is quality.

Chapter 2

VALUE: HOW TO JUDGE AND COMPARE

Value is the second most important factor in successful investing. It spotlights the range in which a stock should be bought or sold, thus providing the basis for investment profits within a finite period of time.

Quality is always the most important criterion for the long run; timing is the most useful for the short term; value is in between. With quality, there should be few mistakes; with value, there can be many errors if the facts are incorrect, no longer relevant, or improperly interpreted.

Value indicates whether or not, and to what extent, a stock is likely to advance or decline from its present price. The projections should be limited to three years and reviewed periodically. For a stock to be regarded as an attractive value, the returns of appreciation and income should be +35% to +50% within twenty-four to thirty months in a normal market; twelve to eighteen months in bull periods.

Value is relative. It can be measured by ratios, current and future, of the stock price to per share earnings, dividends, equity capital and revenues.

Price/Earnings Ratio

This is the current price of the stock divided by the earnings per share, usually for the past twelve months but sometimes for the profits estimated for the current fiscal year. Thus, if a stock trades at 20 and the reported earnings for the past year are $2.00, the P/E ratio is 10. When the time of the calculation is October and the corporate year ends in December with estimated earnings of $2.50 per share, the P/E ratio will be 8.

The P/E ratio reflects the attitude of investors and shows how many dollars they are willing to pay for each dollar of profits. In depression periods, the average P/E for NYSE-listed stocks was under 10; in normal markets, it ranges from 10 to 12; in bull markets, it rises to between 14 and 16. For the Standard & Poor's 500 Stock Composite, here are the high and low multiples:

1976–80	9.1–7.4	1985	14–11
1981–84	11–9.0	mid-1986	16–14

These multiples vary widely according to industry groups because investors are willing to pay more for stocks in highly profitable and/or fast-growing businesses and less for those in pedestrian/low-profit enterprises. In mid-1986, for example, when the overall range was 16–14, these were the P/Es for some major groups:

	P/E Ratio Based on Earnings of:	
Industry	Last 12 Months	Next 12 Months
Beverages	19	17
Chemicals	19	15
Drugs	20	18
Electronics	20	15
Financial	11	10
Oil/Gas	11	10
Recreation/restaurants	24	21
Retailers	21	17
Utilities	11	10

The differences were even more pronounced with specific stocks. With retailers:

	P/E Ratio Based on Earnings of:	
Company	Last 12 Months	Next 12 Months
K-Mart	13	12
Melville Corp.	14	13
Wal-Mart Stores	36	28
Walgreen Co.	20	18

These figures show why value in stocks must be judged in a broad context: vs. similar data in the same industry and, then versus data for the overall market. Aberrations indicate temporary investor attitudes: usually negative when the P/E ratio is below the average; positive when it's above.

Generally, be slow to invest in any stock with a multiple below 8; buy when it's 10–12; check your research when it's over 20; and hardly ever buy when it's over 30. *Note:* I said, "be slow," not "don't."

The P/E ratio can also be valuable in comparisons of:

1. Stocks within an industry group. With electronics in mid-1986, the multiples were AMP, 30; Hewlett-Packard, 22; IBM, 14; Perkin-Elmer, 18; and Raytheon, 14. To a degree, each of these quality companies has different products, but in stock market terms they can be grouped together. Check the ratios in another six months and there may be sharp differences.

2. *Two similar companies.* With Melville Corp. (MES), the P/E was 14 while that of Wal-Mart Stores (WMT) was 36. MES had a return on equity of 22.5%; WMY, 33.8%. To investors, the higher price of WMT was justified by the higher profitability. The price of its stock (adjusted for a split) rose from a low of 11 in 1983 to a high of 53 in 1986; or +380%. In the same period, MES shares increased in value about half as much, from 30 to 73.

Price/Equity Ratio

This is widely used by professionals to check the value of the stock in relation to the value of the corporate assets. Calculation of the price/equity ratio requires two formulas:

$$\frac{CE}{S} = E \qquad \begin{aligned} CE &= \text{Common equity in dollars} \\ S &= \text{Number of common shares} \\ E &= \text{Equity per share} \end{aligned}$$

A good example of its use is with PepsiCo, Inc., before and after its restructuring in 1985–86.

In February 1985, the figures were CE, $1.803,300,000 and S, $93,900,000, so the formula was $1.803 divided by 90,300 to make E equal $19.20 per share. The stock was at 42 ¾.

In April 1986, the data were CE, $1.950,400,000 and S, 90,300,000, so the E was $21.60. PEP stock was at 85 ¾.

The second formula determines the price/equity ratio:

$$PE = \frac{P}{E} \qquad \begin{aligned} PE &= \text{price/equity ratio} \\ P &= \text{price of the stock} \\ E &= \text{equity per share} \end{aligned}$$

$$\underline{1985} \qquad\qquad \underline{1986}$$

$$\frac{42.75}{19.20} = 2.23\% \qquad \frac{85.75}{21.60} = 3.97\%$$

By this checkpoint, PEP stock was undervalued in 1985 and well, if not fully, valued, in 1986.

The key factor is the value of the stock as set by investors. In 1985 they were willing to pay more than twice the net worth per share: the net assets behind each share of stock after subtracting liabilities. That's a high price *unless* there are good prospects for continued high growth, primarily of profits. Of course, a strong market helps.

Back in the boom years of the late 1960s, IBM stock sold at a price/equity ratio of 9.6 because of the company's proven ability and continuing bright prospects to boost sales and profits. As investors began to question Big Blue's ability to maintain such progress in the face of rising competition, the price of its stock fell to more reasonable levels and the price/equity ratio dropped to 3.5.

For most companies, the price/equity ratio is seldom over 1.0. In the 1975–85 period, for the DJIA, it was 1.1. In booming 1986, it rose to 2.0.

The price/equity ratio can be valuable for comparisons between current and past prices if: (1) the profitability and growth are little changed, (2) the ratio is adjusted for basic shifts of the corporation, (3) a further readjustment is made for the ratios of the overall market.

Price/Dividend Ratio (P/D)

This is another double-check, most useful in choosing between similar stocks. It measures the price which investors are willing to pay for each dollar of cash dividends. It is calculated by dividing the price of the stock by the payout per share; i.e., Duke Power, at 41, with a $2.60 per year dividend, has a P/D of 15.8; Southwestern Energy, 9.3; Tucson Electric, 18.2.

For income stocks, especially those that pay out most of their earnings, the P/D can indicate stability. Only when the future outlook is favorable are companies with long records of rising dividends less likely to cut payouts during periods of lower earnings and more likely to raise dividends judiciously.

Companies that pay high dividends that are not always backed by better profits have high P/Ds until management builds a more balanced policy. Their stocks move slowly and are stable only because of flat earnings. Arkla, Inc., is a good example.

With growth companies, the P/D is not significant. Ratios will be very low, but the changes will mark the upward trend in value.

Price/Revenues Ratio (PRR)

This ratio, the market price of the stock divided by the sales or revenues per share, is a favorite of Kenneth Fisher, a well-known and successful analyst. It measures the popularity of the stock. If the company has sales of $100 million and 5 million shares of common stock, the per share sales are $20. If the current price of the stock is 15, the PRR is .75. Usually, a stock can be a good buy when that ratio is under 1.0; a poor choice when it is over 1.5.

The PRR spots stocks of good companies when they are undervalued. When that ratio is low, good news will be translated into higher prices. When the PRR is high, it indicates that the stock is temporarily popular and probably that its price discounts future growth too much. Because there is no distinction between high and low profit margins, this ratio works best with technology companies.

Before getting into categories of value, let's review what we are talking about. Value is not precise nor verifiable. It's a matter of opinion as to the relation of the current price of a security to that projected for the future. For every buyer who thinks a stock is undervalued, there's a seller who thinks its overvalued or at least has poor prospects. In Wall Street jargon, the definition is more complex: "The current price of a stock represents the discounted value of its expected future cash returns: the future stream of dividends and sales price, discounted by the risk-free return on money plus an appropriate premium for risk."

Value is not always what it appears to be. A stock that has been trading at 50 drops to 25. The *true* value has not changed; the difference is in perception. Some institutions have lost confidence in the future of the corporation; they want out. But, at the same time, some other folks bought because they visualized future gains.

These comments get us back to the importance of quality in determining value. All projections of earnings are subject to interpretation and in some cases to manipulation. With quality corporations, profits are real. With speculative, promotion-minded managers, those earnings can be inflated with special adjustments: shift of depreciation policies, inclusion of onetime gains, over-optimistic assumptions, etc. Not all of these are improper, but they distort the true value—unless someone digs beneath the news releases.

Types of Value

To add to the complexity of the analysis and use of value, there are different types based on different data and/or time frames. These are the cores of professional research and are included here to show how complex value can be.

CURRENT VALUE

This is the frame of reference of the ratios outlined earlier. Primarily, they involve recent and current criteria and are most useful for immediate decisions, but they seldom provide the information needed to determine long-term worth.

HISTORIC VALUE

This is identical to current value except that the calculations are based on the past spot or average relationships between corporate value criteria (earnings, dividend, and equity book value) and market price. They are most useful to determine comparatively superior or inferior value. Typically, they cover a period of five or ten years.

Example: a current P/E ratio of 7 versus a ten-year average of 14 would usually be thought of as indicating a 50% reduction in the price per dollar of earnings and therefore a sharp shift in investment value. Such an interpretation may represent the opposite of conclusions reached after a more complete evaluation.

In the 1960s–70s, interest rates doubled and the P/E of the S&P 500 declined from a ten-year average of 17 to 10–7. For a proper calculation, the 1960–69 P/E would have to be reduced in proportion to the lower average multiple (about 50%, from 14 to 7) before there could be a viable comparison with the stock's current P/E of 7.

Even then, the comparison might be misleading if the company had become less profitable. This requires a further adjustment to reduce the P/E in proportion to the decline of the stock's return on equity for, say, the last three years, i.e., an average rate of 8% versus 12% for the base period. This would shrink the historic 1960–69 average P/E (already adjusted to 7 from 14) to 4.6. Thus, the current P/E of 7 would indicate that the stock was a poor value in comparison to its adjusted P/E ratio in the past.

HISTORIC VALUE WEIGHTED

This is a professional's extension that involves complex calculations that give greater emphasis to data of recent years than to those of the past. Wright Investors' Service uses a ten-year span with each succeeding year receiving 15% more weight than the prior year: year 2 has 15% more impact than year 1, etc.

In broad terms, here's how this works. Over the past decade, the P/E ratio for EZ-DOZ-IT has averaged 13, but because of the bear market, erratic profits, etc., the current multiple is only 6, a basic valuation of 2:1. In calculating value, the current P/E of 6 would have twice the weight as that of the ten-year average.

Such a comparison works best when the corporation maintains its original profitability and there have been only modest changes in interest rates. Otherwise, there must be adjustments to take into account the level of return expected by investors at this time; e.g., if yields rose 20% over the decade, the P/E ratio would be reduced by 20%. Well, it's not so complex with a computer!

STANDARD VALUE

This involves the factors that can be expected to apply to the values of the stocks of similar companies. The basic data include the average rate of change in earnings, profitability, dividend payout, and stability as shown by the consistency of performance by management.

These are compared with statistics for:

- All NYSE listed companies.
- Similar companies in the same industry. This will reflect investor prejudices: higher-than-average multiples for electronic firms, lower for stocks of food processors, and so on.
- The cyclical standards shown by corporations whose stock prices fluctuate according to market and economic conditions.
- Favored and unpopular groups at the time; e.g., in 1985, radio and TV broadcasting stocks were +71% while those of electronic systems companies were −11%.

These are difficult computations but once the base data has been computerized, comparisons are relatively easy so the standard value can be used for comparisons.

INTRINSIC VALUE

This is the oldest precept touted by professional analysts and investment book writers: that the intrinsic value of any stock is the sum of all future dividends discounted to the present. It's better for pontification than realistic use because it involves assumptions that may, or may not, continue to be valid:

Assumption 1. The corporation will not be able to maintain the same rate of dividend growth. The question then is when and how much this change will be.

Wright Investors' Service (WIS) takes the pessimistic view that every corporation, no matter how successful today, can be expected to become mediocre (or worse) in about fifty years. Surprisingly, such failures are more frequent than you may think. In my lifetime:

- Great Atlantic & Pacific Tea Co. was for many years *the* dominant food retailer. In the 1970s, after massive store closings, write-offs, and several reorganizations, it was barely solvent. By 1984, it was coming back, slowly.
- International Harvester was once number 1 in farm machinery; today, it's a fraction of its heyday size, has a new name, and is eking out a tiny profit.
- And who remembers stocks of such companies as National Airlines, Hobart Manufacturing, Sheraton Hotels, Howard Johnson, and Food Fair?

In calculating intrinsic value, WIS amortizes profitability, growth, and the percentage of dividend payout from the present rate of mediocrity at the same scale as those of the DJIA over the past fifty years: a normal return on equity of 11%, a dividend payout of 50% and a growth rate for earnings of +5% and for dividends of +5.2%.

Assumption 2. The price of the stock in the future will be at a mediocre multiple of dividends, again using the DJIA as a base. Over the half-century the average yield has been 4%, so the future, mediocre price is set at twenty-five times dividends (the reciprocal of 4%).

At any point between the time of the calculation and fifty years hence, the value of the stock will be proportional to the difference between the present multiple and that of the future.

Assumption 3. At some point it will be necessary to discount the dividend and thus the value of the stock. Forever is forever and you cannot properly compute something that never ends. WIS sets this date at thirty years: the life of a bond issued by the corporation. This time span is flexible and can be twenty-five years for some industries and forty years for utilities.

At the cutoff point the benchmark, for comparison, is a

stock value that is twenty-five times the dividends which can be expected to be paid at that time. This is discounted to the present at the same rate at which all dividends in the interim had been discounted to the present. This final discount factor is the current yield of the bond applied to the price of the stock thirty years from now and will show the current value of the stock in terms of its future potential. The future value of the dividends is then discounted on the basis that the stock will be sold at the same time the bond is redeemed.

The total discounted value of the stock (its future price) will be substantially greater than that of the bond. The total returns from a quality stock will always be greater than those from a debt security bought at the same time.

The point of reference for discounting is a rate that is about 4% higher than that of interest paid on bonds at the time; i.e., bond yields of 10% mean a discount factor of 14%.

Example: assuming that the normal price of the Dow Jones Industrial Average is 1500 but, at this time, it's 1290 (a 14% discount), the normal value of the stock would be determined by that same 14% figure.

PROJECTED VALUE

This is similar to current value except that the computations are based on the projected (five years hence) criteria. The differences are: (1) these data (such as earnings, dividends and book value) are converted to future market prices at their respective current, three-year-average P/Es, P/Ds, PR ratios, each adjusted for changes in profitability during the future period; (2) the actual rate of appreciation, from the current to projected price, plus dividend yield is then used as a measure of comparative value in itself or compared to the current yield to maturity of a bond maturing in five years or with the comparable projected return calculated for a market average.

None of these concepts/calculations of value are definitive. You cannot expect investors to suddenly adopt any one conclusion or even an average, but the comparisons provide a continuing frame of reference. They show the relation of the current stock price to specific values: 10% above the historical normal value, 20% below its intrinsic value, etc. When any stock is clearly below all of these values, it is selling below its true worth. There can be no guarantee that it will not fall lower, but eventually its price will rise and soon exceed those values.

Or vice versa: if a stock is priced well above any or all of these values, be cautious unless the profits are rising at a higher-than-traditional rate and the future is favorable for the company, the industry, and the economy.

To most readers, these explanations are interesting but not always usable. They are included to emphasize the complexity of thorough analysis and to explain the techniques used by successful money managers. Not all professionals go to such lengths in their research, but these are the techniques that make it possible for some major investors to continue to outperform the market over a long period of time.

Understanding Value: How to Avoid Costly Mistakes

By buying stocks when they are undervalued and have sound prospects of appreciation, you can avoid, or at least minimize, one of the major mistakes of investing: *buying a stock near the top of its price range,* when, by definition, it is popular and usually overpriced.

When the inevitable readjustment sets in, the fall can be fast and far, particularly when earnings growth slows. Once a stock drops sharply, it can take years for that stock to get back to the price at which it should have been sold. When Wall Street sours on an industry or company, not even the bluest of Blue Chips can buck such pessimism.

Example: in 1962, IBM topped out at 150 and later that year fell to 78 (not adjusted for the 4–1 stock split). It took two years for this premier stock to get back to 150. And not until 1967 was there a significant price advance, to 324 from the 1966 high of 188.

Investors who bought IBM at its 1962 peak had to wait five years to achieve an adequate gain. With lower-quality securities, the time span is usually longer.

Such unpopularity may or may not be deserved. It may reflect the fact that the stock became vastly overpriced; it may have been caused by lower sales, reduced profits, or investor prejudices, right or wrong. Regardless of the reasons, the value of the stock will decrease in the future. The only sure conclusion is that such declines in stock prices almost always lead to extremes which can be as great on the downside as they have been on the upside. Wall Street always swings from overoptimism to excessive pessimism: from over- to undervaluation. The hanging-on investor will have to wait and wait and wait to break even.

Greater Fool Theory

Another common mistake is to buy stocks on the basis of popularity. This is an error often made by so-called professional money managers such as bank trust officers, directors of pension funds, and decision managers of "conservative" mutual funds. They place their personal desire to be "safe," "comfortable," and "uncriticized" ahead of the best interests of their clients. The feel at ease with such well-known equities as IBM, Polaroid, and Xerox regardless of their real value. They buy and hold big-name stocks without projecting their potential appreciation or depreciation. They buy name and fame, not value.

This happened in the early 1970s with the Nifty Fifties. In 1973, Avon Products was at 120; a year later it was below 20, yet scores of professionals held on. So, too, with Xerox, whose stock price plummeted from around 160 to below 50. Then came a series of up moves (when the company bought more shares) to

70, but soon XRX was down to 46. Later it was up again, to 70, and then down, below 30, in 1982.

These money managers operate on the *Greater Fool Theory:* no matter how overpriced the stock, someone will be foolish enough to buy it. The trouble comes when even these fools recognize reality and there are no more buyers. When any stock rises to a clear overvaluation, sell if you own it and never buy, no matter what. There is no real future in it.

Conversely, it is just as foolish to hold a stock whose price has declined simply in hopes of "breaking even": to stick with Polaroid bought at 150 (which eventually would fall to 15). Yet that's what has been done, and is still being done, by many professionals and too many amateurs. I am constantly amazed to read the annual reports of mutual funds that continue to show ownership of thousands of shares of stocks whose values have fallen over the *years*. If you spot such holdings in the portfolios of funds whose shares you own or plan to buy, call the investment manager and ask for an explanation. My guess is that all you will get is baloney.

And while we are discussing mistakes from overvaluations, keep in mind that there are often times when a group of stocks get out of line with their true worth. In mid-1986, retail stocks were at a temporary peak: Limited Stores at 45 with a P/E of 37; Wal-Mart at 44 with a multiple of 44, etc. These are very high ratios and historically will not be sustained.

The difficulty is that, in the stock market, too few people pay attention to facts. They prefer to let their investment decisions be motivated by rumors, enthusiasm, and unjustified hopes of the upside and by despair and fear on the downside. Greed takes over from common sense.

In investing, patience and facts will eventually win out. Then, the price of the stock is understood to rise or fall in accordance with an intelligent interpretation of corporate earnings and prospects. The only time that any stock sells at its **true value** is when its price is moving from excessive overvaluation to equally excessive undervaluation. Studies show that this norm is usually reached only once every five years!

Investment Criteria

Over fifty years ago, Dr. Benjamin Graham, whose books are still the best guides to successful investing, set down these criteria for judging the quality of a corporation and the value of its common stock. He used these checkpoints to spot good stocks selling at bargain prices (undervalued).

Before you make any major commitments of your savings, compare these checkpoints with those of the company in which you plan to invest. Because of the tremendous rise in the stock market, some of these terms should be revised, but the principles are still valid. *Use 'em.*

- Total debt less than:
  Tangible book value
  Twice net quick liquidation value
- Current ratio (assets to liabilities) of 2:1 or better
- Earnings growth in past ten years of 7% compounded, with no more than two declines of 5% annually
- Stock price ⅔ of:
  Book value
  Net current asset value (current assets less total debt without inclusion of fixed assets)
- Dividend yield two-thirds of that of AAA bonds: when 8%, the dividend should be 5.36%
- Earnings to price yield twice that of AAA bonds: with 8% interest, the required earnings yield would be 16%
- P/E ratio 40% of the highest average P/E in the past five years: if the high multiple was 20, current should be 8

Stock Splits

Theoretically, a stock split or stock dividend does not increase the value of the company's shares. The pie is the same size whether there are four or eight slices. But it does not always work out that way. Extra shares become a favorable force and often push up the value of the stock. Investors view the split as a mark of management's confidence in the future.

This enthusiasm is understandable when the company increases the dividend rate after the stock split/dividend; yet even when there is no higher payout, the sustained climb that preceded the division usually continues, after a short period of fluctuations, at a slower pace.

The impact of a stock split starts about two months before the actual announcement, typically with stocks priced at over $60 per share and with companies that have provided a similar bonus in the past. The surge climaxes during the few days before and after the news. Then there's a decline for a month or two.

When you spot a potential split, *buy* on the basis of quality and value; *sell* immediately after the announcement, or, if you prefer not to cash in fully, sell half of your holdings and be patient.

Reward/Risk Ratio

This is a handy way to calculate reward versus risk. It can provide a frame of reference to determine whether the potential reward from a higher price is greater than the possible loss due to a mistake or unfavorable market/corporate conditions.

Here's how the R/R ratio was used with the stock of Sara Lee Corp. (SLE) in 1983. At that time, SLE stock was trading at 27, about ten times its $2.77 per share earnings. SLE was a quality corporation, rated ABA 10 by Wright and A+ by Standard & Poor's.

Research showed that, over the past five years, earnings rose at an average annual rate of 12%. Being conservative, Fundamentalist Fred projected future gains to be 10% a year so that profits per share might be $3.05, $3.36, $3.70, $4.07, and $4.48 from 1983 through 1987.

TABLE 2-1
Fundamentalist Fred's Projections
for Sarah Lee Corp. (SLE)

Year	Per Share Earnings @ 10% Gain	At These P/Es, Price Will Be 10	12	14
1982	$2.77	28	33	39
1983	3.05	31	37	43
1984	3.36	34	40	47
1985	3.70	37	44	52
1986 (E)	4.07	41	49	57
1987 (E)	4.48	45	54	63

What Happened

Year	Price Range
1983	27–19
1984	35–25
1985	52–37
1986 (Autumn)	72–47

At the same multiple of 10, the price of SLE stock would rise to 45; at a P/E ratio of 12 (possible in a strong market), the price could be 54. There was ample margin for error.

Fred notes that the 1981 low price was 17, so the reward was 27 points up (from 27 to 54) and the risk was 10 points down (from 27 to 17). The reward/risk ratio was 2.7 (27 divided by 10). Any ratio above 1.0 is favorable, so at the time SLE was a buy.

To keep his projections up-to-date, Fred recalculated when the stock reached 44 and the P/E rose to 12. Now the low figure was 40 and the potential high 54: 4 points down and 10 points up, an R/R ratio of 2.5.

By this time the market was booming, food stocks were popular, and SLE moved up to 60. Fred set a stop loss order to protect his profit.

SLE kept rising to over 70 and the P/E ratio was over 15. Fred felt this was too high. Now the reward was small and the risk growing. He sold and almost tripled his money.

Before you buy any stock for growth, write down the R/R ratio based on your analysis of the past performance and future prospects of the company. As a base, use the low price of the last year or so and a target price which you believe can be attained in a normal market. If this is a bull period, keep moving both of these up but keep in mind that as the rewards grow so do the risks.

Chapter 3

TIMING BOOSTS PROFITS, REDUCES LOSSES

Contrary to what some "experts" proclaim, timing is *not* the most important element in stock market success. It is essential in speculation, but only helpful in investing. Quality and value come first and second. The role of timing is to enhance profits and reduce losses.

Basically, timing is a subtle technique that requires accurate measurement of price trends of the stock market generally, and of industry groups and individual stocks specifically. It involves understanding human psychology with special reference to publicly traded securities.

Over the short term, stock movements can be erratic, illogical, and exasperating because they reflect temporary hopes and fears. Over the long run, however, the stock market is rational, generally predictable, and pays a fair price for both debt and equity. Still, it's always a battle. The role of timing is to improve investment performance. Besides, when your timing is good, you'll feel better and be proud of your acumen!

As used in this book, "timing" relates to decisions of when to buy and when to sell and, to a degree, what securities to choose. Broadly speaking, this means to *buy* when the stock is undervalued and starting to move up; to *sell* when the stock becomes fully priced and the risks of retention are greater than the rewards of a sale or, of course, when you made a mistake.

Timing is also valuable in determining the composition of portfolios: when the outlook is bullish, more equities (up to 90%); when business/market prospects are unfavorable, more debt (25% to 30% of current holdings and all new investments). If you, or your spouse, are a worrier, make it 50%. You won't make as much money, but you both will sleep better.

The most important timing involves buying so let's see how this works.

- *Good* timing with a *poor* stock can be temporarily profitable in a strong market, especially when there are "Greater Fools" bidding up an already overpriced stock. Such success is due more to luck than to skill.
- Poor timing with a good stock is upsetting in that the price may drop for a while, but eventually value will be recognized so that there will be gains.
- Poor timing with a poor stock can be disastrous. You may make a quick buck, but soon there will be a sharp decline. Once the enthusiasm fades (why else would you buy it?), there is no realistic possibility of recouping the loss for a long time. Unless you are a seasoned speculator, willing to discipline yourself to sell under a preset schedule, you can lose a bundle. Here's what happened to two "hot" stocks that were touted by brokers in the early 1980s:

Stock	1980	1981	1982	1983	1984	1985	mid-1986
Digicon, Inc.	8	37	16	7	2½	1¾	⅜
Storage Technology	12	36	22	14	8	2	4

The only way to make money with such volatile stocks is to trade: to buy near the low, sell (or sell short) at the high, etc. This is speculating, not investing. Timing is the key because the market prices have little to do with quality and value.

- *Good* timing with a *good* stock is an unbeatable combination as shown throughout this book. Quality stocks bought at the right time will always be profitable sooner or later!

Profitable Timing

The importance of timing is shown by these recommendations by Wright Investors made in January 1985 (Table 3-1): eleven quality stocks for investment growth in the next two years.

With the booming market, the gains came faster and were greater than projected. Within one year the value of a portfolio of 100 shares of each stock rose from $38,198 to $47,659, and seven months later was $58,749. If the investor had timed sales

TABLE 3-1
How Some Quality Stocks Appreciated

	Price			
Stock	January 1985	January 1986	July 1986	High
Alco Standard	31⅝	37⅝	41¼	46¾
Brown Group	28¾	32¾	37½	43⅜
Kroger Co.	38¾	46¾	56⅝	65¾
PepsiCo, Inc.*	14⅛	23⅜	32	35⅝
Procter & Gamble	55½	69¾	77	82½
Raytheon Co.	43	53¾	62⅞	67⅜
Revco (D.S.)	25¼	28	36⅜	39⅞
Snap-On Tools**	17½	21¼	29⅜	29⅞
Stanley Works	27⅜	31⅛	39	46¼
SunTrust	35⅜	37¾	53⅞	56
West Co.	19	26⅜	28⅜	34¼
@ 100 shares each	$38,198	$47,659	$58,749	$64,871

* 3–1 split
** 2—1 split

Source: New York Stock Exchange

at the interim highs, he/she would have pocketed an extra $1,122!

Types of Timing

There are distinct types of timing. Some are easy for the amateur to check; others are more complex and require special analysis, although general trends can be determined from information in the financial press and research reports.

FUNDAMENTAL TIMING

This is basic in that it relates to whether or not it is a good time to invest in common stocks. This is indicated by the movement of the stock market, statements by leading officials such as the chairman of the Federal Reserve Board, the tenor of the business world, and, especially, the trend of interest rates. When these are optimistic, it's time to buy; when they are unfavorable, it's time to sell or at least to delay purchases.

With so many conflicting opinions by self-styled "authorities," most people interpret fundamental timing on the basis of their personal experience and hopes. That's OK until, and unless, they become carried away with their own optimisism or pessimism and ignore or minimize the basic factors of quality and value. The most difficult decisions come when the economy is near its extremes: after the bottom of a recession; before an economic high. That's when it pays to do your homework and follow proven-profitable techniques.

MARKET TIMING

This is closely allied to fundamental timing but is more limited in scope and more precise. It applies to industry groups and sometimes to specific securities. It is a key factor in an investment policy which seeks to buy near cyclical lows and to accelerate profit-taking near cyclical highs. Vice versa for selling.

Execution by market timing alone is difficult. While almost all stocks go up in a bull market, various groups move at different paces. In bear markets, not all groups go down or, at least, fall as much as the overall averages. If we look at winners/losers in recent years, we find there is no set pattern, so market timing, by itself, provides only a background. Data on variations in the gains/losses of industry groups are shown in Table 3-2 and discussed below:

- In 1983, when the S&P 500 rose 15%, trucking stocks skyrocketed 92%, discount stores were up 61% and electronics companies, +56%. Utilities, +13%, stayed close to the average, but metal producers were down 4%, medical suppliers, −3%, and gold producers, −3%.
- In 1984, when the market plateaued at +1%, printers soared 13%, international oils were up 11%, auto parts were flat, S&Ls dropped 15% and metal producers fell 36%.
- In 1985, when the market zoomed 26%, radio/TV stocks jumped 71%, apparel companies were +55% and S&Ls were popular, +51%. Utilities were +24%, but electronics stocks plummeted 11% and steel and cement firms fell 4%.
- In the first six months of ebullient 1986, with the S&P +18%, department store stocks were +62%; defense stocks, +35%; S&Ls, +17%; utilities, +16%; gold producers reversed their fall, moving up 23%, metal producers were −9%, and electronics, −2%.

Since very few groups repeat their triumphs or declines, check data like these, be slow to invest in any group that did well last year, and take a second look at those that faltered.

SECTOR TIMING

This considers specific groups or industries. It is better in theory than in practice. It is useful in choosing groups of stocks but can

TABLE 3-2
How Some Major Groups Fared in the Market

1983		1984		1985		1986 (July)	
S&P 500	+15%		+ 1%		+26%		+18%
Trucking	+92	Printers	+13	Radio/TV	+71	Dept. stores	+62
Discount stores	+61	Inter.Oils	+11	Apparel	+55	Defense	+35
Electronics	+56	Electronics	+ 8	S&Ls	+51	Gold	+23
Utilities	+13	Auto parts	0	Utilities	+24	S&Ls	+17
Metal producers	− 4	S&Ls	−15	Electronics	−11	Utilities	+16
Medical suppl.	− 3	Coal	−16	Steel Cos.	− 4	Electronics	− 2
Gold	− 3	Metal prod.	−36	Cement	− 4	Metal prod.	− 9

Source: Wright Investors' Service

be dangerous because price trends are often the result of overanticipation by investors, especially institutional money managers.

In essence, sector timing concentrates on specific characteristics: high or low growth rates, high or low dividend yields, broad or thin institutional acceptance, cyclical or contracyclical profitability, etc. These can be important, but they are difficult even for professionals to determine. Generally, sector timing requires more research, analysis, and experience than is available to most amateurs.

CORPORATE TIMING

This is keyed to individual stock transactions. It involves a continuous appraisal of the progress and outlook of the corporation in which an investment has been, or may be, made. It measures the recent and prospective trends of earnings and dividends and compares them with those of similar companies. Basically, it means to consider buying after a long downtrend has been reversed and to sell just before or after a price peak. Success requires discipline and adherence to logically determined conclusions rather than to hunches.

Example: in mid-1981, AMP, Inc., was around 50. Profits were slightly higher than those of the year before but, I felt, the long-term future was bright. The company was rated AAA11 by Wright Investors' and continued to be a dominant supplier to the computer/electronics industry. I bought at 51½ with a target price of 100. This was too soon. Annual profits dropped in 1982 to $3.30 from $3.75. The price of the stock fell to 45, just above the stop-loss figure I had set.

In the first quarter of 1983, earnings started to edge up. Investors became confident and, with higher volume, boosted the price of AMP stock to over 200, when I sold.

For a few months, this appeared to be smart as the stock fell, but by spring 1984 it moved up again and in June split 3–1.

After the stock settled down, I considered buying again, but the December quarter earnings slipped to 37¢ from 44¢ per share, forecasting what I considered would be lower profits in 1985. But with the strong market and better earnings, AMP stock started up again and in early 1986 had almost doubled. Well, you can't win 'em all!

Checkpoints

Corporate timing is more precise than other types of timing and relies heavily on keeping abreast of developments such as these criteria from Wright Investors' Service and my comments.

- Quarterly reports of earnings advances and declines are usually anticipated before the data are made public. (In other words, the professionals make their moves before the news is announced.) Price changes seem to reflect projected declines more often, and to a greater extent, than earnings advances; i.e., the reaction to bad news is greater than that to good news.
- The more consistent the gains of quarterly earnings, the greater the price advances. When any company has higher profit gains over four or more quarters, the price of the stock will advance more strongly for the next four quarters. In other words, the money managers go with the winners.
- After a sharp decline in profits after previous superior gains, the price decline comes in the reporting quarter and often may be followed by a partial price recovery; i.e., the professionals take the long view and are not overly concerned with temporary setbacks of quality companies.
- Stocks with the greatest year-to-year declines in earnings for one quarter are likely to perform poorly for several quarters. The institutions want management to prove its ability to come back.
- After several poor earnings quarters, higher profits boost the stock price one quarter before the better earnings are reported. The pros do their homework.

Guidelines for Timing the Purchase of a Specific Stock

Once you are persuaded that the outlook for the stock market and the industry group is favorable, follow these checkpoints to improve your timing of shares of a specific stock:

CORPORATE EARNINGS UP FOR TWO CONSECUTIVE QUARTERS

This applies primarily to companies which are moving back to traditional profitability and growth. It's tempting to buy after one quarter of better earnings, but unless it's a true Blue Chip, three months is not a long enough period of improvement to be sure that the organization is moving ahead.

Even after two good quarters, look for trends and comparisons over the last five years. If the June quarter is usually quite profitable, find out if this year's results are as good as the press release indicates. If the September figures were comparatively strong, were they a bounce-back from a poor period last year because of a previous strike or hurricane? You are committing your savings, so try to keep the odds of success in your favor.

It's natural, and easy, to act on hunches rather than on facts, especially when your broker is optimistic. Strong recommendation by a major brokerage firm or research service can boost the stock price temporarily, but when you are seeking substantial long-term gains, it is wise to wait for confirmation and not make a false start.

COMPARE QUARTERLY EARNINGS

Once you have spotted a company whose profits are rising, check the industry group to see how this earnings increase stacks up against those of similar firms.

Example: in June 1984, Harry Hustle read two articles in business publications. One predicted strong sales for department

TABLE 3-3

Comparing Quarterly Earnings: Department Stores

Company	April 1984	April 1983	January 1984	January 1983	October 1983	October 1982	July 1983	July 1982	P/E Ratio June 1984
Ames	.14	.08	.20	.14	.21	.13	.34	.22	12
Dayton-Hudson	.29	.24	1.54	1.47	.46	.41	.37	.28	11
Federated	.74	.89	4.14	3.55	1.69	.82	.83	.44	8
Wal-Mart	.16	.10	.38	.29	.16	.10	.15	.09	22
Zayre	.20	.13	.65	.56	.34	.27	.17	.06	12

Source: Wright Investors' Service

stores; the other lauded Sam Walton for his success with Wal-Mart Stores in small towns. Harry had a CD coming due and felt that it was time to invest for growth. At the local library, he checked the earnings records of five quality retailers: Ames Department Stores, Dayton-Hudson, Federated Department Stores, Wal-Mart Stores, and Zayre Corp. (Table 3-3).

His research showed that compared to the previous year, every quarter's earnings were higher (except for Federated, which faltered in the April-ended period). The gains were consistent and ample: from about +15% to over +100%. Harry felt that the timing was right and he could double his money.

Now came the hard part: choosing the best of the group. Federated was selling at the lowest multiple of eight-times-earnings because of the poor first quarter (with department stores, the first quarter starts in February). Wal-Mart was at a hefty P/E ratio of 22. The other three were at a reasonable 11–12 times earnings.

Harry split his investments: 100 shares of Wal-Mart at 50 with a target price of 100, and 100 shares of Ames at 26, with a goal of 50, both to be achieved in the next two years.

Harry did well. Both companies split their stock 2 for 1, and by June 1986 (his two-year target date), Ames was at 33 (equivalent to 66 from his 26 cost) and Wal-Mart at 56 (equivalent to 112 from the 50 cost). Since both stocks were priced above his expectations and the P/Es were a sizzling 28 and 42 respectively, Harry sold. As a wise investor, Harry timed his investments successfully. He bought **Up** stocks in an **Up** group in an **Up** market. He sold when the stocks were becoming overpriced.

Watch Out for Wall Street Shenanigans

In most cases, the techniques of timing apply to all equity investments since stocks usually move as a group. There are, however, exceptions, some justified and others the result of professional pique or, occasionally, manipulation.

Quality utilities, with ever-higher dividends, will outpace the averages.

With some industrial stocks, the dividend increase may be more important than rising profits. Usually, the higher payouts tend to slow price gains. Investors consider the stock better for income than for growth.

Or if the dividend holds steady while earnings rise, there may be concern that management is becoming tired, less aggressive, and so worried about the future that it prefers to retain the higher profits for reinvestment. If this plow-back is for research and development, good; if it's added to already ample liquid assets, watch out. The company may be a candidate for a takeover. Such a situation can be profitable but does change the investment value.

The most difficult-for-the-amateur fluctuation is when the price of the stock drops because the earnings gain is less than anticipated by the professionals, not by corporate management; i.e., quarterly profits are +7% versus the projected +10%! With K-Mart, despite higher profits, the price of its stock fell from 42 to 33.

Such pessimism is foolish and uncalled-for especially with a quality corporation, but it's a fact of investment life. Unless there are clear indications, as stated by corporate management, that this lower-than-anticipated gain will continue, there is no logical reason to sell the stock as long as the future prospects are favorable.

How a Professional Handles Timing

To give you an idea of how professional money managers time their transactions, here are excerpts from analyses by Wright Investors' Service. They rely on fundamental analysis and pay little heed to technical indicators. These examples are of stocks already held. The timing of sales occurs when the outlook of the company is unfavorable or it no longer meets investment standards.

On April 16, 1986, the sale recommendation for American Standard Incorporated was as follows:

> AST underwent major changes in 1985 including the acquisition of Trane Co. and the divestiture of a number of businesses. Earnings in 1986 are expected to show a modest increase over 1985's $3.10 per share excluding the $2.54 per share restructuring charge. . . . Reflecting the positive long-term growth potential of these changes, AST shares have advanced 53% in price in the last twelve months, well ahead of the +30% of the S&P 500. At the current price of 44¾, AST shares are valued at 1.9 times beginning-of-the-year shareholders' equity compared to the past five- and ten-year averages of 1.4. Sale of AST is recommended. The company will remain on the Approved Wright Investment List.

Here's a more detailed analysis of PepsiCo, Inc., the giant soft drink/snack food/restaurant company. All of the information was available from corporate reports, news releases, brokerage research reports, and statistical services.

PEP had a high quality rating of ABA5: outstanding market acceptance, strong finances, excellent profitability and stability, and superior growth.

TABLE 3-4 Investment Analysis

PEPSICO, INC. (PEP) — *WRIGHT INVESTMENT ANALYSIS AND EVALUATION*

DIVERSIFIED	FISCAL YEAR ENDS	CAPITALIZATION ($MIL) COMMON EQUITY	L.T. DEBT	PFD STK	CUR-RENT RATIO	COMMON SHARES TOTAL MIL	CLOSELY HELD	TRADING YR-THOU	INST. INVE-STORS	STABILITY EARN-INGS	MKT PRICE	RELATIVITY TO S&P RATIO/RELIABILITY EARNINGS	PRICE	ANNUAL PRICE RANGE	WRIGHT QUALITY RATING
		09/84	09/84	09/84	09/84	10/84	03/84	3YR AVG							
	DEC	1803.3	779.4	NIL	1.4	93.9	NOM	72228	508	76%	79%	.88/70%	.09/58%	18%	ABA5

CAL-ENDAR YEARS	MARKET PRICE HIGH-LOW	LAST	RATIO PRICE TO EARNING HI-LO	EQUITY AVG	DIV YLD AVG	EQUITY CAPITAL EARNED GROWTH	PROFIT RATE	BEGIN OF YR	EARNINGS REPORTED %TAX	12 MOS	% CHG	QUARTERLY MAR	JUNE	SEPT	DEC	DIVIDENDS % OF EARN	LAST 12MO	QTRLY RATE
5-10 YEAR AVERAGES																		
'74-78	28 - 18	S23	15-9.8	2.6	2.9	13.1%	20.6%	8.88	44%	1.83	+17%	.30	.47	.56	.50	37%	.67	.18
'79-83	37 - 27	S32	13-9.2	2.1	4.4	10.0%	19.0%	15.47	39%	2.94	+4%	.52	.86	1.00	.56	48%	1.40	.36
'74-83	33 - 22	S28	14-9.2	2.3	3.7	11.0%	19.5%	12.18	41%	2.38	+10%	.41	.67	.78	.52	44%	1.04	.27
CALENDAR YEARS																		
1974	24 - 9.7	14	20-7.9	2.4	2.5	11.4%	17.5%	P7.01	42%	P1.23	+10%	.21	.30	.37	.35	35%	.43	.12
1975	25 - 14	23	17-9.5	2.6	2.5	12.4%	18.8%	P7.82	44%	P1.47	+20%	.23	.37	.45	.42	34%	.50	.13
1976GK	29 - 23	27	16- 12	2.9	2.4	13.7%	20.7%	HP8.92	45%	BP1.85	+26%	B.29	.49	B.57	.50	34%	.63	.17
1977K	29 - 22	28	13- 10	2.7	3.2	13.5%	22.1%	HP9.75	44%	P2.15	+16%	.36	.56	.66	.57	39%	A.83	.23
1978GK	34 - 23	26	14-9.5	2.7	3.4	13.3%	22.3%	HP10.91	44%	BP2.43	+13%	.41	.64	.74	B.64	40%	.98	.25
1979	29 - 22	25	10-7.7	2.1	4.3	13.9%	22.8%	P12.50	39%	PW2.85	+17%	.48	.78	.86	.73	39%	1.11	.29
1980G	29 - 20	27	9.1-6.3	1.8	5.0	14.0%	23.1%	P13.87	41%	BPW3.20	+12%	.52	.85	.97	B.86	39%	1.26	.33
1981GK	39 - 27	36	12-8.4	2.1	4.3	11.6%	20.7%	P15.58	39%	PWY3.22	+1%	.52	.91	1.03	.76	44%	1.42	.37
1982GK	50 - 31	36	21- 13	2.4	3.9	4.7%	13.8%	HP17.36	43%	PWY2.40	-25%	.69	.97	1.16	BGD.42	66%	1.58	.41
1983	40 - 33	38	13- 11	2.1	4.4	7.7%	16.7%	P18.04	33%	PW3.01	+25%	.40	.79	1.00	.82	54%	1.62	.41
1984	46 - 35	43	22- 17	2.1	4.1			P19.53		BPV2.12		.50	BD.44	1.24		79%	1.67	R.42
1985	44 - 41		21- 19	2.2	3.9													
02/01		42.75	20	2.2	3.9													

WIS APPROVED PROJECTION													
1984	46 - 35	$41	20- 16	2.1	4.1	3.0%	11.5%	19.53	2.25	-25%		74%	1.67
1985	52 - 39	$46	13-9.7	2.3	3.9	11.1%	20.0%	20.11	4.03	+79%		45%	1.80
1986	62 - 45	$54	14- 10	2.4	3.6	11.3%	20.0%	22.34	4.47	+11%		44%	1.95
1989	84 - 56	$70	14-9.1	2.3	3.6	11.8%	20.0%	30.90	6.18	+12%		41%	2.52

COMPARATIVE RETURNS ANNUAL RATES	DIVS GROWTH	EARNS GROWTH	DIVS RINV	EARNED RETURN	AT CURRENT PRICE DIV YLD	ERN YLD	P/E
NEXT 12 MONTHS	+8.1%	+85.4%	+2.8%	+88.2%	'85: 4.2%	9.2%	10.9
NEXT 2 YEARS	+8.2%	+47.8%	+2.7%	+50.5%	'86: 4.6%	10.8%	9.2
NEXT 5 YEARS	+8.6%	+23.4%	+2.7%	+26.1%	'89: 5.9%	14.2%	7.1

COMPARATIVE VALUES	PRICE		EARNINGS		DIVIDENDS	
HISTORIC NORM	40	100%	3.50	100%	1.73	100%
INDICATED MKT	36	88%	3.53	101%	1.70	99%
CURRENT PRICE	43	107%	2.12	61%	1.67	97%
LAST 3 MOS	-3%		+24%	(VS YR AGO)		+4%
YR TO DATE	+0%		-41%	(VS YR AGO)		+3%
LAST 12 MOS	+17%		+20%	(VS YR AGO)		+3%

ANNUAL RETURNS	NORMAL	12MOS	5YR AVG	5YR PROJ
DIV. INCOME	4.3%	3.9%	4.9%	2.7%
EARN. GROWTH	+5.2%	+19.8%	-5.1%	+23.4%
EARNED RETURN	+9.5%	+23.7%	+1.7%	+26.1%
CHG. P/E RATIO		-2.1%	+15.0%	-10.4%
TOTAL RETURN		+21.6%	+16.7%	+15.7%

EXECUTIVE OFFICE: ANDERSON HILL RD, PURCHASE, NY 10577; TELEPHONE: (914) 253-2000; OFFICERS: CHMN/CEO: D.M. KENDALL (63/36/12#), PRES/CHIEF OPTG: D.W. CALLOWAY (49/16/#), EXEC VP/CFO: M.H. JORDAN (48/10/#), VP/SECY: E.V. LAHEY JR. (45/18/10#), VP/TREAS: D. CHRISTOPHERSON (NA/3/#); BUSINESS: 1983 SALES OPTG/INCOME DERIVED FROM BEVERAGES, 38%/20%; FOOD PRODS, 31%/55%; FOOD SERVICE, 19%/24%; TRANSPORTATION, 9%/3%; & SPORTING GOODS, 3%/-2%; PRODUCTS: CONSUMER EXPENDABLES & DURABLES AND SERVICES; DISTRIBUTION: DOMESTIC, 81%; FOREIGN, 19%; EMPLOYEES: 154,000.

ACCOUNTING: INVENTORIES - DOM (60%), LIFO; FOREIGN (40%), FIFO OR AVG COST; INVES. TAX CR - AMOR. LEASES - IN L T D $142.5 MIL. NOTES: (#): KENDALL - CEO SINCE 65, PRES 6 YRS; CALLOWAY - PRES. POS. AS OF JAN 85, EXEC VP/CFO 1 YR; JORDAN - PRES. POS. AS OF JAN 85; LAHEY - SECY SINCE 61; CHRISTOPHERSON - PRES. POS. AS OF SEPT 84; (A): ALL ITEMS ADJ 3:1 IN 77; (B): INCLS $1.27 CHG JUN 84, $.83 CHG IN 82, EXCLS $.19 CHG IN 80, INCLS $.14 PRETAX CR & $.30 PRETAX CHG IN 78, $.06 CHG IN 76; (D): DEFICIT; (G): ADOPTED FASB 52 FOR CURR. TRANS IN 82, INCR EARNS BY $.49, ADOPTED LIFO FOR DOM INV IN 81, RED. EARNS BY $.05; (H): RESTATED TO INCL ACQUIS OR CHNG IN ACCT; (K): ACQ'D 3 COS IN 82, 1 IN 81, 1 IN 78, 1 IN 77, 1 IN 76; (P): BASED ON COM & COM EQUIV SHRS; (R): IND. RATE; (S): AVG OF ANN HI'S & LO'S; (V): INCLS LOSS FROM DISC. OPER OF ($.04) IN 84; (W): INCLS FOR. CURR. GAIN OF $.03 IN 83, $.13 IN 82, $.22 IN 81, $.13 IN 80, $.04 IN 79; (Y): YR & QTRS RESTATED TO CORRECT ACCT IRREG.

FOR EXPLANATION OF HEADINGS SEE *WIS* 1/23/85.

Source: Wright Investors' Service

[*February 6, 1985:*] Following depressed results in 1982 and 1983, PEP is likely to report record earnings for 1984-ended year: \$2.25 to \$2.35 per share . . . +17% to +19% for 1984 and +14% for 1985 . . . [Look for] a 60% increase in the price of PEP shares over the next five years: from 42¾ to 69. Purchase at market.

PEP has cleaned house over the last twelve months . . . sale of North American Van Lines and Lee Way Motor Freight, refranchising of several foreign-owned bottling units and restructuring by Wilson Sporting Goods . . . Taco Bell plans to buy and convert ninety-nine Pup'n Taco stands in California. . . . Earnings should rise \$4.00 to \$4.25 per share in 1985.

Over the next five years, earnings growth can be expected to average +23% compound annual rate from its current low base. Net return on stockholders' equity should average 20%. . . . BUY AT MARKET [about 43].

N.B. Table 3-4 shows a work sheet that is typical of those used by professional money managers. Similar reports are available from Value Line, Standard & Poor's, and brokerage firm research departments. The projections are mechanical, require the use of computers, and are too complex for amateurs who should concentrate on the historical data. You don't have to understand every column, but you should study the trends and relate them to the comments.

Now let's get back to the analysis of PEPSICO to keep tabs on corporate progress (or lack thereof).

[*May 1, 1985:*] Earnings for twelve weeks ended March 23 rose 27% on 5% greater sales; net income, +33% . . . better than expected . . . continue to recommend purchase [stock at 52½].

[*July 31, 1985:*] . . . For second fiscal quarter, earnings per share from continuing operations rose 29% to \$1.25 . . . Total earnings, \$2.68, including \$1.45 gain from sale of North American Van Lines and loss from disposal of Wilson [stock at 56½].

Results: by May 28, 1986, PEP stock was up to 92½. Wright continued to hold, but individual investors might conclude that at twenty times earnings the stock was fairly priced, especially after the announcement of a 3–1 stock split.

> [*August 27, 1986.*] PEP common shares . . . current price/equity multiple of 4.6 is twice the average of the last decade. . . . Potential for superior near-term price gains are less than that of many other AWIL stocks. . . . The proposed acquisition of Kentucky Fried Chicken (for $850 million) will put strain on the company's balance sheet. We are selling . . . but will retain PEP on the Approved List. Stock sold at 32¼. In eighteen months, from an adjusted cost of 14¼ plus $1.76 per share, dividends = +$21.76, a total return of +153% or an annualized rate of total return of over 100%.

This illustrates the why and how of successful investing in Blue Chips!

Doing Your Own Research

Once you become interested in any stock, label a folder with the name of the company and file pertinent facts: corporate reports, news stories, brokerage analyses, etc. Review the file periodically to determine trends and progress (or lack of it). There may be temporary downturns, but as long as the corporation continues to report superior profits, the stock should probably be held.

To double-check and build a visual pattern, add both short- and long-term charts and keep them up-to-date.

Be Realistic; Be Skeptical

Ideally, everyone should do his/her own research and make intelligent decisions. Practically, of course, most people are influenced by the opinions of others: news stories in financial publications, comments of brokers, and reports of analysts/advisers. These sources can be important in timing but also dangerous when not analyzed. It's easy to assume that these conclusions are valid and to act immediately without referring to your checklists. Never be in a hurry to spend your money and always be cautious and usually skeptical.

As you have probably learned to your sorrow, some analysts are past masters in reversing their positions or justifying their errors; most upbeat news stories are initiated by public relations people. These professionals know how to present information about their employer in a favorable context. The publicity may spark a price rise of a few points, but the true measure is the impact in a year or two: will the ultimate result be sustained by higher future profits?

When the news is negative, it may be wise to sell and buy back later when the problems are overcome. When the story is positive, it may be time to buy if the basics are strong and there are logical reasons to expect the forecasts will work out.

Modern business is so competitive that meaningful progress takes time. Usually, this means three to five years for a new product/service to have a significant impact on corporate earnings. And remember that only half of all new products pay off!

There are exceptions, usually the result of hard-to-predict actions such as a takeover which can boost the price of the stock of the target company. In most cases, these are speculations. Not all proposals lead to marriage. That stock can fall as fast as it rose. If you own the stock on its own merits, it is usually wise to sell on the news and take the unexpected gain. Or, at least, set a stop-loss order to lock in your profit.

No matter how enticing the projections, wait for solid confirmation in the uptrend of the price of the stock and, even if it requires patience, the profits of the company. Amateurs time their purchases on hopes, tips, and rumors. Professionals recognize the hype of speculators and take the long view.

Avoiding Losers

Since poor timing with a poor stock can be doubly disastrous, it's important to avoid losers. Stay away from:

1. *Industries severely affected by adverse factors.* Over several years, such problems make it difficult for even a well-managed company to increase earnings. *Examples:* the cement industry in the mid-1970s, the oil industry in the early 1980s, and steel and aluminum firms in recent years.

2. *Quality companies where the anticipated expansion and improved profits will take a year or two.* This applies to corporations which, for competitive reasons, face heavy expenditures for capital improvements, new products, or major acquisitions. This caveat applies especially to takeovers, no matter how friendly or attractive. It takes time for new management to learn the new business, to install the necessary systems and controls, and to develop the personnel to assure that the acquired firm will be as profitable as the parent company. Besides, in most cases the purchase price will be based on future prospects.

3. *Any company where the prospects of the industry are poor or even marginal.* The chances of appreciation are small and unless you are willing to be patient, you cannot look forward to worthwhile gains soon. Always try to keep your money working for the best returns in the near future.

Bear Market Timing

In down markets, timing is more difficult because outside pressures can become more important than facts. Decisions should involve the types of securities to hold. At the outset of a confirmed downturn, it's wise to set up cash reserves and buy for income: bonds and high-dividend-paying stocks such as utilities. Their values will be relatively stable, and usually there will be little or no loss when you want to sell and move back into equities.

The exact amount of reserves depends on how severe and how long you expect the decline to be. As a minimum, for a bear market of six months, set the reserves at 15%. When the downtrend continues, boost these holdings slowly by about 5% per month to 30% or so and to 50% if you become nervous.

At this point, think of your investments as two packages: half-active, half-passive. The action money should be kept in short-term holdings that can be liquidated when buying opportunities occur. The passive funds can be in bonds with short- to intermediate-term maturities.

In timing the switch, start taking profits in stocks most likely to fall: (1) those close to their target highs, (2) those whose prospects for the next year or two are the least favorable.

Be cautious about selling good stocks that are paying adequate dividends and still have strong potential. If you start by selling only winners, you will end up with the worst performers, will constantly erode your capital, and eventually will not be able to reinvest in new, more promising situations.

Never be afraid to take a loss. In investing, it is just as important to keep losses low as to attain high profits. That does not mean that you have to be stubborn and hang on to losers. With quality stocks, the chances of a substantial loss are small. You can hold with confidence that, eventually, the price will rise. But you will do better by selling quickly when you realize that you have made a mistake. As every retailer will tell you, the first markdown is always the cheapest.

On the other hand, don't panic when the price of a ''good'' stock dips suddenly without apparent reason. One institution may unload to balance its portfolio. Other fund managers will see this as a signal for selling, and away they go . . . with no real justification.

Example: in 1979, between January and late February, the stock of Upjohn Co. fell from 50 to 40, then moved up to 46 and back to 42.

This was a surprise as profits continued to rise and management was confident enough to raise the dividend from 33¢ to 38¢ per share. This was an example of unwarranted investor fears of something that never happened.

Proof of this folly came later. The stock came back close to

50 in the summer, moved up erratically, and by early 1986 was over 170 before a split.

Target Selling

One of the best ways to time selling is to set a range of target prices: a spread of 5 to 10 points depending on the anticipated value of the stock, 35% to 50% above your cost. When the price is close to the minimum goal, review corporate prospects with an eye on the trend of the overall market. Usually, there will be no reason to change those goals, but a lot of things can happen in the twelve to eighteen months needed for worthwhile appreciation. Investors may be willing to pay a higher P/E ratio, an industry may become unpopular, or corporate prospects may improve. Or vice versa.

It is always wiser to sell "too soon" than to hang on in hopes of a few more points. Every extra dollar rise increases the downside risk.

Example: in mid-1982, IBM stock was around 60. The prospects for the company were bright and, with a little optimism, the price of the stock could be projected to double, especially in the stronger market. Ray bought 100 shares in the low 60s with a target price of 120.

His forecast proved correct. In less than a year, Big Blue was trading at around 125 so Ray set a stop-loss order at 119½ and let his profits run.

When IBM hit 130, Ray reviewed the situation and calculated that, to achieve the same 100+% gain, the stock would have to move to about 250. This was far above his projection, so he sold, set aside funds to pay the tax, and bought shares of Sara Lee at 25 because his research showed this stock could double soon. (It did).

Ray did well "too soon." IBM kept rising to over 160. But he had an excellent profit and later watched the stock fall to the low 120s. This was good timing with a good stock.

Timing via Price/Earnings Ratio

This is a repetition of a value technique: the use of the price/earnings ratio in timing the sale of a profitable stock. Over the years, with quality stocks, investors are willing to pay about the same times earnings within a fairly set range: for utilities, seven to ten times; for industrials, eight to ten.

When the multiple moves above these ranges, this can be a timing signal, especially when it is a very high ratio. *Remember:* that multiple shows how much investors (or more likely, speculators) are willing to pay for each dollar of earnings. To justify a superhigh stock price, the company must make superhigh profits—an unlikely and unrealistic prospect for large, mature corporations. At some point, major shareholders will start taking their profits and will trigger a sharp, fast drop in the stock price.

In the 1985–86 bull market, the stocks of many retailers soared so that their P/E ratios of 36–42 were twice those of the historical ranges and the current multiple of about 16 for the S&P 500. That was a lot of enthusiasm.

		Price/Earnings Ratio	
Company	Stock Price	Current	10 Years
Charming Shoppes	35	36	18–9
Toys "R" Us	33	36	29–14*
Wal-Mart Stores	52	42	26–14
S&P 500	251	16	10–8.3

* Five years

These stocks were overvalued. At best, they should be sold; at worst, there should be a stop-loss order about 10% below the peak—Wal-Mart at 52.

It can be exciting and profitable when these swingers roar up, but when the decline comes, it can be fast and far. And, in many cases, their recovery will be slow and erratic.

P/E ratios can also be used to spot bargains and to time their purchase. David Dreman, investment counselor, looks for profitable companies whose stocks are selling at low multiples because his studies show they outpace those with high P/Es by a substantial margin.

In normal markets, these bottom fishers look for a dividend-paying stock selling at six times earnings. With the recent bull market, many have raised this ratio to 8.

With Blue Chip stocks, however, this criterion seldom applies because, to meet quality standards, the companies must have high rates of return on equity and wide investment acceptance.

Rules for Selling

Sell when:

- You have made a mistake, even if you discover the error the next day. If there are valid reasons to believe that the stock will not fulfill the original reason for purchase, get out. Forget about the immediate loss. Chances are that when other investors reach the same conclusion, the price of the stock will fall further. Cut your losses. The first loss is almost always the least.
- The price of the stock has doubled. But sell only half of your holdings; you get back your original capital and can still make money with the remaining shares.
- The trend of the chart turns down, unless you are confident of the long-term ability of management to boost profits soon.
- The price/earnings ratio moves well above the high multiple of the past decade.
- The industry becomes unpopular, that is, when the prices of stocks in the group are almost all falling. Don't try to buck Wall Street.
- You feel uncomfortable about the future of the market or the company whose shares you own.

- The price of the stock rises to more than double shareholders' equity at corporate book value per common share. When buyers are willing to pay more than twice the tangible value of the company, they are adding a substantial premium for growth. This applies primarily to shares of manufacturing/transportation companies with large investments in plants and equipment. Drug/service/financial firms usually have small tangible assets in relation to total revenues.
- The dividend yield of income stocks falls below 4%. Utilities should be bought for income with growth a welcome, but secondary, factor.

Never hold a down-moving stock too long in hopes of breaking even. A comeback rarely happens quickly if the decline is justified. All you do is kid yourself (and your spouse). When Wall Street sours on an industry or company, it will take years for the stock to move back to your cost. Don't worry about exact timing. No one can consistently catch the nadir or peak of any stock. Even skilled professionals are satisfied when they come within 10% of those goals. Nor is hitting it on the nose *that* important. When you are shooting for a 50% gain, you can lose the first 10% and still do well. When you already have that 50% profit, there's no need to be greedy.

Technical Analysis (TA) Can be Useful

Technical analysis, when properly interpreted, can improve timing. Its tool—charts, moving averages, ratios, etc.—are used primarily by traders, but they can help investors to catch extra profits at both ends of their transactions: to *buy* when the price of the stock starts to move up; to *sell* near the peak value, before a downturn. TA is a supplement to, not a substitute for, fundamental analysis.

There's a lot of mystery and misinformation about TA (much of it promoted by editors of market letters), but the basic data are readily available and can be easily interpreted (though not always correctly) by individual investors. TA shows what's happening in the stock market by measuring the flow of money into and out of securities with special emphasis on trends and volume.

It is ridiculous to believe, as some technicians assert, that "It's all there" in the price/volume action of the stock or of the market. What is there is only the trading activity of those investors/speculators who participate during any stated period of time. What is *not* there is the attitudes of the majority of investors: those who own the stock and have not sold, and those potential shareholders who may buy the stock in the future.

Investing by timing alone is hazardous. The market timer has to be right twice in a row to be right at all. If he misses the top of a bull market and the bottom of a bear market by 5%, 10% of the spread is gone. Add 2% for commissions and the market has to move 12% for him to break even.

Don't get me wrong. Investment timing is an essential part of portfolio management, but it must be based on proven facts and informed trends, not on temporary aberrations or personal hunches. For successful investing, there are no substitutes for the fundamentals of quality and value, but timing can be improved by technical analysis and, in my experience, can add 5% or more to total returns. Every investor should understand the major technical indicators and how to use them!

What Technical Analysis Is

TA concentrates on what is, not what should be. The technician believes that: (1) the action of the stock market, and of specific stocks, is the best indicator of the immediate future move; (2) 80% of the stock price's movement is due to factors unique to that stock; (3) over a short time (weeks or months), the stock market action is 85% psychological and 15% fundamental.

Some areas of TA are esoteric and more closely related to

crystal balls than to reality, but most techniques rely on facts and logical projections. The goal is to spot trends and to recognize that *a trend in force will persist until a significant change in investor expectations causes it to reverse itself.*

TA involves scores of data and techniques, but these are the most important, the most widely used, and the most readily available for most amateur investors.

Volume. This is always important because it shows the attitudes of major investors. If the price of the stock rises with ever-higher volume (see bottom of Figure 3-1), this is a positive signal and usually the upmove will continue for some time.

If the stock price rises with modest volume, be cautious and buy only when you are convinced that better values are ahead as shown by the fundamentals of higher profits. There's nothing wrong in buying too early, but it can be disappointing not to have

FIGURE 3-1 Chart for AMP, Inc.

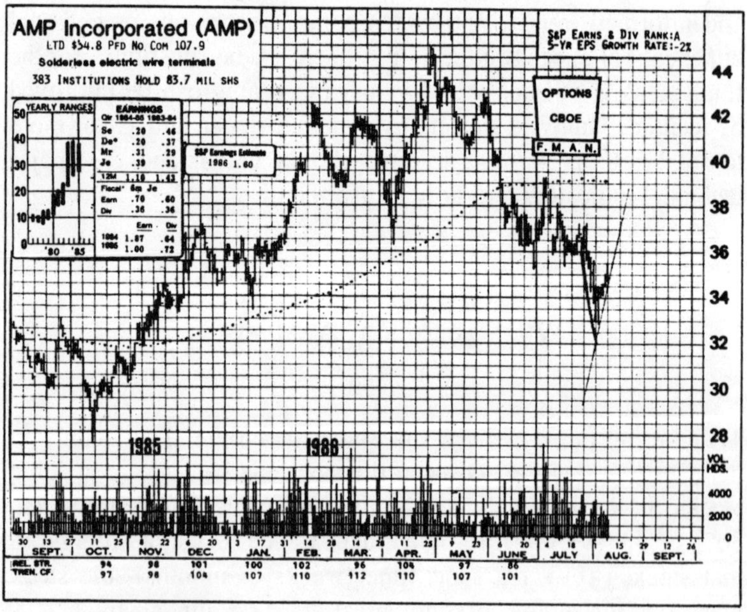

Source: Standard & Poor's Stock Charts

FIGURE 3-2 Long-Term Charts for TECO Energy and AMP, Inc.

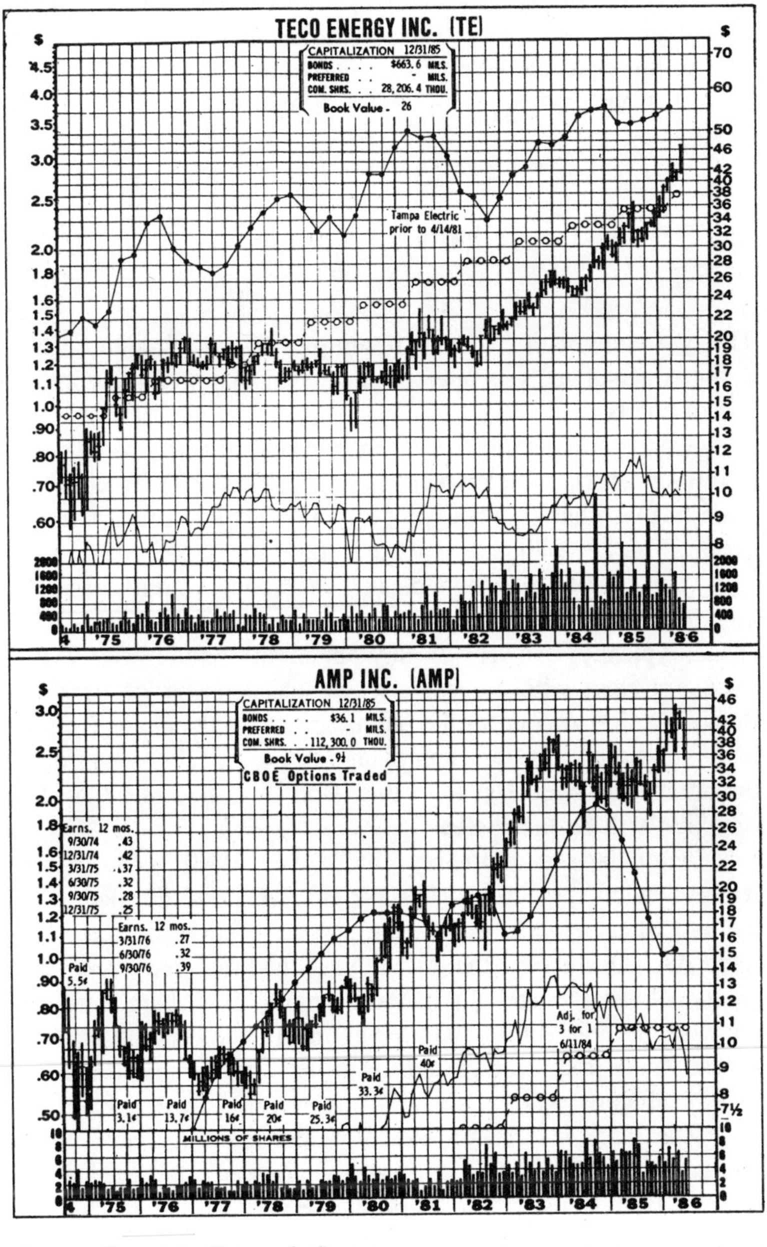

Source: Securities Research Company

your judgment confirmed by others. The best tactic is to wait until other investors show their interest by buying more shares at ever-higher prices. Conversely, when you get ready to sell, delay action as long as the volume is rising with a higher price and act when that uptrend slows and starts to reverse.

Charts for Timing

The best combination for maximum profits and minimum losses is fundamental analysis plus technical analysis, preferably by the use of charts.

Charts are a graphic ticker tape. They measure the attitudes of investors toward the market and/or specific stocks. Technicians believe that charts, when properly interpreted, predict future action. The key indicator is the trend.

You can plot your own data on chart paper, but it's easier to buy them from services. They are available for various time spans, typically, one year, twenty-one months, and twelve years. To use a chart with a specific stock, check the price trend by drawing a line to connect the points shown on the chart. Draw it *at the bottoms* for an upmoving stock, *at the tops* for a downtrending one. Usually, this won't be necessary as the direction will be fairly clear.

Example: In mid-July of 1986, AMP, Inc., was recommended for purchase by Wright Investors' Service. This manufacturer of electrical/electronic connection devices was rated AAA11 and over the last ten years had reported a return on equity of 22.4% and an average annual per share earnings increase of 15%. But in 1985 the company had been hit hard by industrywide price-cutting and lower demand. Its profit rate fell to 12% (Figure 3-1).

The stock was at 36. Research showed that management had taken effective action and that the company appeared ready to come back to its traditional profitable growth. The fundamentals were good. Wright, with its major investments in long-term pension plans, could afford to buy early and wait for the stock price rise: to a target price of about 50 in 1987 and 60 in 1988.

Alert Al, using technical analysis, saw that the chart was unfavorable. The stock price was still trending down (Figure 3-1). Al delayed purchase. After the stock dropped to 33 and then started up, he bought at 34, two points lower than the purchase price of the professional. By mid-September, AMP was up to 38, despite a dip in the overall market.

The risk was that the downtrend would turn suddenly, but this seldom happens. A trend in motion continues until there's a clear reversal, as shown on the chart.

Long-Term Charts

Charts that show the price/volume over a long period of time are also valuable in timing for two reasons:

1. They illustrate the pattern of a stock, which usually tends to be repeated except when there are unusual conditions. A utility stock has a flat pattern until interest rates decline.

Thus, the stock of TECO Energy, the Tampa, Florida, power company, stayed within a fairly narrow range, between 16 and 20, from 1975 to 1980 (with one sharp downturn when profits fell in 1979). Even the subsequent upturn in the early '80's was much the same (Figure 3-2A).

By contrast, AMP, Inc., whose profits are not regulated, had a more erratic pattern: up ten points, down five, etc. Over the years, its price continued to rise because of its high profitability and steady growth (Figure 3-2B).

2. They illustrate when there's a breakthrough to a new high. At this point, the stock usually starts to climb rapidly as investors become more enthusiastic. With AMP, a buy signal came in November 1985 when it broke 100 before a three-for-one split, and again in February 1986 when it pierced the only high around 36. Note that it was still essential to watch for downturns, as came in the spring of 1986. Most quality stocks, as long as they maintain their high rating, move pretty much the same way over the years.

Indicator Digest Composite Index

This type of chart is one of the best ways to follow the market and to catch key trends (Figure 3-3). It is prepared every other week by Indicator Research Group, Palisades Park, NJ 07650. Similar charts are available from other services.

With this indicator, each NYSE stock has the same weight so the chart provides an accurate review of the total market. By contrast, all of the Dow averages are weighted by the market price and number of shares of the component stocks. As a result, these averages have limited accuracy and are useful primarily as points of reference.

As shown on the chart, the Dow Jones Industrial Average (DJIA) has moved more erratically—sharper swings, up and down—than the Indicator Digest Average (IDA). This means that the overall stock market was less volatile than the thirty major stocks. The DJIA may soar twenty points but your stocks will hold steady, or, as we hope, it will be the other way around.

To provide a broader frame of reference, IDA plots a thirty-week moving average (MA). This is just what the name suggests: an average that moves with the unit of time covered. A thirty-week MA is compiled by adding the total prices of all stocks at the close of each week, dividing the total by 30 and plotting the result on the chart. In the thirty-first week, drop week number 1 and add week number 31.

To provide a comparison, this is shown against the IDA line. The technician buys when the MA moves above the IDA; he/she sells when the MA falls below the average. Keep in mind that such decisions will be made daily or weekly so the swings will be pronounced and easier to interpret.

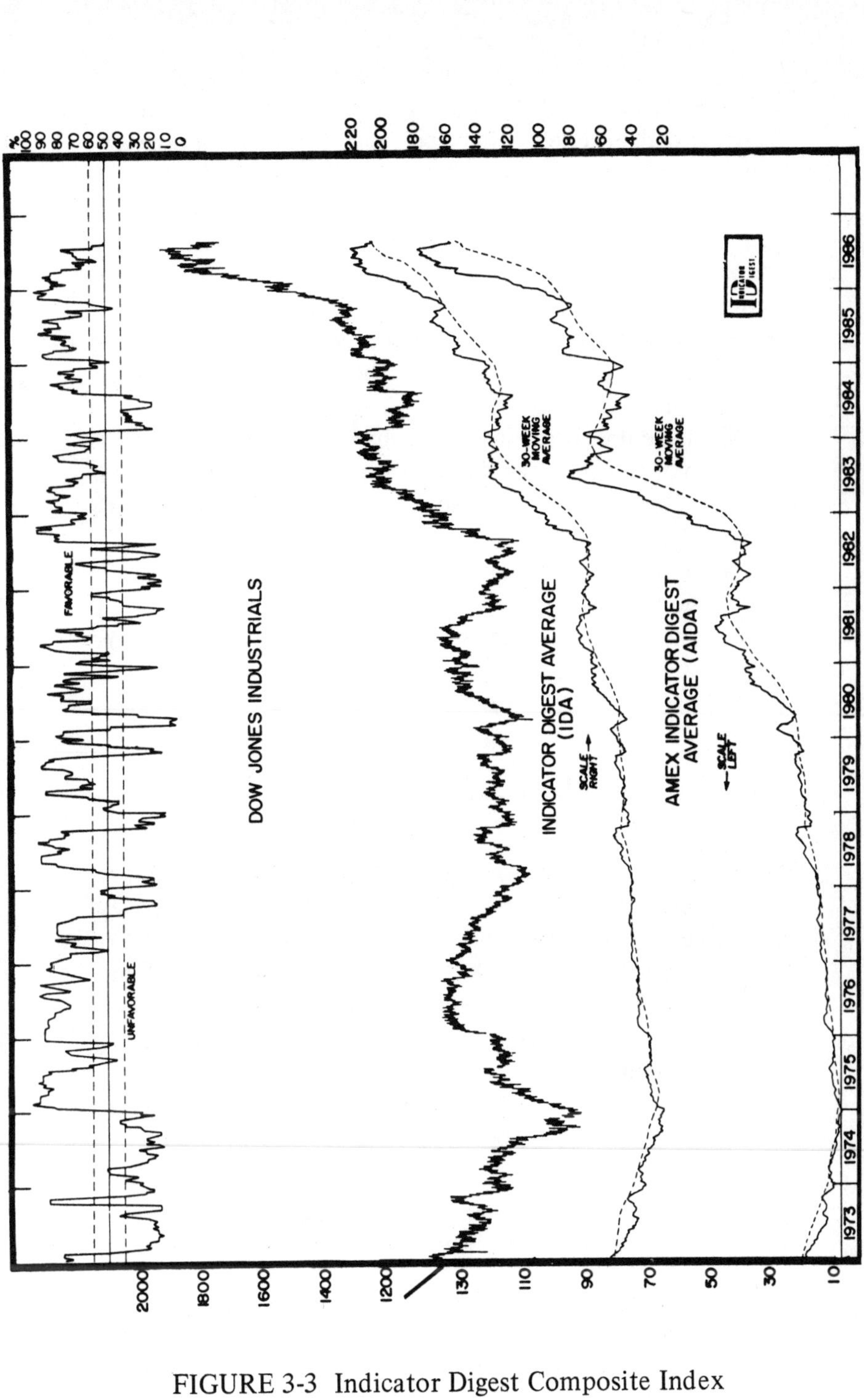

Source: Indicator Research Group

FIGURE 3-3 Indicator Digest Composite Index

At the top of this special chart is a handy trend indicator where the IDA is plotted against percentages indicating favorable or unfavorable buying points. Note that this line reflects short-term projections that may not take place immediately. In early 1984 the indicator was unfavorable, in line with the market decline. It did not move into favorable territory until after the interim rise. And in early August 1986 (the date of this chart), the line was trending down. Yet, on the next Monday the DJIA soared thirty points. A month later, the market dropped over a hundred points.

To make it easy for investors, there's an index from 0% to 100% (top of chart). When the line moves over 60, the market is favorable; between 60 and 40, it's neutral; below 40, it's unfavorable.

Note that the IDA moves more sharply than the DJIA. In June 1986 the IDA was moving down while the DJIA was still soaring. The break came in the next two weeks. By following the IDA, the smart investor knew when to bail out.

Using the Averages

No market indexes/averages represent overall institutional performance because they show only the action of a relatively few equities and do not reflect the varied and changing strategies of diversification between stocks and fixed income investments, money management policies which call for temporary switching of some funds into cash equivalents or the use of program trading via futures contracts.

Any and all of these indicators can be valuable to catch trends and make comparisons.

CATCHING TRENDS

When the final figure keeps moving up, investors are still optimistic. Always check the volume and look for other types of confirmation. If the market goes up with heavy turnover, it means that the professionals expect higher prices for the immediate future.

If the gains come with lower volume, be cautious. This signals a period of indecision about either the interest rate, governmental action, or the direction and degree of the next market move.

If the volume is high and prices drop, watch out! This may be the start of a decline. At this point, if you have a welcome gain, it's probably wise to sell or, at least, to set a stop-loss order. But it's usually wise to wait for confirmation over two or three days or, with speculative holdings, a week or two. With quality stocks, however, be patient. Sooner or later, their values will assure higher prices.

These days, the volume of the market is so high and the price movements so broad that some of the old checkpoints have to be reexamined. Still, the basic concepts are valid: a trend in motion will continue until there is a clear reversal.

Whenever there's a significant shift in any major average (and generally they move together), review all equity holdings to see whether, and how soon, the prices of your stock holdings follow suit. If it's a bull market signal, it may be time to buy more; if its a bear market, get out or, if you are experienced, sell short. Take advantage of the information flashed by these indicators.

MAKING COMPARISONS

Compare the percentage profits or losses of your portfolios in relation to that of an appropriate average. For example, at the end of June 1986, from the start of that year, the DJIA was +22%; the S&P 500, +18%; Value Line, +13%; and the NASDAQ Composite, +24%. If the values of your common stocks rose more than 25%, you were beating the market. If they were up 20%, you did OK. But if your gains were lower, find the laggards and determine whether their future prospects are strong enough to warrant retention.

Clearly, this period was one where the best performers were shares of major corporations. If you hold Sexy Electronics or Star War Toys, it's time to sell such speculative stocks. That trend in motion must be interpreted!

Other Technical Indicators

There are scores of other tools of TA. They range from projections based on the length of women's skirts to the winner of the Superbowl football game. The credible indicators are most valuable when used in connection with charts to provide a background or, better yet, to confirm a trend. The basic information is available in the financial press with such data as:

ADVANCES/DECLINES (A/Ds)

These figures (Table 3-5) highlight the weekly action of the market by the number of stocks whose prices rose, fell, or remained unchanged. The overall market, as measured by the DJIA for the period in mid-September 1986, was relatively flat, with a swing of about fifteen points (1%) from a Tuesday high of 1778 to a Friday low of 1763.

Almost the same number of issues were traded daily. There was a strong advance on Wednesday to 982 stocks from 646 on Tuesday. The declines were much the same in reverse: heavy on Tuesday and light on Wednesday. But note that on Friday, when the Dow dropped, the advances, declines, and unchanged held within a narrow range. Investors were uncertain.

NEW HIGHS/LOWS

New highs/lows for the last twelve months were not overly significant except that on Tuesday, when the Dow rose, the number of new lows also increased.

TABLE 3-5
NYSE Advances/Declines, Highs/Lows

DJIA Close	Mon. 1767.58	Tues. 1778.54	Wed. 1769.40	Thurs. 1774.18	Fri. 1762.65
Issues traded	2,018	1,999	1,995	1,982	1,974
Advances	801	646	982	704	775
Declines	837	940	627	821	793
Unchanged	380	413	386	457	406
New highs	6	7	12	12	9
New lows	19	37	27	22	18
Sales (000) shares	177,912	153,253	165,707	155 123	192,677

Source: Barron's

The best way to use A/Ds is to plot them on a chart against the DJIA. Near market peaks, the A/D lines will almost always top out and start declining before the stock market average. Again, use A/Ds for confirmation of other technical trends.

MOST ACTIVE STOCKS

This table can be found at the top of most financial pages. It's a good place to spot winners and losers. When there's unusual activity in any stock, or group of stocks, something is happening. At the time the move may be for the wrong reasons, but then again, it may reflect information of which you are not yet aware.

In most cases, volume precedes price. Some major money managers are making a move and, in a few days, the direction of that move will become apparent. Professionals act as a herd. When one or two major institutions start buying, this will alert other money managers who, anxious to get on the bandwagon, follow these leaders. The volume soars and up goes the stock, usually for a short time. Increasingly, the action will be triggered by computers which are set to buy, or sell, at a specific price. First come the professional leaders; then the professional followers and, finally, the public.

When the high volume comes with lower prices, action can be very rapid—too fast for most amateurs. That's why a stop-loss order can be valuable, especially with volatile issues. As an amateur, you are competing with sophisticated, computerized professionals and, unless you are alert, can be clobbered.

With the most-active stocks, look for groups rather than companies. If there are four or five oil companies with heavy volume, institutions are interested: favorably if the prices rise; unfavorably when they decline.

Check the list daily to find the same companies or groups. Then, get information on the winners and start selling the losers. Take your time and wait for confirmation. Do your homework and try to determine the reasons for this extra activity. (That's what a broker is for). If the long-term prospects are good, hold or consider buying.

Forecasting: Seasonal Patterns Can Improve Timing

Projections in Wall Street can never be exact, because the stock market is a moving mirror image of the excesses of man and the extremes of human optimism and pessimism. It reflects investor expectations for the stock market as a whole and for securities of individual corporations. These attitudes are the result of hope and fear, of opinions of domestic and international developments, of money and credit of corporate earnings and dividends, of politics and policies, and, most important, of prejudices based partly on facts and mostly on fancy.

Still, there are forecasts that can provide background for timing. They are based on the belief that what has happened before is likely to occur again, and because they are well documented over the years, they can be considered reasonably reliable.

These seasonal patterns are not always accurate nor supported by facts, but in an atmosphere so subject to rumors and dreams, anything that people believe tends to become self-fulfilling—to a degree. The most widely used are:

JANUARY INDICATOR

The first month is almost always a signal of what's ahead for the full year. Some professionals try to beat the crowd by relying on the action of the first five days but, in recent years, with the frantic stock market, this has not been overly reliable.

The market move in January has predicted that of the full year 80% of the time. If the market is up in the first month, the year will probably end at a higher level—but not always. In 1982 and 1984 the market slipped in January but ended December at a higher level. The key checkpoint is the trend, not the percentage of the rise or fall.

Keep in mind that there are other factors that have an impact. In the presidential year of 1984, the average was down in January but the year ended on the plus side.

SUMMER RALLY

Regardless of the previous trend, the stock market usually moves up in the summer, from a low close in May/June to a higher mark in August/September. Over the past decade, the average annual gain has been 9.38%: an ebullient +21.03% in 1980 (from a May 12 low of 805.20 to a September 22 high of 974.57) to a barely ahead +0.44% in 1981 (May 11 low of 963.33 to a late summer high of 967.66).

YEAR-END RALLY

Since 1955 the stock market has been higher in December/January than in November. As measured by the DJIA, the difference between the low closing price of the last two months of each year and that of the first month has averaged about +10%

in the past decade. The gains have ranged from a tiny +0.86% in 1968 to a whopping +22.2% in 1974. Usually, the lows came in November and the highs in January.

Under the old tax law, long-term capital gains were taxed at the lowest rate, so year-end sales, at a profit, were often wise. Now, with uniform tax levies ahead for both gains and income, it may pay to delay profitable sales until January to catch the higher prices.

Summary

For major investments, wait to see what happens in January. If the market moves up in the first five days, be optimistic. If this rise continues for the next few weeks, invest fully. If it fluctuates, wait a bit. If the trend is down, invest defensively and hold a portion of your funds in liquid assets as reserves to be used for buying opportunities later, probably in June to catch the summer rise.

Chapter 4

FIXED ASSETS/ INCOME SECURITIES FOR SAFETY/ DIVERSIFICATION/ TAX BENEFITS

In all portfolios, there's a time and place for investments in debt: *to preserve capital,* fixed assets such as savings accounts and money market funds; *to assure income* and, at times, provide appreciation, fixed income holdings such as bonds, both taxable and tax-exempt.

Most of these debt investments are safe. Bank accounts are federally insured up to $100,000; bills, notes and bonds issued or guaranteed by the U.S. government are the best you can buy; and bonds issued by Blue Chip corporations, institutions, and governments are sure to pay interest and be redeemed at par. But with the tremendous demand for capital, especially for takeovers and restructuring, an increasing number of debt securities involve greater risks than stocks.

In both personal and fiduciary portfolios, the types of debt investments should vary with your resources, goals, and risk levels; the amount of debt holdings should be related to the economy, the cost of money, and the outlook for the stock market. When interest rates are high, the smart investor locks in

TABLE 4-1
Comparative Investment Returns

Period	Stocks: Total % Change	Average Compound Annual Rates: Stocks	Bonds	90-Day T-Bills	Inflation GNP Deflator*
1900–09	+145.9%	+ 9.4%	+ 4.2%	+ 5.7%	+2.1%
1910–19	+167.4	+10.3	+ 2.6	+ 5.3	+7.2
1920–29	+281.8	+14.3	+ 6.4	+ 3.9	−1.4
1930–39	−0.3	0	+ 3.1	+ 0.6	−1.5
1940–49	+125.5	+ 8.5	+ 3.8	+ 0.5	+6.4
1950–59	+464.6	+18.9	+ 1.1	+ 2.0	+2.7
1960–69	+67.2	+ 5.3	+ 2.9	+ 4.0	+2.7
1970–79	+ 65.8	+ 5.2	+ 7.5	+ 6.4	+6.6
1980–86**	+198.6	+17.7	+14.5	+10.0	+5.4
1900–86	+263,719%	+ 9.5%	+ 4.7%	+ 4.0%	+3.2%

* Gross national product
** Through September
Source: Wright Investors' Service

high yields; when interest rates fall, he/she scores capital gains and shifts to stocks.

Only rarely should debt securities account for more than 35% of total holdings. Historically, quality common stocks have grown faster and, over the years, provided more income and more appreciation than fixed income securities. Table 4-1 shows how investment returns (price appreciation plus income) changed over eighty-six and a half years, between 1900 and mid-1986. Stocks returned 263,719%—an average annual rate of return, with reinvestments, of 9.5%—while bonds returned +4.7% and T-bills, +4.0%. The inflation deflator was +3.2%.

There were decades when bonds were more profitable, for example, in 1930–39, when they returned +3.1% while stocks plateaued; and in 1970–79, when bonds rose at an average compound annual rate of +7.5% versus 5.2% for stocks. T-bills were more profitable in 1930–39, when their return was +0.6% versus zero for stocks, and in 1970–79, when they returned about 25% more than stocks.

When you play the debt market, you should be nimble and relatively quick: selling stocks for capital gains and buying bonds for income and most appreciation.

With fixed asset investments, such as bank accounts, CDs, and money market funds, the principal remains the same and the income varies with the interest rate; with fixed income holdings, the interest is usually set for the life of the investment but the market value shifts with the cost of money—**up** when interest rates decline, **down** when they rise.

Strategy and Policy

The bond market is huge—in the trillions of dollars—and dominated by professionals who consider the purchase of 100 bonds ($100,000) a small lot. That's why it's necessary to understand how they operate. Here's a digest of the approaches used.

STRATEGY

This is the overall investment plan: (1) the percentage of assets to be allocated to fixed income securities in relation to those used to buy equities; (2) the choice of maturities: long-term debt due in more than ten years; medium-term, two to ten years; and short-term, less than two years; (3) total returns: income plus projected appreciation with comparisons of the advantages of long- versus short-term maturities; current income versus yields to maturity; and discounted low coupon issues versus higher yielding new issues; and in all cases (4), the potential changes in interest rates and future trends of the economy.

With short-term investments—Treasury bills, CDs, etc.—the decision relates to the types of securities or to the type of fund in which these are held. These are always considered as temporary reserves which should be readily available for more permanent holdings.

With medium- and long-term issues, the yardstick is total returns, taking into account the possibility that the issue will be called.

POLICY

This is based on an analysis of the one-to-five-year outlook for interest rates rather than the three-to-six-month projection which often turns out to be misleading. The objective is to determine whether and when to shift from one group to another: from corporates to governments, from long to intermediate term, and so forth.

Timing is critical with long-term debt. It's easy to get into bonds but hard to get out, at a profit. That's why many professional managers are slow to buy new bond issues. These may pay a higher yield, but their appreciation is limited by the call price which typically is less than 8% above cost: $1,080 versus $1,000 purchase price. Such a small profit is less than can be expected and usually achieved with quality stocks over the five or ten years of call protection.

With utility stocks, for example, the dividend yield will be close to that of the bond interest rate plus the probability of a rise in the stock value and payout so that the long-term returns can be more than the bond's coupon rate.

What to Do

Keeping in mind that bonds are a professional's market, the amateur must accept this situation and tailor decisions accordingly. First, however, one comment that relates to the title of this book: the idea that bonds are safer than quality stocks is not true. The shares of many Blue Chip, established, financially strong, well-managed corporations fulfill every criteria of long-term investment safety: regular returns, maintenance of principal plus steady growth and ever-higher values. There will, of course, be temporary fluctuations, and for a short period of time the value of some quality stocks may decline, but over the long term of a true investment program, their market worth will be greater than that of the best-rated bonds. Stocks are live, growing investments; fixed income holdings are "dead" holdings over the long term.

Still, debt issues do provide a base and a balance, and at times can be holdings as good as or better than stocks, especially when yields are ample and equities are bouncing around.

Fixed Assets Investments

With these, the principal stays the same, but the income fluctuates with the interest rate. These investments should be limited except in times of high yields. They are more convenient than profitable. For most investors, $5,000 to $10,000 should be the maximum commitment. This is more than enough to pay for emergencies, and you can always use credit cards for air tickets and major prepayments. I never cease to be amazed at how many senior citizens complain that their income is so limited that they can never buy a steak or see a movie. Yet, too often, they have $50,000 (or more) in a bank account/savings certificate paying less than 6%: $3,000 a year. If they invested $40,000 of these funds in a mutual fund, they could count on at least $4,000 from this source alone. If you have an older relative who is so foolish, try to explain the facts of financial life and turn fear into joy.

Keep Your Money Working

Investment money should work 365 days a year. These days, this is easier than in the past; many checking accounts pay interest, and most brokerage firms have money market funds into which dividends, interest, and proceeds of sales can be swept. The yields are small but every penny counts.

With these short-term holdings, the choice should not be on the basis of extracting the last fraction of a percentage point of interest (by sending your money to Texas or Australia) but on the ability to cash in quickly for new opportunities. No investment decision should have to be delayed until the interest qualification date or the maturity of the holding, as with, for example, a bank account that requires a minimum balance for thirty days or a CD that has to be held for six months.

Changes in the prices of publicly traded securities, especially common stocks, can occur rapidly. The stakes involved are much greater than the accrued interest that might be obtained. When a stock-buying decision has to be made, the necessary funds should be available within five business days, the time span set by the NYSE between the date of the stock purchase and that of final payment.

The arithmetic is clear: ½ of 1% interest a year is equal to a price change of one-quarter of a point on a $50 per share stock. In a busy market, an undervalued stock can move up a full point in a few hours!

SAVINGS ACCOUNTS

These are deposits in financial institutions where interest is paid at a base rate, typically about 5% but occasionally a bit more. Your money is safe because each depositor's funds are insured up to $100,000 by an agency of the federal government. If the bank/thrift goes bust, you will have to wait for your money.

Always check the terms. With a mandated minimum balance of $2,500 and an average interest rate of 5.0%, the annual income will be $125. If your balance dips below this floor, there may be a monthly service fee of $10. This means that, over a year with six lean months, the net income will drop to a measly 2.5% rate of return.

Similarly, high bank fees can cut your stated yield. With a minimum balance of $2,500, the interest rate of 6.0% will provide an apparent return of $150, but when there's a $5 monthly ($60 a year), the income will be $90 for a 3.6% yield.

CERTIFICATES OF DEPOSIT (CDs)

These are special types of bank/thrift deposits that pay a stated yield for a stated term, usually a minimum of three months and a maximum of three years, but, for large sums, up to ten years. Most are insured, to a maximum of $100,000, by a federal agency. They can be purchased for as little as $1,000 or for as much as $100,000.

The interest rate is tied to that of six-month Treasury bills so it was over 11% in 1985 but recently was down below 7%. In their ads, the banks/thrifts emphasize the compounded rate of return.

Time	Stated Yield	Compounded Yield
3 months	6.50%	6.81%
6 months	6.90	7.25
12 months	7.30	7.68
30 months	7.70	8.12

But, as explained in small type, the total yield is based on daily compounding of interest and assumes principal and interest remain on deposit a full year.

With CDs, there are penalties for early withdrawal: a minimum loss of one month's interest for a CD maturing in one year or less and of three month's interest for longer term CDs.

N.B. The institution may set a higher "mark to market" penalty. This is the difference between the rate on your CD and the current market rate of a similar CD.

Example: Conservative Connie, anxious to lock in what she felt was a high yield, invested $10,000 in a ten-year CD yielding 10%. To her surprise, the interest rate zoomed to 13% so, at the end of three and a half years, she wants to switch and take a loss of $250 interest. But the bank says the penalty will be $1,950. This is calculated as follows: the difference between the stated rate (10%) and the current rate (13%) is multiplied by the number of years to maturity (6.5) to determine the percentage penalty on the amount withdrawn (19.5%) to get $8,050, a penalty of $1,950, not the anticipated $250. The only solace: this $1,950 is fully deductible as an adjustment to gross income.

When the CD is in an IRA and the saver is over age fifty-nine and a half, there's no penalty.

CDs are for convenience, not profit. Some folks are so anxious to get the highest yield that they send their money to out-of-state banks. Most of these are in Texas, where the economy has been so devastated by the oil-price slump that many are—and will be—in default. How stupid can you get?

Sure, you can count on the government insurance, but such repayments take time during which you will lose income. And there will be extra costs for postage/phone calls, etc. **Do your homework:** a difference of 1% on $10,000 is $100 a year, slightly more with daily compounding. This "reward" is not worth the risk.

SHORT-TERM NOTES

These are debt obligations, usually of the U.S. government, with maturities up to three years. They are available in units of $1,000. Their interest rates are slightly less than those of T-bills and they are substantially more than those of savings accounts/CDs.

These short-term instruments should be held as a matter of strategy when wisdom calls for a substantial portion of funds in reserves. They will provide ample returns and can be rolled over at maturity.

They should not be held as a matter of policy because, by definition, you know that at some point in the relatively near future you would need the money to buy quality stocks. You would have to sell in the open market and, since there is a substantial spread between bid and asked prices, might lose money. As a rule of thumb, if you expect to use the money in sixty to ninety days, you should keep your money in a money market fund.

COMMERCIAL PAPER

These are short-term corporate notes. They have a ready market and relatively short maturities, seldom more than nine months. The primary consideration is always the liquidity, but never the yield alone. Quality is always essential. They are rated, by Standard & Poor's, for example, A, A-1, A-2, A-3, B, etc. Buy only those with an A in their quality. Bear in mind, however, that they are bought primarily by institutions and professionals.

U.S. SAVINGS BONDS

These are excellent investments for small sums and good holdings for a portion of pension plan assets. They are 100% safe, can be bought without commissions and redeemed quickly, usually at cost plus interest.

EEs are available at 50% of face value, e.g., a $50 bond costs $25. HH bonds sell in denominations of $500 and $1,000. You can buy either through a payroll savings plan, at local financial institutions, or, by mail, from Federal Reserve banks, or the Bureau of Public Debt, Washington, DC 20239–0001.

When held for at least five years (ten-year maturity), EE bonds bought after November 1986 earn 6% interest or 85% of the average yield of Treasury notes and bonds with five-year maturities. Those purchased earlier continue to pay up to 7.5%. This interest (actually appreciation) is exempt from state and local taxes and accumulates tax-free until the bonds are cashed in. You can defer taxes by converting the EEs into HHs after six months. These pay 7.5% interest semiannually . . . taxable.

With EEs, after eighteen months, interest is credited the first of each month, so buy at the end of the previous month to get the maximum return.

TREASURY BILLS (T-BILLS)

These are short-term debt obligations of Uncle Sam. They are equivalent to cash and assure modest to high yields depending on the current cost of money.

T-bills are available for 90 and 180 days and one year. The first two maturities are auctioned weekly, the last once a month. All issues are actively traded with daily prices reported in the financial press.

The minimum original purchase unit is $10,000, but you can buy or sell smaller amounts in the after-market. As these are favorite investments for major institutions/corporations, a purchase of $100,000 is regarded as a small lot.

All T-bills are sold at a discount that reflects the interest to maturity. Thus, a 360-day 7% bill would cost $9,300 and a year later would be cashed in for $10,000. The actual yield, on cost, would be 7.53%. The $700 gain is considered interest so, for federal income tax returns, is taxable at the full rate. This gain is not subject to state and local income levies.

T-bills can be bought directly by a bid on a form available from a Federal Reserve Bank. With your application, you send in a check for either: (1) the full face value and get back a check for the difference between your cost and $10,000, or (2) 5% of the total, with the balance to be paid on notification of acceptance, directly or through an account established for this purpose. Each purchase is acknowledged with a receipt. At maturity, you can roll them over (exchange old for new bills) or redeem them at a commercial bank.

Or you can deal through a banker or broker at a cost of about $25 for the purchase and $15 for a rollover. For information, request *Basic Information on Treasury Bills* from your nearest Federal Reserve Bank.

T-bills are excellent temporary investments for both individual and fiduciary funds. You never have to worry about quality, value, or timing. But they may not always provide maximum flexibility or returns.

MONEY MARKET ACCOUNTS/FUNDS

These are available from almost every financial entity: bank, thrift, brokerage firm, credit union, insurance company, and investment management organization. They invest in liquid assets such as Treasury bills and notes, certificates of deposit, commercial paper, repurchase agreements and so forth. They pay daily interest that is compounded, permit sales or purchases at net asset value, and charge management fees that appear modest but can add up to profitable sums for management. Their yields move with interest rates on short-term Treasuries and have ranged from over 15% in the early 1980s to less than 7% recently.

These are convenient parking places for cash reserves, not investments in the truest sense. For modest savings, they are better than T-bills: minimum purchase of about $1,000 with no fees for additions but the loss of about seven days' interest while your check clears. By contrast, the minimum cost of a T-bill is about $9,400 ($10,000 face value less current yield of 6%) and, when bought through a bank, a fee of $25. All income is fully taxable.

With a brokerage account, money markets are useful to sweep over interest, dividends, and proceeds of sales of securities while waiting for new opportunities. Set up such an account with your broker with all portfolios of over $10,000. See Table 4-2.

Timing tip: buy new shares of MM funds after noon, so that you will get interest for that day.

In selecting a money market fund, check the assets as to:

Type. The safest debt securities are federal government obligations; the riskiest are CDs of small banks and thrifts and repos (repurchase agreements) where the seller of the short-term debt agrees to repurchase at a set future date and a set profit for the buyer. Be wary of aggressive funds that deal with other lenders under the same management. Despite state supervision, some institutions have been unable to fulfill their commitments and gone bankrupt.

Diversification. This means variation among debt issues, with the greatest concentration in federal obligations. When any fund has heavy holdings in foreign securities, the yields may be higher but so are the risks.

Maturities. The shorter the average time to redemption, the more conservative the management, since short-term holdings insulate

TABLE 4-2
Typical Money Market Fund Quotations

Fund	Assets	Average Maturity	7-Day Average Yield % Return	% Compounded
Dreyfus Liquid Assets	$ 7,749	45 days	6.4%	6.6%
Fidelity Cash Reserves	4,398	55	6.5	6.7
Lehman Cash Reserves	277	35	6.5	6.7
Merrill Lynch Cash M'g't	18,410	47	6.7	6.9
Scudder Cash Investment	1,217	40	6.3	6.5
Vanguard Prime	1,915	36	6.5	6.7
Donoghue's Money Fund Average of 268 funds		44	6.19	6.38

30-day average yield: 6.24%

During the week ended May 27, 1986, the seven-day average yield remained the same at 6.19%; the thirty-day average yield decreased to 6.24% from 6.29%; and the average maturity shortened by one day to forty-four days. The professionals did not anticipate major changes in interest rates.

investors against sharp movement in interest rates. Longer maturities can provide higher returns, but they will be offset by a decline in value if the cost of money rises suddenly.

Forget about the seven-day yield and concentrate on: (1) the thirty-day rate of return because usually you will not withdraw earlier, (2) the average maturity because this indicates how long the current yield can be maintained. When management looks for lower interest rates, new money will be invested at a lower yield so it will try to extend current maturities, occasionally as long as sixty days. Vice versa: when the outlook is for a higher cost of money, maturities will be shortened to be ready to benefit from the future rise.

Like many Wall Street figures, such averages are better for conversation than profit. The time spread between different funds is seldom significant except in erratic markets. The yield of one fund may be ½ of 1% higher and the average maturity ten days longer, but on $10,000 that's only about $2 a week more. Over a period of time, most money market funds will report about the same returns. For most investors, the primary consideration should be convenience and service.

Determining Yields

In real life, the stated yields are not always comparable because of different methods of computation.

Fund A uses a "mark to market" method based on a constant net value. Each day, a "pure interest" yield is computed to reflect the interest income earned on the portfolio. Then, the manager: (1) marks assets to the day's closing prices, (2) determines the capital appreciation/depreciation per share, (3) adds or subtracts the gain or loss from the "pure interest" yield to arrive at an "actual yield."

Fund B marks to market on a variable net asset value. The manager does not factor capital gains/losses into the interest but adjusts the net asset value of the shares to the $1 per share cost.

Fund C uses "straight line accrual," which recognizes pure interest only, so that the principal and yield remain stable.

Over a short time period, one fund may report a slightly higher yield, but in six months or so there will be little difference because the money managers are all buying the same assets in a competitive market. There are printed bulletins that report weekly yields of money market funds (and other types of short-term investments), but unless you enjoy telephoning and switching, the extra interest will not be enough to pay for the cost of the subscription, postage, phone calls, and scratch paper.

Investing in Bonds

As noted earlier, some bonds should be included in every portfolio with reasonable assets, say $20,000 or more. These debt issues provide modest income, possible appreciation, and preservation of capital. The percentage of fixed income securities depends on the type of portfolio, your investment goals, and your (and your spouse's) sleep-well level.

When you buy any type of fixed income security, you are loaning money. In return, you receive a preset payment of interest and, at some future date, the return of the principal. That the yield is certain does not mean that the prices of bonds will remain stable. Their market values reflect the current cost of money.

Forty years ago (the life span of some utility bonds), the interest rate for well-rated bonds was about 2% a year. Their prices dropped as interest rates rose so that when the cost of money was 15%, each $1,000 par value bond was trading at about $300.

On the other hand, bonds floated with a 15% yield rose to $1,500 when interest rates fell 10%.

A second drawback with bonds, etc., is that the income can be eroded by inflation. At a 4% rate (lower than the average of the past decade but probably higher than can be expected in the future), the purchasing power of the $1,000 redemption value will be cut to about $700.

This brings us back to the premise of this book: that, over the life of a true investment program, quality stocks are more rewarding than debt securities. But there are periods when debt holdings are more profitable.

Between 1970 and mid-1986: the average dividend of the Dow Jones Industrial stocks was between 40% and 50% of the yield to maturity of the Dow Jones Corporate Bond Average. However, the market prices fluctuated widely: annually, for stocks, as high as +45% in 1975 and as low as −4% in 1981; for bonds, from −13.2% in 1980 to +23.6% in 1982. That's why, for maximum returns, bonds have to be managed as carefully as stocks.

That's not easy for the amateur. When interest rates rise, the values of outstanding bonds decline until the new higher-paying issues dominate the market. The smart investor cashes in with the peak prices and reinvests the proceeds in more rewarding debt.

Similarly, when interest rates fall, as in 1985 and early 1986, it's a signal to buy discount bonds—old, low-coupon issues selling below par—and hold to maturity for excellent total returns.

In investing in bonds, it is important to: (1) think in terms of the entire portfolio, not just one or two debt issues/funds, (2) consider the probability of changes in the interest rate, (3) concentrate on total returns over the next three to five years, (4) manage the portfolio in terms of fundamental investing, not trading. No bond portfolio should have a turnover above 10% a year.

Definitions

Most corporate bonds are sold in minimum units of $5,000, but the trading prices are quoted in units of $1,000, as a percentage of market value. Thus, at 70, the bond price is $700. Short-term T-bills and almost all tax-exempts are quoted on a yield basis. For a one-year T-bill offered at 8.7%, this would mean a market price of $9,130. For Washington State General Obligation bonds, 8%, due in 1909 and trading at 101⅜, a yield of 8.87%.

Interest is calculated on a daily basis of a 360-day year of twelve thirty-day months with the exception of U.S. government issues other than Treasury bills. With these, the interest is calculated on the exact number of days of a 365-day year.

In most cases, when you buy any fixed income security in the open market, you pay all of the accrued interest to the seller. For a $1,000 9% bond, bought at 98 on the fifteenth day after issue, your cost is $983.75, the $980 price plus a half month's interest at $3.75.

Quality is even more important with debt issues than with stocks. Since you are lending your money, you want to be sure you will be paid interest promptly, can buy and sell in an active market, and, at maturity, will get back the face value of the bill, note, bond, preferred stock, etc. Some professionals set their own standards, but the most convenient references are the rat-

TABLE 4-3
Ratings: Bonds/Commercial Paper/Notes

Taxable/ Tax-exempts	Moody's	S&P	Pretax Interest Coverage
Highest quality	Aaa	AAA	12.82X
High quality	Aa	AA	9.50X
Upper medium	A	A	6.65X
Medium	Baa	BBB	4.41X
Speculative	Ba	BB	3.14X
Undesirable	B	B	2.13X
Poor quality	Caa	CCC	

Commercial paper: maturity less than 365 days

The letter indicates capacity for timely payment; the number, the relative degree of safety and capacity to pay.

Highest	A
Very strong	A-1
Strong	A-2
Satisfactory	A-3
Adequate capacity	B
Doubtful capacity	C

Municipal notes: liquidity and degree of market risk

Strong and safe	SP-1
Satisfactory	SP-2
Speculative	SP-3

ings set by Moody's Investors Service and Standard & Poor's (Table 4-3).

For investments, never buy any bonds rated below BBB. A lower classification, no matter how famous the corporation, is a speculation. Watch for potential or actual changes in ratings: the S&P Creditwatch focuses on bonds of companies that may be affected by new events or trends: mergers, voter referenda, regulations, etc. When a bond is downgraded, that's a sign of trouble and unless the bond is near maturity, it should be sold. When it's upgraded, it's a favorable sign of greater financial strength. The table also lists the pretax interest coverage: the multiple of earnings available for debt payments. AAA bonds have profits almost thirteen times the money need to meet the semiannual interest charges.

The debt of quality corporations is suitable for fixed income holdings. The professionals often have a supplementary list of major companies whose credit is adequate so that the interest and priciple can be expected to be met without question, but whose records of growth and profitability are not attractive enough to warrant inclusion on the approved stock list.

Examples: Dow Chemical would not be acceptable for equity investments because of its high debt—about 54% of total capital. But as long as the company continues its profitable growth, its bonds can be worthwhile investments.

McDonald's Corporation, the fast-food chain, is another company not on the Approved Wright Investment List because its debt/equity ratio is over 50%, reflecting the large real estate lease obligations. Yet, there is no reason to fear that the company will be unable to meet interest payments, because its return on equity has been a high 22% a year.

How Bonds Are Traded

Buying and selling bonds can be more complex and costly than trading stocks. Debt issues of a few hundred large corporations are listed on the NYSE and AMEX. These daily quotations show volume but report trades of nine bonds or more. These are handled under an automated system so can be checked in the financial press. The minimum commission is $2.50 each, but most brokers and dealers charge $5 to $10 per $1,000, typically with a minimum of $25. For the small investor, each transaction costs one-half to one point, added to the cost and subtracted from the sale proceeds.

Most corporate and almost all U.S. government bonds and tax-exempt issues are traded over the counter on a bid and asked basis. Generally, the bid price is one quarter or one half a point ($2.50 to $5.00) below the asked price. This spread represents the dealer's profit.

Trading Tips

Accurate prices for a small lot of bonds (less than fifty) are difficult to obtain. That's why it is smart to set a specific price or narrow range to buy or sell.

With unlisted issues, you can tell your securities dealer to ask bond brokers to obtain bids by asking, "Put my bonds out with a broker." This has two advantages: (1) you will be certain that many market professionals will know about the bonds; (2) you will probably obtain the best possible price at that time.

The bid process is computerized so that your request is transmitted to hundreds of brokers throughout the nation. If you are dealing in units of fifty or more, a conscientious broker will call dealers whom he believes have a special interest in your type of bonds to ascertain if they want to bid to acquire the bonds for subsequent resale or to fulfill a specific order.

Well, that's what the brokers tell you but, it seems to me, the best tactic is to try to buy from your broker's inventory. Tell him the quality and approximate maturity you want and hope he has some leftovers in stock. This will save you a few points because the firm seldom wants to hold odd lots.

Table 4-4 shows the weekly transactions for typical corporate bonds listed on the NYSE. Here's the interpretation:

In the past year, the prices ranged widely and at this time are close to their highs. The swings have been about fourteen points ($140) for the bonds due in the next few years but almost twenty-four points ($240) for the long-term Indiana Bell bonds.

The only currently competitive yield, 8.9%, was that of Indiana Bell, due in thirty-one years. Amoco pays a high 13%, but in the next five years the investor will lose $120 as its price will drop from 112 to 100.

TABLE 4-4

How Bonds Are Quoted*

New York Stock Exchange: Taxable Bonds

	52 Weeks			Current	Sales	Weekly		Net	
Rating**	High	Low	Name/Coupon	Yield	$1,000	High	Low	Last	Change
AA	91	77¾	ATT 3⅞, 90	4.3	184	90⅛	89⅛	89⅛	. . .
AAA	113⅞	108½	Amoco 14, 91	13	130	112	111½	112	+2½
BB+	82⅞	67	BethSt 4½, 90	5.8	29	79⅛	78⅛	78⅛	−3⅜
CCC	75⅝	62⅜	McCrory 7½, 94	10	10	73⅝	73½	73⅝	+¼
AAA	95	71½	IndBell 8⅛, 17	8.9	5	91½	91½	91½	+1⅛

* For Week Ended May 30, 1986

** Not shown on the quotations in the financial press; for reference only.

Conversely, the ATT and Bethlehem Steel bonds have low current yields but rewarding yields to maturity due to appreciation to par: about ten points for high-rated Ma Bell and over twenty points for riskier Bessie.

Compared to stocks, the volume was thin: a high of 184 sales for ATT, a low of 5 for Indiana Bell. Note that the widest change was thirty-three points for Bethlehem Steel (showing why it's smart to give your broker orders within a narrow range).

The price changes were erratic—a spread between the weekly high and low of +2½ points ($25) for Amoco and of −3¾ ($375) for Bessie.

The real market for bonds is over the counter: almost all government issues, direct obligations, and those of federal agencies; tax-exempts of major issuers; and loans of thousands of smaller corporations. Transactions of the first two groups are published in daily newspapers but information on the others is available primarily in special publications.

Most of these bonds are traded on a bid and asked basis. Typically, the bid price is one-fourth to one-half a point ($2.50 to $5) below the asked price. This spread represents the dealer's profit. This varies: (1) according to the time to maturity, (2) according to the character and quality of the security, (3) inversely to the degree of activity and size of the market for that particular debt, (4) according to the inventory of the dealer. Active issues, nearing redemption, have the smallest spread; less-traded, long-term securities have the widest gap.

Watch out for thinly traded issues and always get more than one quotation on the same or similar debt.

Examples: In the spring of 1986, a physician friend asked me about American Hospital Supply 7⅞, 2007. His office was next door to a branch of a national brokerage firm, so I checked prices. The bid was 82⅝; the asked 91, a spread of almost $100.

A student in my investment course for senior citizens showed me a slip from her broker offering to buy $25,000 of New York State Dormitory Authority, Long Island Jewish Hospital, GNMA collateralized bonds, 10⅜, 2012 at 114.90. (GNMA means a guarantee of payment of interest and principal by Uncle Sam.) I checked with a New York bond dealer who came up with a price of 116: $275 more!

Advice for Bond Investors

- Be Scroogy with bonds. A spread of one fourth of a point on each side of a transaction can make a worthwhile difference. Check with two dealers when you are involved with sizable investments.
- Ask your bank to handle the deal. If you are a good customer, they will handle the details and probably get a better price.
- Tell your dealer to ask bond brokers to obtain bids by saying, "Put my bonds out with a broker." This has two advantages: (1) you will be certain that many market professionals will know about the bonds; (2) you should get the best possible price at that time.

  The bid process is computerized so that your request is transmitted to hundreds of brokers, some of whom may have a special interest in your type of bonds.
- Enter your order at a narrow price range and be willing to wait a week or two.
- Determine the maturity date, quality rating you want, and amount you plan to invest and ask your dealer to try to meet these criteria. As noted before, with odd lots you may pick up bargains, but when you sell you may get less.
- Learn to understand the importance of yields: from the summary herewith, from your dealer, or from a library book on bonds.

The Importance of Yields

To professionals, the current price of the bond is important only in relation to yields and, for long-term holdings, to future value when interest rates change. These are the different types of yields with explanations based on Table 4-5.

Coupon yield is the interest rate stated on the face of the debt issue: 11¾%, 3½%, etc. For each $1,000 bond, the holder will

TABLE 4-5
Quotations and Yield Calculations: Treasury Bonds

Security	High	Last	Current Yield	YTM
11¾, May 1989	110.25	110.6	10.62%	7.82%
14⅝, Feb. 1992	130.5	128.28	11.40	8.19
3½, Nov. 1998	93.9	92.30	3.79	4.24
7⅞, Nov. 2002–07	98.21	95.22	8.27	8.31

N.B. These figures are not what you find in the press but are revised for illustration. Current yield is based on closing price.

receive interest, usually semiannually, totaling $117.50 and $35 respectively.

Yield on purchase prices is the annual rate of return based on the price paid for the bond. This is higher than the coupon yield when the bond is bought below par; lower when acquired at a premium. For that 11¾% bond, the yield on purchase price is 13.05% if the bond was bought at 90 ($900).

Current yield is the rate of return at the last quoted price of the bond. This is higher than the yield on purchase price if there has been a decline in value since purchase: for the 7⅞% bond at 95.22: 8.28%; for the 14⅝% issue at 128.28, 11.40% versus coupon yield of 14⅝%.

Yield to Maturity (YTM). This measures the annual return on investment until the security comes due. It is the sum of the total interest and a proportionate share of the appreciation (when bought at a discount) or depreciation (when purchased at a premium).

Since the 11¾% bond is selling above par and will lose value at maturity, the YTM is 7.82%, well below the current yield of 10.62%. But the YTM of the low coupon issue is 4.24%

versus yield of 3.5% on purchase price at par and above the current yield of 3.79%.

Here's how to approximate the YTM for a discount bond: 5.95%, due in ten years, and trading at 85 ($850), par value $1,000.

1. Subtract the current bond price from face value:
   $1,000 − $850 = $150
2. Divide this figure by the number of years to redemption:
   150 ÷ 10 = 15
3. Add the total interest payments:
   $59.50 × 10 = $595, so 15 + 595 = 610
4. Add current price to face amount and divide by 2:
   850 + 1,000 = 1,850 ÷ 2 = 925
5. Divide step 3 by step 4:
   610 ÷ 925 = 6.59%

   YTM is about 6.59%.

For true YTM, check statistical reports.

Calculation of Future Value

When you buy a bond at par, you want to project its future value if the cost of money changes over the year. This formula reflects the inverse relation between the price and yield:

$$\frac{AIP}{CY} = MP$$

AIP = Annual interest payment
CY = Current yield
MP = Market price

With a new $1,000, 8% bond, maturing in twenty years, the market price is $1,000, the annual interest is $80, and the current yield the stated 8%:

$$\frac{\$80}{8} = 100\ (1{,}000)$$

If interest rates rise to 9%:

$$\frac{90}{9} = \$888.88$$

If interest rates fall to 7%:

$$\frac{80}{7} = \$1,142.86$$

Bond Provisions to Check

With almost all debt issues, there may be special terms that affect the longevity, and to a degree the income, of the issue. They can be found in the prospectus of new offerings and should be included in the information furnished by the broker/dealer.

SINKING FUND

As the name implies, a sinking fund aims to sink corporate debt by setting aside cash that can be used by the trustee to buy back bonds periodically: in the open market when the bond price is below par; by lot when it's above par. Here are the advantages:

To the corporation. A sinking fund shortens the average life of the debt issue and provides greater market stability.

To the investor. The plus is that this reserve reduces the risk by steadily lowering the total debt and thus provides support for the market price of the bonds. The negative is that the bonds may be retired early so that the investor will have to find new investments, possibly when interest rates are lower than had been projected.

Example: in 1976, Enserch Corporation, then known as Lone Star Gas Company, sold $50 million of 8.75% debentures due in 2001. With a sinking fund to start in 1981, the company planned to acquire $1,875,000 worth of bonds annually. This meant that 75% of the issue would be retired before the final maturity and that the average life of the bonds would be 17.1

years, not the twenty-five years that the 2001 maturity date suggested. Enserch would pay less interest than with a non-purchasable bond and the investor would face the possibility of holding a short-term investment—five, six, or seven years.

A sinking fund does carry extra protection but if you are investing, especially fiduciary funds, for twenty-five years, why get involved in a situation where you must accept repayment in eighteen years?

Call Protection

Many bonds and some preferred stocks can be called (redeemed) at the option of the corporation before the stated maturity date at a price above face value. This early redemption often takes place when the company can borrow at a cheaper rate than that of the original debt. In most cases there is call protection, that is, no redemption for ten years or so. For example, Commonwealth Edison 15⅜, 2012 in 1982, were not callable until August 1987 and then at 112.41.

After this grace period, if interest rates have declined, it's important to check all holdings as usually there are special provisions listed, in small type, in Bond Guides.

A quick gauge for the probability that the call will be exercised is to divide the coupon interest rate by the call price: 15.37 ÷ 113.24 = 13.6%. When this quotient is higher than the current interest rate on similar bonds and there are still many years to maturity, chances are that you will have to cash in—at a profit above the issuing cost but below the market price (about 115 recently), when new debt paid about 9+%.

Yield Curve

Interest rate levels, direction and patterns involve three categories of debt maturities: short-term (under one year), medium-term (five to ten years), and long-term (ten to thirty years). Over time, each group has distinct characteristics: short-term rates fluctuate more widely than do long-terms; long-term prices fluctuate more than short-term prices.

For investors, the important factor is the future cost of money. When investors look for interest rates to drop, they buy bonds with longer maturities, usually due in the next five to ten years, or if they want to lock in higher yields, they go farther out, to twenty years or more. Similarly, when they expect higher interest rates, they do the opposite—to a degree.

One of the most widely used forecasting tools is the yield curve (Table 4-5). The shape of that curve shows investor expectations of the future cost of money. The chart illustrates the relationship between the rates of return of fixed income securities of similar quality with different maturities ranging from ninety days to thirty years. The chart is plotted from the left with the shortest maturities and continues to the long-term ones on the right. The important factor is the trend.

Interpreting the Yield Curve

On the charts, the focal point is the crosshatched area. At the top is the situation in 1984 when yields were high—long and wide; in 1985 (second from top) the critical area had narrowed; in January 1986 (third from top) the hatched area was expanding and by August that year was about the same except that short-term debt was wider and long-term narrower. As shown in Figure 4-1, yields declined significantly in 1984–85 and stabilized in 1986.

Here's what these tables showed (remember, view them as forecasters):

February 17, 1984. The trend is upward as shown by the rise in the yields of the one-to-five-year debt. Interest rates can be expected to rise within the next six months: for short-term debt, sharply; for long-term, modestly. This was the time to buy/hold

TABLE 4-6
Yields on U.S. Debt Securities

Date	Maturity by Years 1	5	10	20	30
2/17/84	11.99%	12.07%	12.33%	12.31%	12.20%
8/30/85	7.53	8.78	10.32	10.64	10.46
1/31/86	5.67	8.51	9.20	9.46	9.33
8/26/86	5.84	7.29	7.58	8.04	7.62

Source: Wright Investors' Service

short- to medium-term issues and be cautious about long-term holdings.

August 30, 1985. The curve is flattening, indicating that investors anticipate the same or lower rates soon. The spread between the short- and long-term rates narrowed.

January 31, 1986. The short-term trend is up but the long-term line is plateauing. Time to lock in higher long-term returns.

August 29, 1986. The curve continues to narrow and project lower yields with an advantage for medium-term holdings: as shown in Table 4-6, 8.04% for twenty-year bonds versus 7.29% for five-year debt and a low 7.62% for thirty-year issues.

As with most technical tools, this type of chart may not always be correct at any one point, but it will show the trend so that when you switch from equities to debt, you can buy the bonds that will pay more and probably be worth more when you switch back to stocks . . . or hold to maturity.

To better understand how to use the yield curve, ask your broker to dig up old charts and historical data on interest rates. By making comparisons with those forecasts and what actually happened, you will understand why so many professionals rely on this type of chart. Besides, even if you are not heavily in bonds, it's important to know what the experts look for in the

FIGURE 4-1 Yield Curves for Debt Securities

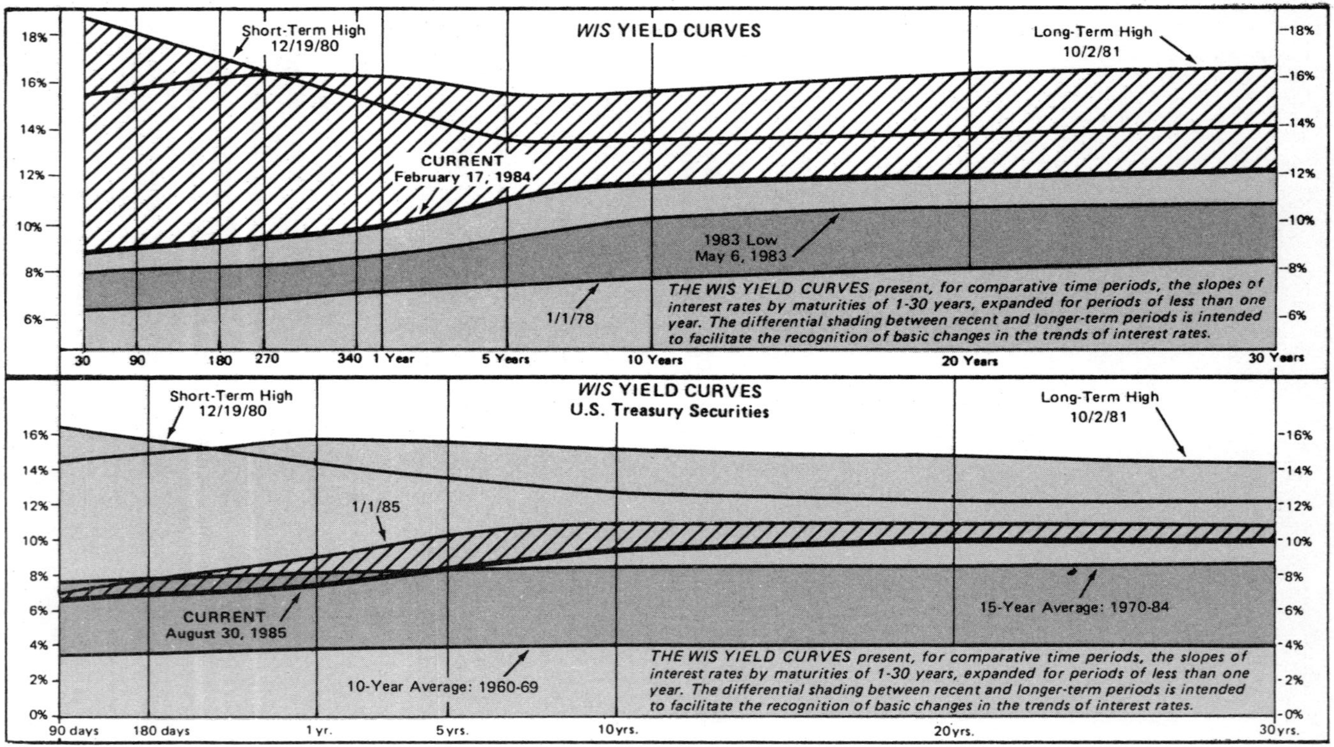

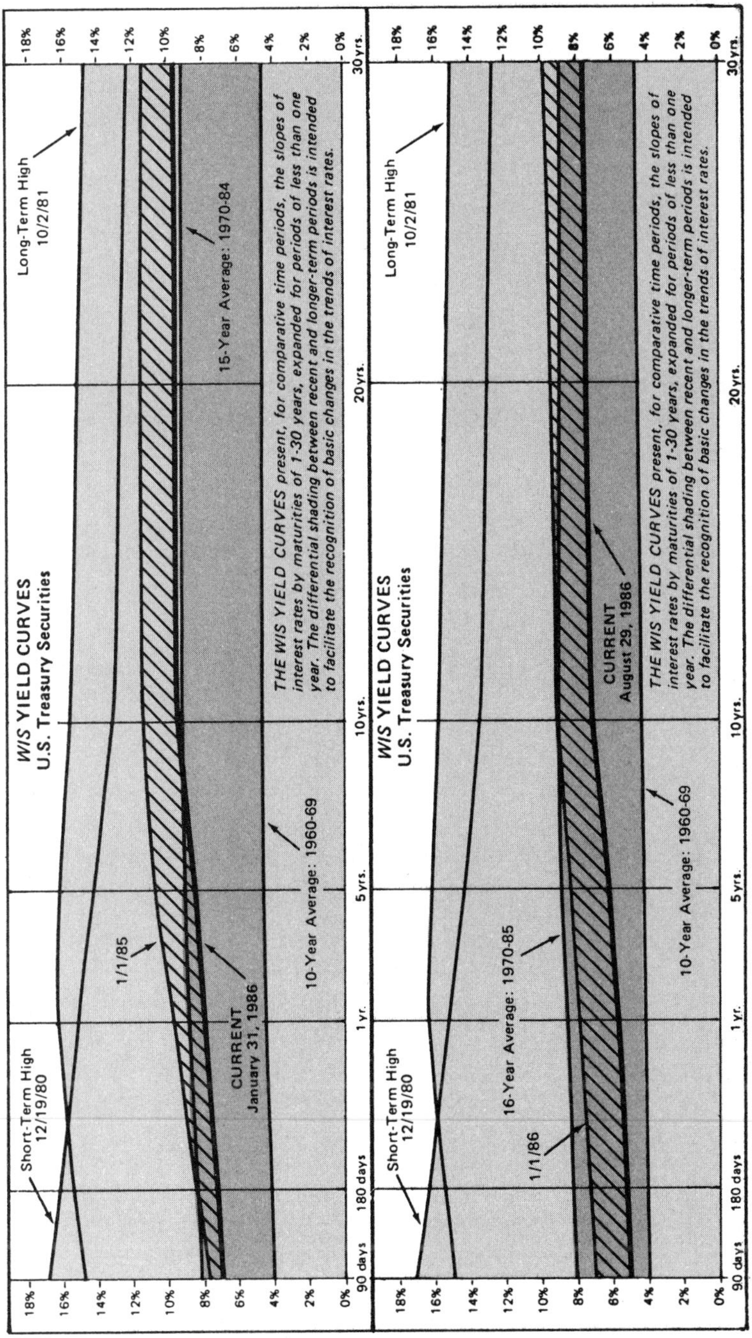

Source: Wright Investors' Service

future. Interest rates are always significant with security investments.

What to Do with High-Yielding Bonds

Since the prices of bonds move opposite to interest rates, there will be capital gains when the cost of money drops as it did when the yields of the Dow Jones Bond Average fell from 14% in 1981 to 9.3% in late 1986. Thus, bonds issued in 1982 and 1983 with coupons of 14% to 16% rose sharply by 1986.

These high-interest bonds can be temporarily rewarding if there are a few years to maturity or the bonds are trading close to the call price. But when the redemption price is much lower, you will lose money as the market value declines. Thus, there's a trade-off between income and capital loss.

Security	S&P Rating	Year Issue	1986 Price	Call Price	Current Yield
Com.Edison 16, '90	A	1982	108	103	14.8%
Humana 13¾, '13	A	1983	114	111 100*	12.1

*Call price drops in September 1993

Commonwealth Edison debt, at 108, yields 14.8%. The bond is callable at 103 in early 1987 and matures in four years. With such a short time frame, the utility may prefer to skip the early call, so the total income per bond will be $640. If competitive new bonds pay 10%, their income will be $400 so the high yield pays $240 more. There will be a capital loss: a possible $50 with the early call; a sure $80 if held to maturity. The net returns will be a potential +$160 or a sure $80 . . . not overwhelming profits.

With Humana, in the next seven years (when the call price drops to 100), the interest will total $962.50 (7 × $137.50). If the competitive yield is 10% ($700 total), the Humana income will be $262.50 more. If the bond is called in 1993, the capital

TABLE 4-7

Comparative One-Year Rates of Total Investment Return for U.S. Treasury Securities

To	If Interest Rates Decline			If Yield Curve	If Interest Rates Increase		
Maturity	1½%	1%	½%	Remains Unchanged	½%	1%	1½%
90 days	5.3%	5.5%	5.7%	5.9%	6.1%	6.3%	6.5%
1 year	6.1%	6.1%	6.1%	6.1%	6.1%	6.1%	6.1%
2 years	7.9%	7.4%	6.9%	6.6%	6.0%	5.6%	5.1%
3 years	9.4%	8.5%	7.7%	7.0%	6.0%	5.2%	4.4%
4 years	11.2%	9.9%	8.6%	7.2%	6.1%	4.9%	3.6%
5 years	11.8%	10.2%	8.7%	7.3%	5.7%	4.2%	2.8%
10 years	17.5%	14.0%	10.6%	7.3%	4.3%	1.3%	−1.6%
15 years	20.2%	15.9%	11.9%	8.1%	4.4%	1.0%	−2.2%
20 years	23.3%	17.8%	12.6%	7.9%	3.3%	−0.9%	−4.8%
30 years	28.3%	20.7%	13.8%	7.4%	1.9%	−3.2%	−7.9%

loss, from 114 to 100, will be $140, so the extra net is $122.50 If the bond is called earlier, at 111, the loss will be $30 but the high income ceases.

In the unlikely event that the bonds are not called, there will be a $140 loss but the high income will continue.

Whether you own or buy such bonds, do your homework to weigh the rewards versus the risks.

The Impact of Shifts in Interest Rates

Changes in the cost of money are reflected *immediately* in the prices of actively traded debt issues and *soon* with all types of fixed income securities. Table 4-7 shows projections in August 1986.

Corporate Versus Utilities

Portfolios of taxable bonds should be diversified by: (1) types: corporates, utilities, and governments, and (2) maturities: seldom less than ten or more than twenty years. These are general guidelines and should be reviewed separately according to goals and needs: your own or of a beneficiary.

There's a distinction between corporate and utility debt issues. Both must meet quality standards so there's little likelihood of default. But many utility bonds have longer maturities than those of industrial corporations: generally, twenty to twenty-five years for corporate and up to forty years for utilities.

Forty years is a long time during which vast changes can occur, especially when the energy companies are subject to greater political and governmental pressures than are most industries. Add the recent trend to diversification—FPL Group (the old Florida Power & Light) buying Colonial Penn Insurance

Co. and Pacific Lighting acquiring Thrifty Drugs—and there's no way you can be sure of the future. True, a careful analyst can catch deterioration before it becomes dangerous, but with utility debt the risks can become greater than the rewards.

Special Types of Bonds

As debt, bonds can be tailored to meet the needs of the borrower or, more likely, packaged to attract more investors: variable interest rates, extendable maturities, shares in pools of loans, etc. Some of these may be useful for special situations, but, because of their trick provisions, most do not qualify as Blue Chip investments. There are, however, several types that can be worthwhile holdings under certain conditions for certain situations.

Zero Bonds

ZERO COUPON BONDS

These are a special type of debt that can be excellent for long-term investments in a pension plan portfolio but are not suitable for personal savings. As always, the number 1 criterion should be the quality of the issuer.

These bonds are sold at prices far below their face values, pay no interest, and are redeemed, at par, at some specified future date, up to thirty years hence. This appreciation works out to an average annual rate of return that is competitive with the debt yields at the time of issue. Typically, when interest rates are 9%, a $1,000 zero due in twenty years would cost $172; one that matures in ten years, $415 (Table 4-8).

TABLE 4-8
Zero Coupon Bonds; Value per $1,000

Years to Maturity	Interest Rate 9%	10%	11%	12%
20	$ 172	$ 142	$ 117	$ 97
15	267	231	201	174
12	348	310	277	247
10	415	377	343	312
7	540	505	489	442
5	644	614	600	558
0	1000	1000	1000	1000

Zeros are *excellent* for pension funds where all taxes are deferred until withdrawal; *good* for small trust accounts for children/parents with income tax exemptions: *terrible* for personal savings because the investor must pay federal taxes on the imputed interest: the annual increase in market value which he/she does not receive. And there may also be state levies: New York and California follow the U.S. laws; Massachusetts and Pennsylvania exact a tax when the bond matures or is cashed in.

Zeros are issued by the U.S. Treasury and by corporations which need immediate cash, prefer not to pay out interest regularly, and anticipate that they can use the money so effectively that they will have ample assets to repay the loan at maturity (or earlier, if subject to call).

Or they can be stripped: the interest-bearing coupons are removed from the principal certificates, and each portion is sold separately. They are available from the U.S. Treasury as STRIPS or from brokerage firms in packaged form such as CATS (Certificates of Treasury Securities), TGRs (Treasury Investment Growth Receipts), and Early Bird Receipts.

With the first two, the actual certificates are held in an irrevocable trust by a custodian bank. If the selling sponsor should run into trouble, the bonds will be redeemed by the bank.

Early Birds are like shares in a mutual fund. They represent ownership of the future interest and principal payments of the bonds in which the sponsor has invested. *Big plus:* they can be converted into direct obligations of Uncle Sam.

There are also special deals such as GAINS (Growth and Income Securities) where the zeros become straight bonds after several years.

Example: A 9.55% coupon zero with a $5,000 face value costs $1,632. After twelve and a half years, it will be converted into a regular bond paying that same 9.55% to maturity in another fifteen years. These could be good if interest rates fall but risky if they should rise.

Zeros can also be used for financial planning: Bill Bizness borrows $50,000 for ten years at 11%. He gets this low rate because he accepts another $12,000, which he uses to buy $25,000 in STRIPS. By the time the loan is due, the zeros will be worth $73,725, almost enough to repay the debt.

The best zeros are those of the U.S. government because they are 100% safe. They do pay a slightly lower yield (or cost more) but that's little enough to pay for assurance that there will always be money at redemption time.

ZERO MUNICIPALS

There are also tax-exempt zeros issued by states and local governments/authorities. They are suitable for personal portfolios because all appreciation is tax-free. Usually, these are subject to early call. Thus, a twenty-year bond might turn into a ten-year security. But the yield could be more rewarding.

Example: Dr. D buys a twenty-year, $1,000 zero coupon municipal bond for $117.50. This works out to a yield to maturity of 11%, but, since the bond can be redeemed in ten years at 103% of par ($342.80), the yield to call is 11.31%. Now you have to reinvest the money, possibly at a lower rate of return.

MUTUAL FUNDS

Zeros, both taxable and tax-exempt, are available through mutual funds. For a small investment, you can diversify your holdings and can arrange to add small sums or, if necessary, withdraw all or part of these savings. Compared to direct holdings, these pooled investments may provide a better price if you cash in early. But this benefit is offset by the hefty management fees: a 0.7% expense sounds low but over twenty years is equivalent to paying a front-end load of 13%. In effect, you could pay $10,000 for $8,700 worth of bonds.

PLUSES AND MINUSES OF ZEROS

Pluses

- The yield to maturity is locked in so there's no reinvestment risk. This is valuable when the cost of money declines. With straight debt, you might have to reinvest at a lower return.
- The cost is low so zeros can be useful for small investments and comparatively large appreciation.
- For the investor who expects interest rates to decline, zeros provide an opportunity for capital gains since their values rise faster than those of current debt issues.

Minuses

- The market is volatile because, when interest rates shift, the market value of a twenty-year zero yielding 10% will move about two and a half times as fast as a twenty-year, 10% straight bond.
- Risk is greater than with regular bonds in that if a default should occur, the investor receives nothing. By contrast, after ten years the holder of a twenty-year, 10% bond would get back 61.4% of invested money. Similarly, if the credit of the issuer declines, the market value of the zero will fall faster than that of a straight debt issue.
- If there is a call provision, the investor will get less with zeros than with straight debt because most of the zeros' appreciation takes place in the last years of the total maturity.

- As a percentage of investment, the acquisition cost of a zero is high. The commission is about the same whether the bond sells at $250 or $1,000.

ZEROS CAN BEAT CDS

For tax-sheltered savings, such as the income portion of a pension plan, zero coupon bonds can be more rewarding than CDs. Since the zeros are bought at discount and pay a set sum at maturity, the annualized yield, reflecting automatic compounding of interest, is locked in.

If you invest in short-term bank certificates and roll them over at maturity, you can't tell what your long-term yield will be because you don't know how interest rates will fluctuate. Over the years, you will win if the cost of money rises (and the new CD pays more) but will lose when it falls. Usually, the interest rate on a long-term CD will be lower than that of the same maturity zero.

Table 4-9 compares yields when six-month CDs were paying 8%.

Junk Bonds

These are low-grade bonds (rated BB or lower by Standard & Poor's) with coupons as much as five percentage points higher than A-rated issues, currently, up to 15% (Table 4-10). They are used primarily for takeovers and leveraged buyouts. Their volume has quadrupled since 1979 and in 1985 made up nearly 20% of all new corporate debt issues.

For the issuer, junk bonds are a means to shift payments to Uncle Sam. The interest is tax-deductible as a business expense, and when the proceeds are used to acquire companies that pay dividends, there are extra benefits since 85% of that income is tax-exempt to the corporation.

In the early years, most junk bonds were relatively safe and led to the assertion by their sponsors that they were only slightly

TABLE 4-9
Total Returns: Tax-Sheltered Investment of $67,684

	Rate	Value at Maturity
6-month CD rolled over 8 times	8.00%	$ 93,206
1-year CD rolled over 4 times	8.50	95,089
4-year CD	9.50	98,968
4-year zero coupon bond	10.00	100,000

Source: Gabriele, Heuglin & Cashman, Inc.

more risky than regular corporate debt. The truth is more persuasive: from 1977 to 1985 the default rate on high-yield debt was more than twenty times that of all corporate bonds, 3.2% versus 0.13%. Since the majority of these junk bonds were floated after 1982, most issues have not had time to go sour!

Once the acquisitors have taken over, they hope to reduce the massive debt by selling off assets. But if these sales cannot be made, or only at bargain prices, there's real trouble and usually bankruptcy.

TABLE 4-10
Comparison of Bond Yields

Bond Rating	Yield
U.S. Treasury	10%
AAA	10¼
AA	10¾
A	11¼
BBB	11¾
BB	12¾
B	13¾
Below B	15

Still, Wall Street, eager to collect huge fees—as much as $10 million per deal—keeps developing new ways to sell even more debt: "death-backed" bonds based on pools of life insurance policies and time-sharing units such as used with condominiums. The gullible public keeps buying, and so far, there have been no effective controls. Greed continues to dominate common sense.

The sale pitch is that, with such high yields, you can afford one or two failures. Maybe so, if the company hangs in there, but in the interim there are market risks: junk bonds react quickly to shifts in interest rates and to adverse corporate developments so that their prices can fall three or four points ($30 to $40) in one day.

One alternative: buy shares of mutual funds specializing in these speculative issues. These provide diversification, are liquid, and, when half of the total holdings are in "honest" debt, may be business risks. Most of these are load funds so that 8.5% of your money goes to the promoters, not for "investments."

Regardless of the sales pitch of your broker, junk bonds are just that: trash. Some issues may have some merit, and if you are lucky enough long enough, that 15% yield may be enough to offset the probably long-term losses.

Special Bonds

These are Wall Street creations that may have some use to some investors under some circumstances. They are usually better for speculations than investments. Here are some typical "opportunities":

PUT BONDS

These are debt issues that can be cashed in, before maturity, at full value. If interest rates rise, you have the opportunity to reinvest the proceeds at a higher return. Or, if interest rates slide, you can sell at a profit in the open market. Usually, the "opportunity" occurs at specific time intervals, three to eleven years out.

In effect, the put provision transforms a long-term maturity into an intermediate-term investment. Meanwhile, you receive a higher yield than you would from a regular bond of comparable maturity.

Since the coupons, at issue, are lower than those of straight bonds, corporations save money. But if interest rates fall, investors will keep the bonds and prevent money-saving refinancing.

EXTENDABLE NOTES

At set future dates, the interest rate is changed to a preset percentage of the prevailing yield of U.S. Treasuries. Thus, over ten years, you can buy ten-year debt in five two-year bits. These may have some value in periods of rising interest rates but not when yields are falling. They are always better for the issuer than the investor.

With few exceptions, these special bonds are designed for institutional investors who trade in large lots. Often, their terms include special clauses that permit the issuer special privileges, which, of course, are seldom beneficial to the buyer. Only rarely are any special bonds suitable for amateurs and, then, should be chosen with expert advice. Why worry when you can be safe and sure with regular debt issues?

BONDS FOR SWINGERS

Swingers' bonds include: (1) government plus bond funds and (2) SPINS.

1. Government Plus bond funds. To add to their income, the managers write options on the bonds in their portfolios and trade interest rate futures. If the calls are exercised, the proceeds of the sales may have to be reinvested at lower yields and, of course, such activities involve commissions and management fees.

Always check the *real* returns. Some funds advertise the yields of the past year or, if more favorable, of the last three months. That means that when interest rates are dropping, the implied promises are overly optimistic. And when they buy bonds at a premium, these extra costs are not amortized or deducted until the sales/redemptions. Thus, you could end up with a loss or, if there should be a profit, this may be taxable in some states.

2. *SPINS* (*2% Standard & Poor's 500 Index Subordinated Notes*). The individual purchases four-year notes that pay 2% interest annually in minimum units of $1,000. In 1990, if the S&P 500 has risen enough above a predetermined level, investors will receive an additional amount based on that increase. If the index is the same or lower, they get back their original commitment. For bullish speculators only!

Mortgage-Backed Securities

These are packages of mortgage debt whose interest, amortization, and repayments are passed through to investors. They can be bought directly or through shares of mutual funds . . . in most cases.

The primary types are: Ginnie Maes, Freddie Macs, Fannie Maes, and collateralized mortgage obligations.

GINNIE MAES (GOVERNMENT NATIONAL MORTGAGE ASSOCIATION)

These are pools of mortgages insured by Uncle Sam and guaranteed by the Federal Housing Administration, Veterans Administration, and, occasionally, Farmers Home Loan Association. The investor receives a share of the payments of interest and amortization and, when there is a repayment or refinancing, a portion of those dollars.

Currently, the yields are the highest of any government debt security: from about 9% to 11%. With direct purchases, the minimum investment is about $25,000, but you can buy shares of mutual funds for $1,000. Most of the mortgages are for thirty years but, practically, with repayments, the average life of the pool is twelve to fifteen years.

That's why mortgage-backed securities should be bought primarily for pension funds or by individuals over age seventy with life expectancies of 11.5 years for a male and 15.2 for a female. If the investor lives longer, there must be additional assets to replace the previous income.

The prices of Ginnie Maes and similar securities reflects the interest rate of the underlying mortgages, the current cost of money, and the life of the loans in the pool. With an average twelve-year life: an 8% pool unit trades at about 94 ($940 per $1,000 face value) for a yield of 8.85%; a 10% pool, at 103 for a yield of 9.66%; a 12% pool, at 106 for an 11.14% return. Always get full information on all of these factors before you buy.

Mortgage-backed securities appear simple but actually are complex. Information is available through prospectuses but most dealers/brokers are not overly knowledgeable and are reluctant, or unable, to explain the details. Here are some of the factors that are skipped over. In general terms, the same comments apply to all mortgage-based pools but for convenience let's concentrate on Ginnie Maes.

All Ginnie Maes are issued with thirty-year "due dates," but the yardsticks are "average life" and "half-life".

Average life is the time it takes to receive back the average dollar of principal. It is weighted for time by multiplying each dollar of principal by the number of years it is expected to remain outstanding.

Half-life is the time which elapses before half of the principal is returned. It treats every dollar of principal return equally, regardless of when it is received. Because it does not give extra weight to cash flow in the distant future, it will usually

TABLE 4-11
Work Sheet for a Ginnie Mae

Item	Best Case: 120% FHA	Average: 85% FHA	Worst Case: 50% FHA
Cash flow yield	9.43%	9.44%	9.45%
Bond equivalent yield	9.62	9.63	9.63
Average life	11.3 years	13.3 years	16.0 years
Half-life	9.4 "	12.3 "	16.5 "
Principal and interest paid			
Next 12 months	$13,301	$12,369	$11,420
Next 5 years	70,846	65,570	59,714
Next 10 years	120,918	116,754	111,280

Source: Gabriele, Heuglin & Cashman, New York

be about two years shorter than average life. Both of these factors are considered by professionals in comparing Ginnie Maes with different issues and with corporate/government bonds.

The payments are made on the fifteenth of each month. With a $100,000 Ginnie Mae with 9.5% interest, the interest will be $791.66 and the minimum principal repayment, $44.24; a guaranteed total return of $835.90.

A typical pool, at the start of the eleventh year, would pay $727: $412 interest and $315 principal. At this point the cash flow, on the balance, would be 13.9%. But when interest rates drop, the check might be bigger because of early repayments.

Table 4-11 is a work sheet for a 9.5% Ginnie Mae issued in May 1986 with a $2 million total and an investment of $100,000. (FHA refers to the experience figures of the Federal Housing Administration).

As with a home mortgage, the cash flow remains constant even though the value of the principal declines. But the mortgage service fee, based on the outstanding balance, edges downward. The cash flow percentage increases as the same payment applies against a lower base.

The yield equivalent to that of a similar bond is higher because payments are made monthly rather than semiannually.

The quoted value of the holding will fluctuate with interest rates. When these fall, more homeowners refinance their loans so the fund managers have to reinvest those dollars at a lower yield. Roughly, Ginnie Maes pay 1% to 2% more than Treasury bonds. In early 1986, part of this premium was due to the huge demand for home mortgages which forced the agency up to its legal $65 billion ceiling. This pressure kept returns high and provided many investors with capital gains. Such fortunate conditions are not likely to occur frequently.

Taxwise, the interest of Ginnie Maes (and other mortgage pass-throughs) is taxable, but the extra cash from repayment of the principal, when the security was purchased at par, is not subject to income tax because it is a return of capital.

There are also similar pass-through pools:

FREDDIE MACS

These represent units of pools owned by the Federal Home Loan Mortgage Corporation, a financial entity owned by savings and loan associations. It buys fifteen-year mortgages from the originating lenders, who continue to service the loans. The agency packages the mortgages and sells certificates for $25,000 or, in special deals, with shares at $1,000 each.

Because the loans are guaranteed, as to timely payments of interest and principal, by the agency, not the federal government, the yields are slightly higher than those of Ginnie Maes. But the short life reduces the likelihood of prepayments.

FANNIE MAES

These are pools sponsored by the Federal National Mortgage Association. They are designed for major investors with minimum units of $25,000. The agency is the guarantor.

COLLATERALIZED MORTGAGE OBLIGATIONS (CMOS)

These are bonds backed by pass-through certificates or mortgage pools such as Ginnie Maes, Freddie Macs, Fannie Maes, and conventional mortgages made by financial institutions.

CMOs come in three or four tranches, or series. Initially, number 1 receives both interest and principal until retired. Number 2 receives interest and principal; the other two receive only interest. After the first group is retired, the next is elevated to receive principal as well as interest until completely paid off, etc.

On the average, the life of number 1 is two to three years; number 2, five to seven years; number three, ten to twelve years; number 4, fifteen years or longer.

When the portfolio of the CMO contains a majority of government-guaranteed mortgages, they may be worthwhile investments. But the larger the percentage of nonguaranteed, noninsured loans made by the banking institution, the greater the risk. There is no way the investor can know the true value of the underlying properties. You are taking the word of the sponsor, often with no professional verification. One major bank sold millions of dollars of certificates on condominiums that were unrented and in poor repair.

The yields of such CMOs are higher than those of government-backed securities, but the risks are far greater. Older folks will remember a similar rip-off in the late 1920s when New York banks valued their real estate holdings far above their true worth when they sold participations to the public. Such chicanery was a primary cause for the bankruptcy of several major financial institutions.

MUTUAL FUNDS

As with bond funds, there are two types of mortgage pass-through funds, primarily with Ginnie Maes.

Unit trusts, which invest in a basket of securities and so can advertise a high yield. But the small type in the prospectus notes that the value of the shares will decline if interest rates rise. Here again, if interest rates fall, a high-paying portfolio is vulnerable to early prepayments so that the proceeds will have to be reinvested at a lower rate of return. But the initial interest rate is maintained for a limited number of years.

TABLE 4-12
How Ginnie Maes Are Quoted

	Prices in 32nds			Bond Equivalent Yields 12 Years	
	Bid	Asked	Change	Avg. Life	Cash Flow
8s	98–00	98–04	+44	8.33	8.38
10s	106–08	106–16	+32	9.18	9.16
12s	107–30	108–06	. . . .	10.92	10.70

Source: Barrons

Mutual funds where the managers trade their portfolios in anticipation of changes in the cost of money. If they guess right, they can outperform the fixed portfolios. When they miss the shift in interest rates, the investor loses money.

With both types of funds, there are useful extras: periodic payments of set sums; compounding of reinvested income; easy withdrawal of assets; opportunity to add new deposits; accurate records for tax purposes, and prompt sale of shares.

Again, be wary of the claims by aggressive dealers/brokers. All types of mortgage pass-throughs can provide regular income and, comparatively, high yields, but, at the end, there will be nothing left! With straight debt, you will get lower yields, but at maturity you will get back your principal.

Preferred Stocks

These are "middle" securities, halfway between a bond and common stock. They have preference on all income available after the payment of bond interest and before dividends on the common stock. Most preferreds are cumulative; i.e., if the company fails to make enough money to pay the preferred dividends in one year, the payment due is added to the total and, if possible, paid later.

Compared to common stocks, preferreds are safer but, unless convertible, do not provide the higher income of common stocks of profitable corporations. *Most important:* because the dividend is fixed, the market values fluctuate like bonds: down when interest rates rise; up when they fall.

For *individual and pension/trust portfolios*, preferreds are convenient, inexpensive investments for fixed income. Their cost is low: from $25 to $100 per share (versus $1,000 for a bond); their payments are quarterly; and when listed on major stock exchanges, their shares are easy to buy and sell.

For *corporations*, preferred stocks have an extra plus: 85% of their income is tax-deductible so a corporation in the 34% tax bracket (under the new tax law) chalks up an after-tax return of 94.9%. But investment losses cannot be written off against other corporate income/earnings.

Preferred stocks are excellent investments for the income portion of portfolios, especially for small sums: leftovers from the proceeds of sales or new savings.

One easy way to choose preferreds is to find a quality utility and work backwards: match your savings to the price of 100 shares of preferred; e.g. if you have $2,100, look for preferreds selling around 20.

Company	Stock	Price	Yield
Commonwealth Edison	$1.90	19½	9.7%
rated A–	2.00	20½	9.7
	8.38	84	10.0
	2.37	25	9.5
	2.87	27	9.4

Checkpoints for Preferred Stocks

In choosing preferred stocks, analyze these factors:

Quality: companies rated BBB or higher by Standard & Poor's. You want preservation of capital first, then income.

Low debt: capitalization with debt less than 40%. Bond interest must be paid first so the lower the debt, the safer the preferred stock.

Interest coverage: income double the interest charges. Ask your broker for such data.

Call provision: no terms for early redemption to permit the company to buy back the stock at a few dollars above par (a price that may mean a loss for unwary investors). This is important with issues that were floated some years ago when interest rates were higher. When the cost of money declines, it pays the corporation to redeem the shares with extra cash or a new, lower-coupon issue. Have your broker double-check this provision as some utilities can use funds no longer needed for construction—often under an obscure provision in small type.

Sinking fund. This permits the corporation to buy back shares each year: from surplus funds when there are ample assets; by open market purchase when the market price is below par. Typically, this might permit the purchase of 5% of the shares after the first five years. Thus the stock you expected to hold for twenty years may turn into a ten-year holding.

Marketability. Compared to common stocks, the trading of preferreds is limited so prices can swing two to three points a day. As a general rule, place your order to buy or sell within a narrow range based on the closing price of the day before.

Full voting rights. The NYSE lists only preferreds with the right to vote if the corporation gets into trouble. Unlisted preferreds do not always carry this privilege.

Favorable restrictions. (1) Dividends payable to common stockholders are restricted so that the preferred stockholders will be paid first; (2) Managements cannot issue new preferreds or bonds without approval of two-thirds of preferred owners.

Premiums. Dividends on preferred stocks should be 20% greater than the yield of the bonds of the same or similar corporation. As Benjamin Graham cautions: "The preferred holder lacks both the legal claim of the bondholder and the profit possibilities of a common stockholder."

Experienced broker. When you plan large investments in preferreds, deal with a brokerage firm that has a research department that follows preferreds. Most brokers are not well versed in this area.

Trick preferreds. These are convertible/redeemable preferreds that pay a regular dividend for the first five years and then can be converted into common stock at a discount. They include:

- Variable rate preferreds, where the dividend is pegged to the current highest rate of Treasury ninety-day bills, ten-year notes or twenty-year bonds. These may be worthwhile when interest rates are rising, but they can be costly when they fall.
- Participating preferreds, where the dividend is set in dollars but, when the dividends on the common stock rise above that figure, the preferred gets the same payout as the common stockholders.

With all of these special "opportunities," there are extra risks. In Wall Street, there's no free lunch. These deals may be suitable for speculations, but they are seldom as safe or as profitable as straight preferreds.

Do's and Don'ts of Bonds

Do consider your own, and your clients', needs. If income is paramount, select bonds with high current yields and relatively short maturities, typically about ten years. This will enable you to remain flexible and be in a position to shift to longer maturities when interest rates become substantially higher.

If total returns are important—as with a trust where one person is the beneficiary of the income and other heirs are to inherit the principal—look for discount bonds with a competitive yield to maturity. Keep the spread between the current yield and YTM relatively small.

Don't trade bonds. This is speculating, not investing. The fundamental investor does not move in and out of the bond market or sell and buy every time there is sharp shift in market prices. Sure, smart traders can make a lot of money by frequent swaps, but that's a special business not suitable for amateurs or for managers of fiduciary funds. And judging from the results of managed bond funds that do trade for extra profits, there are more failures than successes—over time.

There are occasions when interest rates keep soaring—e.g., 1980 to 1984, when trading was profitable—but only rarely do the rewards of such activity justify the risks. In investing, the role of fixed income securities is to preserve capital and to provide steady income.

Do manage bonds. Debt issues should be bought for specific maturities and sold only when the quality of the corporation deteriorates, investment goals change, or there are significantly more rewarding opportunities elsewhere.

With substantial portfolios, it is wise to revise holdings to achieve greater total returns. At that time, the decision should be made on the basis of five-year projections to determine whether the new purchases will provide substantially greater total returns than can be anticipated with current holdings. As a rule of thumb, for most amateurs such action is too expensive and should be made only when the interest rate advantage is about 2%.

Don't lock bonds away. Too many investors buy bonds and hold them until maturity. This assures peace of mind but little else. With all investments, there should be a continuous and, at maximum, annual reevaluation of the quality and prospects of the issuer. Has the company increased its debt excessively? Is profitability still high? Is growth lagging? Was it necessary for the company to borrow money or defer charges to meet the interest on the old debt when new bonds were issued?

One of the greatest errors in money management is made by trustees of corporate pension plans and college endowment funds when they invest heavily in fixed income securities. These portfolios must have ready cash to meet their ongoing obligations. During a depression/recession, this lack of diversification can be disastrous. When the managers need cash, they have to sell bonds at heavy losses.

Do deal with knowledgeable brokers/dealers. Only a handful of firms meet basic requirements: to make markets, to maintain inventories, and to know where specific types of bonds can be obtained. Set specific criteria and try to buy the bonds you want, not only those the dealer has to offer. Of course, if you can afford only small purchases, the details are not overly significant. You can stick to quality and service.

In buying a number of bonds, look for dealers who maintain an inventory and have been in business for many years. To obtain the best prices: (1) check bonds of similar quality with competitive yields—within a range of .05 basis points ($5 per bond); (2) get prices from three dealers/brokers; (3) choose the bonds best suited to your investment objectives.

Do look for total returns as projected for the next five years. This should be an average annual rate comparable to current yields, preferably at least 10%. If interest rates drop, sell the bonds and reinvest the proceeds on the basis of the future outlook: long-term, if you expect interest rates to drop; short-term, if you expect them to rise.

Do diversify. For taxable investments: 50% utilities, 25% industrials, 25% U.S. governments. Or if assets justify a wider range: 40% utilities, 15% industrials, 15% financial institutions, and 30% U.S. Treasuries.

Do be cautious with new issues. If there should be a significant drop in interest rates and the call protection is limited, you may be forced to turn in the bonds at lower-than-market prices.

Do concentrate on short/intermediate-term bonds with personal investments. Their values may fall a bit but since they will be redeemed soon, you will get back the par price.

Don't rule out long-term bonds, especially for pension funds. A surprising number of people shy away from long-term bonds, those maturing in twenty to thirty years. They feel that once a purchase is made, the investor must be locked in to maturity. This might be true with debt of small companies with thin markets but it is false with bonds of well-known firms. These issues can always be sold quickly.

The judgment as to which maturities to choose does not depend on what you think the economy will be many years hence or even the profitability of the issuing corporation. The key factor is always the future cost of money. If the original debt carries a low coupon, chances are that its price will decline because, historically, interest rates will rise over the years (and probably drop later). If the original yield is ample, you are locking in a welcome rate of return, and when interest rates decline, the value of the bond will rise.

That's why it's smart to mix your debt portfolio: short-term bills, intermediate-term bonds/notes, and long-term bonds selling at a discount or with high yields and adequate call protection.

The current yield of discount bonds may be slightly lower than can be obtained with new bonds, but you will have the benefit of appreciation to maturity.

Example: In mid-1986, new bonds with twenty-year maturities were paying about 8%. But you could do better with discount bonds, e.g., GMA (General Motors Acceptance) AA+ rated, 8½, '06, were selling at 91 ($910), a yield of 9.3%. At maturity, you could count on a nine-point ($90 per bond) gain. Each year, the price of this bond will move up and, if interest rates decline, that upmove will be faster. If you expect interest rates to go to 7% in another couple of years, do not wait. Buy the GMA bond now.

Or you could buy Bell of Pennsylvania 9¼, '19, at 100. The current yield will be slightly more than the GMA debt, but you will have to wait longer for redemption. There could be an added plus if the cost of money falls well below 7%: the telephone bond might be called at 108.63 ($1,066) for an extra profit.

Part 3

SPECIAL SECURITIES/ SITUATIONS

Now that we've discussed the primary types of stock market investments, let's take a look at some areas/techniques that are usually best for more adventuresome, experienced investors:

Convertibles: securities that combine the income of debt with the potential appreciation of equities. As with most compromises, you have to settle for less so these hybrids are useful primarily for special situations: for trust funds where the beneficiaries want some income now and can wait for capital gains; for cautious investors who prefer to let market forces make their decisions.

Options: for extra income by selling calls on owned stocks. This is a sound, almost risk-free tactic when you are willing to accept limited returns. It is not to be confused with speculating by buying options for quick profits (and inevitable losses).

Overseas investments: shares of foreign-based corporations, where high returns have often been more illusory than real because of inadequate information, creative corporate accounting, and market values subject to external forces over which the investor has no control.

With all of these, the quality of the corporation whose securities are involved is the key criterion. With Blue Chips, values can be easily determined and their prospects projected with reasonable accuracy. With marginal and low-grade firms you are speculating, not investing.

Chapter 5

CONVERTIBLES FOR SPECIAL SITUATIONS

One of the most widely held misconceptions in Wall Street is that convertible securities (CVs) provide the best of two worlds: (1) the income and safety of bonds and preferred stocks and (2) the price appreciation and growth of common stocks. Under some conditions there is some truth in these concepts, but in most cases common stocks of the same companies will be more rewarding.

CVs are usually better for speculation than for investment if only because they are seldom issued by quality corporations and, then, primarily in periods of corporate financial stringency. The majority of these hybrid securities involve takeovers, reorganizations, and small, new firms. They can be useful for special situations but, for best returns, require more research/analysis and sharper timing than straight debt or equity securities.

Convertibles are fixed income securities which can be converted into equity through an exchange for shares of the common stock of the same company or, occasionally, of an allied/subsidiary corporation. The swap is made at a specific ration, usually until a specified expiration date. There are two major types:

- **Convertible bonds** (*debentures*), which represent debt of the issuing company. Typically, they are sold in units of $1,000 and pay interest semiannually.
- **Convertible preferreds** (*stocks*), which are sold in units of $100 and pay dividends quarterly.

These hybrids have two values:

- **Investment value:** their theoretical worth as a conventional bond or preferred stock without consideration of the benefits of conversion. This is the basis for the adage that predicates that, in bear markets, the yield provides downside protection by setting a floor for the CV price; i.e., when the prevailing interest rate is 10%, the lowest value for a 7% CV debenture will be 70 ($700).
- **Conversion value:** the amount the CV would be worth if exchanged for shares of the common stock; i.e., a $1,000 CV that can be converted into fifty shares of common stock will be worth $1,500 when the stock trades at 30.

Usually, a CV sells at the higher of its two values and, often, at a premium. In bear markets, investors like the high yield; in bull markets, speculators become excited about the possible gains from a price rise of the stock.

The truth is that things do not always work out as projected. In down markets the floor is broken; in up markets the CVs rarely appreciate faster than the common stock.

As so often happens in Wall Street, when enough people believe something is true, no amount of logic or facts makes much difference. The biggest reason for the popularity of CVs is that the demand, encouraged by aggressive brokers, tends to exceed the supply so that their prices are often higher than their true value by either criteria.

Keep in mind that CVs are a form of common stock based on debt (not the other way around). They are a loan with a warrant to buy the common stock. That means that the ultimate value will reflect the profitable growth of the issuing company. In buying CVs, it is also important to consider why they were offered and how they benefit the corporation. With CVs, a company can:

- *Borrow money at a lower rate* than can be obtained with straight debt. Interest rates of new CVs can be 2% to 4% below those of regular bonds, a savings, to the borrower, of $20,000 to $40,000 a year on every borrowed million dollars for as long as twenty years.
- *Sell stock at a higher price* than can be obtained with a straight offering. To raise $20 million through an equity issue, a company would have to sell a million shares of common stock at $20 (disregarding financing costs). Since the typical CV commands a 15% premium, the same amount can be raised by selling CVs at 115. There would be no dilution of equity, and conversion would require about 174,000 shares of new common stock.

As prime investments, CVs leave much to be desired. Only a handful are listed on major stock exchanges and their markets are thin. It's not unusual to have successive closing prices vary as much as three points ($30 on a $1,000 face value debenture).

CVs of quality corporations can be, or become, investments. Those of small, unseasoned firms are speculations. To attract capital, these new companies have to offer something extra so they use CVs with a "sure" yield and the lure of an equity position. As long as the firm stays solvent, there will be income, but the payout from conversion requires substantially higher earnings. Since only one of three new corporations survive, the risks are high.

Calculating the Premium

The premium is the percentage difference between the conversion value and the market price of the CV. To calculate, use this formula:

$$PC = \text{Price of the common stock}$$
$$SC = \text{Number of shares by conversion}$$
$$PV = \text{Current price of the convertible}$$
$$SP = \text{Dollar premium you pay}$$
$$CV = \text{Conversion value of the convertible}$$
$$P = \text{Percentage of premium}$$
$$CV = PC \times SC$$
$$PV - CV = SP$$
$$\frac{SP}{CV} = P$$

Example: MoneyMaker, Inc., convertible debenture 7%, maturing in 2006, rated A, is issued at 100 ($1,000). Each bond is convertible into 20 shares of common stock which is selling at 40. To find the percentage of premium:

$$CV = 40 \times 20 = \$800$$
$$1000 - 800 = 200$$
$$\frac{200}{800} = 25\%$$

This is a high premium and justified only when the company is well known and financially strong, and has excellent prospects for profitable growth.

Guidelines for suitable premiums:

- Less than 15%: small risk with quality companies
- 15% to 20%: attractive but still risky
- 25% or higher: the yield of the CV should be close to that of bonds and corporate prospects should be bright. Just be sure that those projections are based on facts, not on hope or hype.

So much for the risks. The rewards may be different than anticipated because of external factors such as the cost of money and internal failures such as lower-than-projected increases in corporate earnings and dividends.

As fixed income securities, CVs move, in price, with interest rates. When these drop, the investment values rise so that the current yields are much less than those of other debt holdings. The conversion value (supposedly the extra attraction) will increase only when the corporate dividends are raised to total more than the fixed income. This is the basis for a higher premium.

Selling Versus Converting

As shown in Table 5-1, in bull markets, the values of CVs can soar because of the high yield and/or better earnings. Usually, this is the time to sell rather than to convert: (1) you have a hefty gain; (2) the yield to maturity of the CV is below that of other debt issues (for Allied Stores, 3.51%; for Corning, 4.15%); (3) the premium is almost gone; (4) there's still a wide gap between the interest of the debt and the dividend income of the stock if

TABLE 5-1

Typical Convertible Debentures of Major Corporations

Company/Security	S&P Rating	Recent Price CV	Recent Price Stock	Shares per $1,000 Bond	Conversion Premium	Annual Income CV	Annual Income Stock
Allied Stores 8¾ '09	A−	182	48⅞	$36.62	1%	$ 87.50	$42.48
Corning Glass 8¼, '07	A−	157½	59¼	43.98	1	82.50	36.72
Macmillan, Inc. 7½, '10	BBB+	129	47	23.95	14	75.00	14.37
Texas Eastern 12, '09	BBB−	108½	25¼	24.84	72	120.00	54.65
Zayre Corp. 7¼, '10	BBB+	121	34⅜	28.41	24	72.50	9.09

Source: Standard & Poor's

converted (for Corning, $82.50 versus $36.72); (5) the original attraction of the dual potential of the security is minimal.

Other Criteria

As with all investments, the primary consideration should be the quality of the issuing corporation: a rating of B+ or higher. Other points to consider:

BREAK-EVEN POINT

This measures how long it will take for the yield of the CV to pay back the premium paid at purchase. The shorter the break-even time, the less the risk and the greater will be the potential rewards.

Example: a 7% debenture is trading at 70 ($700)—a yield of 10%. Each CV can be converted into twenty-five shares of common stock, so when the stock is at 30 the conversion value is $750. The difference is $50.

Since the interest is $70 and the dividends on the stock total $30, there's a spread of $40. Divide 100 by 40 to get 2.5. That's the number of years it will take for the extra income from the interest to make up the conversion premium. That's an acceptable premium as most professionals look for the break-even point to occur in three to four years.

LENGTH OF THE CONVERSION PRIVILEGE

As a rule of thumb, the duration of the conversion period should be at least five years. A shorter period does not allow sufficient time for profits to rise enough (and thus the price of the common stock) to make swapping worthwhile.

TIMING OF PURCHASE

New CVs are usually offered at par without commission (the company pays the broker). But this savings will probably be offset by a higher price and premium. The best bet is usually a CV trading at a discount. The yield will be relatively high and the premium relatively low. While waiting for the common stock to appreciate, you can count on a good yield.

CALL PROVISION

Typically, a CV cannot be redeemed for five or ten years. This provides protection but also reduces profits if the price of the stock, and CV, should move up sharply. Usually, it is wiser to sell than redeem.

A better buy is a CV with a sinking fund, primarily with debentures, whereby the company agrees to retire a portion of the debt annually: at par when the price of the CV is high; by purchase in the open market when it's low. There are not many of these available because such terms lower the attraction of the issue.

TIMING OF CONVERSION

Keeping in mind that a CV is a version of the common stock, swapping makes sense when the income from the stock is greater than the interest/dividends of the CV.

Example: Hoopla, Inc., 6% convertible, due in the year 2000 and rated A, can be swapped for thirty shares of common. The interest is $60 a year so when the dividend is $1.50 per share, that income will be $45. There's no reason to convert. When the dividend rises to $2.05 per share, the stock income will be $61.15 and it may be time to make the exchange. There's no tax until the stock is sold.

When CVs Can Be Useful

There are two special situations where CVs can be useful investments:

1. IN CERTAIN TRUST FUNDS

Some trusts funds require that all investments be made in bonds. This restriction limits income and, over the years, inflation will decrease the real value of the principal. By buying CVs in such trust funds, the trustee can fulfill the legal requirements and still maintain, and possibly enhance, the value and income of the fund.

Example: Dr. Yes sets up a trust for his wife and children. With no provision for invasion of principal, the income from 9% bonds would be a steady $9,000 on every $100,000. In ten years, the purchasing power of this income would be cut about one-quarter with inflation at 3% annually.

If the same sum were invested in 7% convertible debentures of a quality corporation, the steady income would be less—$7,000 a year. But if the company continued to raise its dividends, the bonds would be converted to stock, the income would rise, and there would also be substantial capital gains. In five years or so, the family could count on $10,000 or more income.

2. TO PROVIDE INCOME FOR OLDER PEOPLE

CVs can provide retired people with income to live on and can enable them to eventually leave potentially more valuable assets to their heirs. Again, this requires investment in a quality corporation.

Checkpoints for Convertibles

- Buy CVs only of quality companies, preferably those growing at an above-average rate.
- Invest for a minimum of five years so that there's a good chance that the value of the common stock will rise (and dividends increase) enough to justify conversion.
- Buy only when the premium is less than 15% (Table 5-1).
- Be slow to buy new CVs. There's no commission but they are likely to be overpriced. Otherwise, why would the company offer them?
- Look for bargains in the after-market. Shortly after the new issue has been sold, the CVs will settle down to a competitive level, usually below par. By buying at a discount, you get the benefit of a long-term appreciation to maturity even if the price of the common stock is slow to move up.
- Place your order, for both listed and unlisted CVs, at a set price a few points below the last closing quotation. In a dull market, you may save money.
- Be wary when the price of the CV, as measured by the yield, is higher than that of straight bonds of the same or a comparable company.

  Select only issues where the interest/dividends are amply covered by corporate earnings. Back in the takeover years, conglomerates often issued CVs with fixed payments which were so high that their payment required the sale of assets. That's not exactly a constructive policy.

Investment Companies

If you are puzzled by CVs or have limited capital, take a look at mutual funds that invest primarily in CVs. Most of these are closed-end funds whose shares often sell at discounts. When they can be bought below NAV (net asset value), you get a double benefit: a higher rate of return and the possibility of appreciation. If the fund pays 8% and its shares trade at a 20% discount, your return will be about 10%. And if the discount narrows, you will have welcome capital gains.

Chapter 6

OPTIONS FOR EXTRA INCOME

Options, whether involving stocks, futures, indexes, commodities, or foreign currencies are primarily speculations, not investments. Under certain conditions, investors who sell options on quality stocks which they own can add extra income of 10% to 15% annually. Such success requires careful selection, sharp timing, and strict discipline. Before you venture into any type of options with your personal or pension assets, discuss your plans with a seasoned broker and paper-test your projections for at least one month.

The Options Market

Options are a cross between dealing in stocks and trading in commodities. They permit holders to control a relatively large contract for a small amount of money, e.g., for a premium of $150, 100 shares of IBM worth $15,000 for up to nine months.

Options are rights to buy or sell a specified number of shares of stocks/futures/indexes at a specified price up to a specified date. If the price of the contract moves as projected, you make money; if you guess wrong, your loss can be limited to the amount of your commitment.

The most widely used and best-for-investors option is a *call:* the right to buy the underlying securities/contract at a certain price, called the strike price or striking price, at or before the expiration date. The seller of the call collects a premium and comes out ahead if the price of the stock falls or stays below the strike price. The buyer of the call is betting that the price of the stock will go up above that strike price and is willing to pay for the right to buy at the strike price. With stocks, the unit is usually 100 shares.

A *put* is the opposite: the right to sell the securities at a set price at or before the expiration date. If the price of the stock falls, the holder of the put can acquire the stock at the lower market price. You buy a put when you are bearish. The seller wins if the stock price rises or stays the same.

For traders, there are combinations: spreads, strips, straps, and straddles. They are complex, involve careful calculations, and, to be profitable, require substantial sums.

Options are traded on major stock exchanges with prices of the premium (the dollars paid per 100 shares) quoted in the financial press. These vary with the duration of the contract, the type of security, corporate prospects, and the activity/trend of the stock market.

The base points are:

- *The striking price,* at which the holder of the option must sell or can buy. These are usually quoted at five-point intervals: 35, 40, 45, etc. When the stock is selling at over $100 per share, the quotations may be at 10-point intervals.
- *The expiration month,* after which the option cannot be exercised. This is usually listed quarterly: January/April/July/October, February/May/August/November, and so forth. The quotations are for the first three periods to a

maximum of nine months. For a few popular stocks, the quotations may be monthly.

- *The expiration date,* the Saturday following the third Friday of the stated month. As we'll see, that can be a wild day on Wall Street.

Table 6-1 shows typical quotations for calls. In the press, the prices of puts are shown with a *p* after the first column. Since puts are used primarily for hedging and speculations, their prices are not shown or discussed here.

Thus, in early September, with RR stock at 40, the calls for December, at the strike price of 40, traded from a high of 3 ($300) to a low of 1¾ ($175) and closed at 2⅝ ($262.50).

Generally, the value of the call moves with the price of the related stock, by about half as many points as the stock price changes, i.e., if an option with a strike price of 30 is worth 3 when the stock is at 30, it will trade at 1½ when the stock is at 25.

With active options, however, the professionals create their own markets and near the expiration date will shift prices sharply in hopes of profiting with their personal positions.

How to Make Money Writing Calls

Investors can make extra money by writing (selling) calls on stocks they own. These are covered calls. The strategy depends on your objectives. Table 6-2 shows these choices with 300 shares of RR stock bought at 40 in early September. The total cost was $12,150: $12,000 plus $150 commission.

If you want income, you sell on-the-money calls at the strike price of 40 with an exercise date in March. Assuming you sell at the daily high, the premium is a hefty 3¾ points ($375): for 300 shares, $1,125 which, minus commission, nets $1,075. This brings the cost to $11,075, in case you want to enhance your returns with a bit of bookkeeping.

TABLE 6-1

How Call Options Are Quoted (Weeks Trading) in September

Stock, Expiration Date, Strike Price	High	Low	Last	Stock Price
RR Sep. 35	5	3¼	4⅝	40
EE Sep. 40	1 15/16	⅝	1 7/16	40
RR Dec. 40	3	1¾	2⅝	40
EE Mar. 40	3¾	2½	3½	40
RR Mar. 45	1½	1¼	1½	40

In October and January, RR pays a dividend of 75¢ per share to add $450 income.

On March 21, RR stock is up to 46, so the calls are exercised and the stock is sold at 40: $12,000 minus $150 commission to net $11,850.

In a pension fund, where there are no immediate taxes to pay, the total income is $1,525: $1,075 from the premium plus $450 dividends minus $300 commissions, to net $1,225. This is a 10.5% rate of return in about six months or, annualized, +21%—about twice as much as could be obtained with straight debt securities.

In a personal portfolio, the profit would be reduced, at a 28% tax rate, by $343 to $862, for a 7.2% rate of return in about six months, or 14.4% annualized—not too shabby for an almost risk-free operation.

When you write on-the-money calls, you get immediate, sure income but you lose the chance of potential appreciation: from 40 to 46. For the conservative investor, this technique can be safe and profitable. If the stock price dips below 40, there will be no real loss until it breaks 37, thanks to that 3¾ point premium.

For Total Returns

For the aggressive investor, writing out-of-the-money calls can be worthwhile, especially in a slowly rising market. In this case,

TABLE 6-2
Writing Calls for the Investor

September 9: Buy 300 RR common stock at $40 per share: $12,000 + $150 commission = $12,150.

FOR INCOME: Selling on-the-Money Calls

Sell 3 March calls at a strike price of 40 for 3¾ ($375) premium = $1,125 − $50 commission = $1,075.

March 21: RR stock at 45, so options are called at 40 and stock sold: $12,000 − $150 commission = $11,850. Dividends: two at 75¢ per share per quarter: + $450.

Since there are no taxes to pay in a pension plan, the total income is $1,525: $1,075 from the premiums plus $450 from dividends minus $300 for commissions, to net $1,225.

Percentagewise, this is a 10.5% rate of return in about six months or an annualized rate of 21%. If the transaction had been with shares in a personal portfolio, the profit would be reduced, at a 28% tax rate, by $343 to $882 for a 7.26% rate of return: 14.52% annualized.

FOR TOTAL RETURNS: Selling out-of-the-Money Calls

Sell 3 March calls at a strike price of 45 at 1 ($100): $300 minus $50 commission, to net $250.

March 21: RR stock at 46 so options are exercised and stock sold at 45: $13,500 − $150 commission = $13,350.

In a tax-deferred pension plan, total income would be $1,930: capital gain of $1,230 + $250 premiums + $450 dividends: a 15.9% return in about six months or an annual return of 31.8%. In a personal portfolio, with a 28% tax, this would be reduced by $540.40 to $1,389.60. Percentagewise, this is a 10.4% rate of return, or an annualized rate of about 20.4%.

Source: Dean Witter Reynolds, Inc.

you sell March 45 calls for a premium of 1 ($100) each for $300 income. After commission, this nets $250, so the out-of-pocket cost for the purchase of the stock is cut to $11,900.

In March, when RR stock is at 46, the calls will be exercised and you will have to sell the 300 shares at 45: $13,500 minus $150 commission for a net of $13,350. In a tax-deferred pension plan, total income will be $1,930: capital gain of $1,230 + $250 net premiums plus $450 dividends. This is a 15.9% rate of return in about half a year, or 31.8% annualized.

In a personal portfolio, with a 28% tax, this would be reduced by $540.40 to $1,389.60. Percentagewise, this is a 10.4% rate of return, or almost 21% annualized.

The bad news is that if you had not written the calls, your profit would have been greater: $1,800 capital gains versus $1,750 received. If the stock soared to 48, the "loss" would be more. If the stock had not reached 45 by late March, you could keep the premium and the shares and start writing new calls, hopefully at a strike price of 50.

Here's another technique that can be used if the stock takes off and zooms into the 50s. You buy back the original calls, at a loss, and write new ones at a higher, farther-out strike price. This sets up a tax loss which can be used with your federal tax return, up to a maximum of $3,000 a year.

Example: when RR stock moves up to 44 in February, the premium for the March 45 call is 1½ and for the August 50 call, 1. You buy back the 45 call at a loss of a half point plus commission and sell the 50 call for 1 (minus commission) in hopes of a five-point gain. But it's no fun when the stock skyrockets!

Example (at another time period as this is a true situation): In September 1985, Ida Investor bought 300 shares of Wal-Mart Stores (WMT) at 50¾, a total cost of $15,447. At the same time, she sold three March 55 calls at 2⅛ for a net of $595. She calculated that this was a smart move as she could look forward to a $1,490 return: net gain of 853 plus $595 premium plus $42 from three dividends. This would be +9.1% "yield" on her investment, or an annualized rate of about 16%—her overall target.

But WMT soared, split two for one so that she now owned 600 shares and was liable for six calls trading at 4¼. By January, Ida was convinced that in the roaring market WMT would continue to rise, so she bought back six calls at a cost of $2,638 and established a short-term loss of $2,042. This was deductible on her income tax return.

Then, she sold six September 35 calls at 2¼ with a net of $1,276. For about $1,400, she boosted the strike price by five points ($1,500 total).

But, unfortunately for Ida, the stock kept soaring and by midsummer was at 48, with those calls trading at 14. She still had a substantial profit with WMT but, because she wrote calls, this was limited and far below what she might have achieved by owning the stock and not writing the calls.

Checkpoints for Writing Calls

Once you understand the rewards and risks, writing covered calls can provide extra returns of 10% to 15% a year *if* you do your homework, deal with a knowledgeable broker, review your position frequently, and follow rules like these:

Define your goal. If you want safety plus income, concentrate on stable quality stocks that pay fair dividends of 3% to 4% and write close-to-the-money calls.

If you opt for high total returns, look for rising stocks, write out-of-the-money calls, and hope for 2% dividends, 7% premiums, and potential appreciation of over 7%: all for a total of 16%.

Try to work with units of 300 shares so that the commissions will not cut too deeply into your returns. If you become experienced, work with a discount broker or arrange for a better deal from your regular registered representative.

Concentrate on stocks you would like to own on their own merits, not those with high premiums. Quality stocks are excellent because their potential can be projected with reasonable accuracy and usually their price movements will be slow and steady.

For extra profits, look for stocks of companies that will pay three dividends during the holding period. This income will lower your net cost. Buy American Home Products in early May and write January calls. The ex-dividend dates will be around May 7, August 7, and January 7.

Sell calls in flat markets. This will give you a better chance for price appreciation with out-of-the-money calls.

Use margin when you feel that you understand what you're doing. Under current rules that apply, this is 50% so you can buy $2 worth of stocks for every $1 investment, and that 7% premium will mean a 14% rate of return minus a few dollars interest.

Be persistent. Once you have decided to write options as part of your investment program, keep doing so regardless of what the stock market does. You may lose a few points when a stock soars, but overall, in a year or two, you can double your investment returns.

Write options on stocks in your pension fund. Since there are no taxes to pay, all of the profits will build your assets.

Keep a separate bookkeeping system for your personal portfolio. This will make it easier for your accountant to prepare your tax return and to provide proof to the IRS.

Writing calls can be a profitable investment technique, but almost all other uses of options (buying for quick profits or to hedge positions) are speculative. That's why they are not discussed here.

Options on Stock Indexes

The latest gimmicks to attract speculators are options on stock indexes. They are *not* for investors, but everyone who is involved with the stock market should be familiar with the concept of these prepackaged units, understand how they are traded (and, often, manipulated), and be aware of their impact on the stock market, especially near the monthly expiration dates.

A stock index is another triumph for Wall Street packaging. It makes it possible to play the stock market without owning a single share of stock. Also, this vehicle combines the growth potential of equities with the speculative hopes of commodities, and, though touted as an "investment tool," is one of the riskiest speculations of all.

A stock index is a futures contract on a group of stocks of a market average or industry group. For $3,500 or less, you can control as much as $100,000 worth of securities. You are speculating on the future movement of the underlying index. This index, in varying degrees, reflects what is happening with the component stocks. If the value of the index shifts as you anticipate, a 10% move can mean a profit of as much as 100% in one day, week, or month. If the change is opposite to your projection, the loss will usually (but not always) be limited to your "investment."

For superswingers there are options on these futures. As with calls/puts on stocks, for a small premium these speculators acquire the right to buy or sell the contract at a set price for a set period of time. Again, a correct guess as to the price movement of the index can bring quick profits.

Even Wall Street admits the risks of indexes, and most brokerage firms screen all clients and insist that they have: (1) a net worth of $100,000 exclusive of home and life insurance, (2) the right risk temperament, the ability to deal with losses, because, as David Dreman, columnist for *Forbes* magazine, warns ". . . a mere hiccup in the market can wipe out 100% of your capital."

Major Indexes

Currently, there are futures indexes on the overall stock market such as Standard & Poor's 500, Standard & Poor's 100, NYSE Composite Index, AMEX Major Market Index, and Value Line, and half a dozen special industry groups such as oils, computer technology, gold/silver, etc.

The acquisition costs are low because the price of the index is a fraction of the total worth: with S&P 500, each full point is valued at $500, so a quotation of 250 means the unit represents $125,000 in stocks. The minimum price change for a contract is 0.05, or $25.

In early July when the S&P 500 is at about 250, Cedric buys five September 260 calls at 4 ($400 each): $2,000 plus commission. Three weeks later, in a strong market, the contract is up to 6 ($600) so Cedric sells for a two-point profit: $3,000 gross, or a profit of $1,000 on his $2,000 commitment (remember, that's not an investment).

More than likely, however, Cedric, being the aggressive type, buys on margin so his outlay is far less (as little as $200) and his profit greater.

But if Cedric guessed wrong and the market fell so that in September the index was at 245, he would lose all of his capital. At 255 close, he would get back some of his money but still sustain a loss.

Trading in indexes, directly or by options, is a zero-sum game even before commissions. The buyer or seller makes money only at the expense of the other party. For amateurs it's doubly risky because, with limited capital and even more limited knowledge, they are trying to compete with professionals.

Indexes for Investors

One thing about Wall Street is that its marketing managers are imaginative and are experts at rationalizing irrational concepts.

Stock index contracts are visualized as "an opportunity to protect portfolio values in bear markets. By buying puts on these market indicators, you will make money enough to offset the losses on your stocks."

Here's the sales pitch (under the old maximum 50% tax rate):

In April, Cautious Cal is happy because his personal investments have risen from $38,000 to $48,000 in three months. But now he is nervous because he anticipated a dip in the market and wants to protect his gains. If he sells, his tax will be at the 50% rate.

At the suggestion of his friendly broker, Cal sets up a hedge with options on the AMEX Major Market Index, currently quoted at 120. He buys four July 120 puts, representing about $48,000 in securities, for 2⅞ premium, or a cost of $1,150.

Cal's pessimism is justified. The market drops 10% so the value of his portfolio is down $4,800 and the MMI falls to 108. Cal sells the puts for 12 ($4,800) and writes off the $1,150 premium as an insurance cost (not counting commissions).

If Cal had been wrong and the market rose 10%, the MMI would be at 132 so the puts would expire worthless. But his portfolio would be +$4,800 so that, even after the $1,150 cost of the puts, his gain would be about $3,650.

Under the new tax law, the tax benefit would be less but the concept is valid.

All these manipulations sound great: easy, profitable, simple, and exciting—but, realistically, they involve tension, research, close supervision, hard work, and, most important, luck. If the movement is halfway, you're trading dollars and wasting time. Such hedging tactics make sense with multimillion, professionally managed portfolios but rarely for individuals.

What your broker doesn't stress is that, with indexes, swings can be amazingly rapid. One Friday afternoon, when the Federal Reserve Board reported an unexpected $2 billion decline in the M-1 component of the money supply, the prices of futures contracts fell sharply. Two minutes later, when the FRB announced a ½% cut in the discount rate, the indexes jumped twice as much as their previous decline.

Such price volatility can make a whopping difference to the speculator with small margin. By exchanges rules, all futures contracts prices are marked to market each night (calculated as to their closing values). Excess gains can be withdrawn, but losses may require additional collateral. If this is not forthcoming, the account can be sold out the next morning. With options, of course, there is no need for extra margin. The maximum loss will be the cost of the premium.

Basis Trading

Few amateur investors have sufficient assets to play this game, but its impact can be so great, even devastating, that this technique should be understood by everyone who owns common stocks.

Basis trading is another form of hedging that permits institutional investors to lock in profits regardless of the movements of the stock market. The decisions to buy or sell pay little attention to the health of the economy, outlook for corporate profits, etc., and are based on projections (a fancy name for guessing) of the values of two items: a stock market index, usually the S&P 500, and a futures or option contract that represents the right to buy that index at a future expiration date.

As with all options/futures, there's a price to pay for this right: the premium (basis) that is based on the difference between the price of the index and the price of the futures contract. There must be two participants, each taking the opposite side. By buying one side and selling the other, the professional sets up a hedge and makes money whether the market goes up or down over the selected time period because, on the day that the contracts expire, its value must equal the value of the index. With basis trading, the spreads reflect the profits.

The big trading comes at the "witching hour" four times a year: at the end-of-the-quarter expiration date. This is the time when the premium disappears and contracts must be closed out. Trading of the options/futures and major stocks of the index can be wild and woolly as outlined elsewhere. Table 6-3 gives an example of basis trading:

TABLE 6-3

How the Pros Make Money with Basis Trading

May 10, 1985: S&P 500 at 184.28; September 180 futures at 189.25: a high spread of 4.97 points	
BUY stocks to duplicate S&P 500	−$9,210,000
Sell 100 September 180 futures on S&P: 500 × 189.25	+ 9,462,500
September 20: S&P: 500 at 180:	
SELL stocks	+ 9,424,000
Loss	− 214,000
BUY futures at 180: $9,000,000 from sale at $9,462,500	+ 462,500
Dividends from stocks	+ 151,500
Profit	+ 400,000
Annualized rate of return: 11.9%	
September 20: S&P 500 at 190:	
SELL stocks at $9,496,000 from cost of $9,210,000	+ 286,000
BUY futures at 190: $9,500,00 minus sale price of $9,462,500	− 37,500
Dividends from stocks	+ 151,500
Profit	+ $400,000
Annualized rate of return: 11.9%	

On May 10, 1985, the S&P 500 is at 184.28. September 180 futures contracts are at 189.25, a hefty 4.97-point spread. Speculators are bullish.

On that day, fund A buys a basket of stocks that duplicate those of the S&P 500 for $9,210,000. At the same time, the manager sells 100 September 180 futures at 189.25 × 500 to collect $9,462,500. Here are the scenarios on the September 20 expiration date:

- *If the S&P is at 180,* the stocks are sold for $9,424,000, for a loss of $214,000, and the futures are bought back at

180 ($9,000,000), for a profit of $462,500. Now the net gain is $248,500. Add dividends from the stocks of $151,500 and the total profit is $400,000, an annualized rate of return of 11.9%.

- *If the S&P is up to 190,* the stocks are sold for $9,496,000, for a gain of $286,000 (cost of $9,210,000). Now the fund buys back the futures at 190 ($9,500,000), which, from the original sale price of $9,462,500, creates a loss of $37,500. Since the dividends from the stocks are $151,500, the total profit is $400,000: $286,000–$37,500 + $151,500.

Theoretically, it is possible for the amateur to follow this pattern. Realistically, the investor must have a very large portfolio because of the need for diversification to match the index and, of course, the substantial commissions.

Expiration Date Turmoil

The madness and disruption of the market starts on Wednesday of the week when contracts and options expire, accelerates on Thursday, and becomes frenzied on Friday. This surge comes from two sources:

1. Megabuck investors who are forced to buy stocks as part of their intricate trading schemes built around stock index options and futures that will expire. The target is the price disparity. One group sells short in expectation of a drop in the prices of the stocks that would mirror the movements of the index. Earlier, they hedged their short position by buying futures and options on the indexes with the goal of modest +12% to +20% returns. They earned interest on the cash from the short sales—less the cost of options of futures. And because of the price disparity, traders make more on their long positions in futures and options than they lose on short sales.

To make the scheme work, the professionals have to cover their short positions: buy back the stocks sold short before the expiration at the end of the week.

2. *Professional traders who concentrate on the options markets.* Typically, the options crowd in Chicago want stock prices to rise so that they can sell their calls at a profit or let their puts expire worthless; the New York operators strive to depress the stock prices so their calls won't be exercised or their puts will be profitable.

These shrewd professionals deal in fractions of a point, which can be significant when they own or are involved with thousands of options or shares of stock. This is no time or place for amateurs. **Never** buy or sell securities in the last three days of an expiration week. Prices have little relation to reality.

Chapter 7

OVERSEAS INVESTMENTS

Foreign securities have been more profitable than those of American corporations . . . at times. In 1984, when the American stock market rose only slightly, British stocks were up 31.8%; in 1985, when the DJIA jumped 27.6%, Austrian stocks skyrocketed 112.8%—all percentages in local currency.

But before you hock the family jewels to buy shares of European or Asian companies, you should understand that there are extra risks.

Risks of Foreign Investment

INADEQUATE OR LIMITED INFORMATION

Abroad, there is no SEC to set standards of accounting or reporting financial data. In Germany, depreciation and reserves make earnings almost meaningless, and companies show only enough profits to cover dividends. In England, under their depreciation schedules, accountants put British Oxygen Group's 1983 earnings at £55 million; by U.S. standards, they would have been £93 million.

HIGH COSTS AND EXECUTION DELAYS

Foreign transactions involve high costs and, often, delays in the execution of orders and the delivery of shares. With direct purchases, there are two brokerage commissions and there are foul-ups in 40% of transactions compared to 1% for U.S. stocks. In Italy, the average time for clearing was three months in a year when the local market soared 100%.

DIFFERENT RULES/REGULATIONS

In Japan, stop-loss orders are not permitted and foreigners cannot sell short. The nonresident must appoint a Japanese broker with authority to act on the investor's behalf. Dividends, usually two a year, are paid annually about three months after the record date.

ADDED TAXES

These are often levies by the foreign government; e.g., in Japan, all income from Japanese securities is subject to a 15% withholding.

PERILS OF FOREIGN EXCHANGE

These occur when: (1) income/gains are translated into dollars (that +31.8% for British stocks, in dollars, dropped the profit to Americans to +5.2%; (2) there's government intervention—the intentional buying or selling of a particular currency by a nation's central bank to sway exchange rates; (3) the national government devalues its currency (e.g., when Mexico reduced the worth of the peso, the high yields of bank savings accounts were wiped out).

Foreign Investment Possibilities

EUROBONDS

With bonds, there can be additional difficulties because of the terms of the debt and the rules of the exchanges. The bonds are denominated in a variety of ways, usually in round numbers such as 100,000 Japanese yen, 1,000 Swiss francs, or 100 British pounds. Most Americans have enough trouble understanding the differences in quotations of Treasury and corporate bonds!

There are, however, more convenient opportunities with Eurobonds, which are sold outside the country of issuance. They are denominated in dollars, yen, marks, etc., or, to minimize exchange fluctuations, in European Currency Units. This ECU is a weighted average of the currencies of members of the European Economic Community. These special bonds have no withholding tax on interest, and there are no records kept of buyers—just in case you want to hide some deals from your ever-loving partner.

This field of direct purchase is improving rapidly as industrial and financial corporations expand their markets, but it's still structured for large investments.

AMERICAN DEPOSITARY RECEIPTS (ADRS)

These are negotiable receipts representing ownership of shares of a foreign corporation. They are issued by an American bank against securities held abroad, usually by a bank located in the country where the foreign corporation is headquartered. ADRs enable foreign companies to tap American capital and American

TABLE 7-1

Typical ADRs Traded in America

Company	Nation	Company	Nation
AEG Telefunken	Germany	Ericsson Telephone	Sweden
L'Air Liquide	France	Heineken	Netherlands
Am. Israel Paper**	Israel	Marks & Spencer	UK
Anglo-American	S. Africa	Mitsubishi Bank	Japan
Bowater Corp.	UK	Pirelli	Italy
British Petroleum*	UK	Plessey*	UK
Broker Hill Prop.	Australia	Royal Dutch	Netherlands
Buffelsfontein Gold	S. Africa	Swire Pacific	Hong Kong
Canon	Japan	Tokyo Marine & Fire	Japan
Deutsche Bank	Germany	Toyota Motors	Japan

N.B. All securities not marked by asterisks are traded over the counter.
* New York Stock Exchange
** American Stock Exchange

investors to sell profits abroad. They are traded like stocks: a few on the NYSE, many on the AMEX, and most OTC (Table 7-1).

Each ADR is a contract between the holder and the bank. The U.S. purchaser pays in dollars and receives dividend and interest in dollars. The bank handles all mechanical details, reports, stockholder voting, etc.

To qualify for ADRs, the foreign company must submit its financial statements to the SEC so the investor can count on accurate (though not always complete) information. This is a costly and time-consuming process so that usually only the largest of foreign firms are willing to incur the expense and hassle.

ADRs are a convenient way to buy into foreign businesses, but their market values are subject to the same pressures of regular stocks. In 1983, the ADRs of Glaxo, the British pharmaceutical firm, were trading at 14. Two years later, despite rising earnings and a 30% increase in the price of the base stock in

London, the American substitute was down to 12. Reason: rising dollar, falling pound.

MULTINATIONAL AMERICAN CORPORATIONS

These are not exactly overseas investments but there are many major corporations which derive over 30% of their revenues and profits from foreign operations: Coca-Cola, Dow, IBM, J&J, Merck, Pfizer, Warner-Lambert, and Xerox, for example.

FOREIGN MUTUAL FUNDS

These are available in three general types:

Global funds, where investments are made in any country, including the U.S.A. This provides excellent diversification and the opportunity to switch holdings to take advantage of the falling dollar, e.g., to U.S. companies that now face less competition from abroad: the paper industry, furniture manufacturers, and producers of specialty machinery.

International funds, where investments are made only in foreign firms but can be concentrated in the most rewarding countries: in mid-1986, out of Japan into Germany, France, and Great Britain.

Country-specific funds, where investments are made in one or a related group of countries: Japan Fund, Korea Fund, Scandinavian Fund. Here, timing is important because domestic economies can rise and fall quickly.

Spread Your Risks

For most amateurs, the best way to invest overseas is in a mutual fund. There are no hassles with commissions, holdings are diversified, and the professional managers have access to corporate and economic information so are in a position to project the strength of the dollar versus foreign currencies. Typically, two-thirds of gains (losses) with foreign holdings come from share-price appreciation (depreciation) and one-third from swings between the relative-to-the-dollar values of currencies.

Best bet: pick two or three of the best-performing funds and split your investments. But limit your total foreign holdings to 15% of your total portfolio, unless and until you are in a position to keep abreast of new developments. It's tough enough to make money with securities of companies that provide full information and whose fortunes are followed in the financial press. When you move out of your field of knowledge and experience, you are taking extra risks so that the potential rewards should be double those available with American securities.

But, in another few years, as world markets become more closely integrated and better, more reliable information becomes available, it may be worthwhile to expand those overseas commitments.

Impact of Fluctuations in the Value of the Dollar

The most critical factor in overseas investments is the value of the U.S. dollar because:

- *Investment income and profits (losses) must be converted from foreign currencies to U.S. dollars.* When the dollar rises, the earnings from foreign holdings buy fewer dollars on the foreign exchange market so the true returns will be lower. Vice versa when the dollar falls.
- *The profits of foreign firms usually depend, to a large degree, on the ability of the company to sell in the American market.* With a weak dollar, they do well; when the dollar rises in value, they sell fewer goods in America and lose market share.

In the early 1980s, when the dollar's worth was declining, overseas investments were more rewarding than those of many U.S. stocks, but since 1985, with a 60% rise in the dollar, foreign holdings have been less attractive.

At this time, the impact of the stronger dollar is greatest in Japan, somewhat detrimental for European firms, and of minimal consequence in Hong Kong, Singapore, and Korea, where the values of their currencies are tied to the U.S. dollar.

There are, of course, other factors in currency fluctuations: lower interest rates, oil prices, and inflation have boosted European economies so that there has been an explosion of spending for consumer goods and investments. But these same factors have been bad for countries like Australia and Canada, which depend heavily on the exportation of raw materials such as oil, lumber, metals, and paper.

With most foreign investments, if you select wisely and well, you may make more than you could with U.S. stocks. However, if you guess wrong, you face double trouble: your losses can double from the failure of the corporation to perform as expected and from currency conversion. By American standards, few foreign companies are Blue Chips.

Part 4

PROFESSIONAL MONEY MANAGEMENT

The two chapters that make up this section describe the techniques and tactics of professional investors: how they manage large sums in pooled funds and in the portfolios of wealthy individuals.

Chapter 8 deals with mutual funds whose shares can be bought by individuals. It includes an explanation of the services, tactics, and costs, plus a checklist to help you find the best performers. With their vast resources and skilled analysts, some of these money managers can afford to gather the information needed to make judgments on secondary stocks, to speculate in specific areas, and to take positions that would be difficult, and, probably, dangerous for amateurs. A few of these speculative funds will report high returns for a year or two, but, over the years of up and down markets, the winners are those which stick to the fundamentals outlined in this book.

Chapter 9 discusses the specific steps a typical professional takes in comparing quality and nonquality corporations. This will show you how easy it can be to choose Blue Chips and to avoid "poor" companies that are always losers.

Chapter 8

MUTUAL FUNDS: BEST FOR CONVENIENCE AND SMALL INVESTORS

For the investor with limited time, money, and knowledge, shares of mutual funds offer an opportunity to participate in the stock market and, with careful selection and patience, to achieve total returns as good as, and occasionally, better than those of stock market averages. Add convenience, services, and accurate reports and these pooled funds can be useful for almost any type of investment goals. But you will lose the fun and excitement of making your own decisions!

These funds sell shares to investors and use the proceeds to buy securities designed to meet specific goals: income, growth, or balance and, with special types, to provide extra benefits in income or tax breaks. These funds are managed by investment companies which are business enterprises seeking the highest returns on their dollars and management. Since 1980 their popularity has soared so that in 1986 their assets were $581 billion, four times those of 1980. Most significant has been the change in operation, from investment vehicles where money flowed in or out according to performance to today's funds, where marketing is the primary force. To many investors, the packaging is more important than the results and it's *caveat emptor*. There are still funds whose management maintains integrity but too often the sponsors are promoters selling the sizzle and neglecting the steak.

Take your time in choosing mutual funds. These should be long-term holdings that should be sold only when you need money, change objectives, or conclude that the performance/service is inferior. Concentrate on the fundamentals: your goals, the character of the management company, and the proven ability of these professionals to make more money over time. Forget about the temporary (one- or two-year) records of superior performance heavily promoted by brokers and some financial publications. Most important, be comfortable and use your common sense.

The same principles of quality and value that apply to personal investments mark the best funds. Beware of name and fame and buy and hold shares in Blue Chip organizations whose managers attain average annual total returns 2% better than those of the DJIA or S&P 500. That's a worthwhile benefit for a management fee of ½ of 1% of the value of the total portfolio. This +2% should be a net figure, after deductions for commissions, administration, promotional costs, and extra fees for reinvestment of dividends and/or early redemption.

In bull markets, most funds will report superior results, but what you want is a record that continues to beat the averages: higher gains in up periods; lower losses in down markets. Those goals are not easy because institutional investors are the market since they account for 70% of all transactions on the NYSE. As proven by Wright Investors' Service, there are professional organizations that manage money successfully—year after year. Invest the majority of your savings in quality funds and, if you want to take a fling, speculate with the balance . . . and buy a rabbit's foot.

Definitions

On Wall Street, all investment companies are called "mutual funds" although legally this appellation applies only to open-end funds that offer and redeem their shares at net asset value (NAV), the worth of the underlying securities.

Mutual funds are pooled investments in securities, debt issues, limited partnerships, and so forth. The management firm sells shares to the public and invests the proceeds for a fee and generally distributes the income and realized appreciation to shareholders. In effect, these shares are service contracts to intermingle and invest your money in various types of financial instruments.

Broadly speaking, investment companies can be categorized by their methods of selling and investing, by their structure, by their objectives, and by the types of securities they buy and sell.

In *selling,* there are two groups: load and no-load.

LOAD

These are funds that are sold through brokers, dealers, and special representatives. The load is the commission, ranging from about 8.5% for small purchases down to 2% for large, usually contractual, commitments. This fee is deducted from the investment so that less money goes to work for the shareholder: with a 8.5% load, $91.50 of every $100 invested. Thus, the actual cost is 9.3%. But the salesman handles all details.

NO-LOAD

These are funds that are bought directly from the sponsoring firm without commission. All of your money is invested, but you must do all the work: setting up the account, mailing your checks, arranging for income to be reinvested or paid to you, etc.

Example: With two funds each yielding 10% a year, a $10,000 investment in a no-load increases to $11,000 in year 1 and to $12,100 in year 2. With a load fund with an 8.5% commission, you start with $9,150 and have $10,065 in one year and $11,072 in two years: $1,028 less. In ten years, at the same 10% return, no-load assets will be $25,939: $2,024 more than the

$23,939 for the load fund. Some load funds have outperformed no-loads, but they are the exception rather than the rule. You pay for convenience.

With both types of funds, there are additional charges that can affect the long-term returns because they reduce the amount of money on which gains can be compounded:

- *Management fee*. Depending on the fund, fees run from 0.5% to 2.0% of net assets. Be wary of any fund that has administration costs above 1.85% of your money and look elsewhere when they hit 2.00% unless the performance is supersuperior.
- *Back-end loads*. These are also called deferred sales charges. They are deducted from your investment when you cash in your shares. They start at 4% to 6% on withdrawals during the first year and gradually decline to zero about the fifth year.
- *Levy for reinvestment of dividends/interest*. This is widely used with bond funds and maybe as much as 1.25%, so a 10% yield will be cut to 8.75%.
- *Marketing costs*. Under SEC Rule 12b-1, mutual funds can dip into assets to pay certain promotional expenses. The idea was to help small funds grow by increasing sales to offset redemptions. By interpreting this provision liberally, many management firms now deduct costs of literature and mailing and even incentive payments to brokers.

With one major government securities fund, expenses were 1.30% of average net assets with 0.73% paid in 12b-1 fees. The average expense ratio of bond funds, without these paid-by-shareholder items, was 0.89%. Worse yet, this fund gained 14% in that year versus an average of 20% for all bond funds!

N.B. Fees are based on net asset value (NAV) but are also related to income earned. Thus, if the NAV is $10 and the management fee is ½ of 1% (50¢), a 20% appreciation ($2) raises the market value of each share to $12 and the fee to 60¢.

In *investing*, there are two broad groups:

OPEN-END

Open-end shares can be purchased from, or sold back to, the fund at the daily NAV: the total of the cash and market value of the securities held. When demand warrants, new shares are issued.

CLOSED-END

These are similar to regular corporations in that the capitalization and number of shares are fixed. When you buy, someone else has to sell. Many are listed on the NYSE so can be bought and sold like regular stocks, through brokers, at standard commissions.

Usually, shares of closed-end funds sell at a discount, apparently because investors realize that to make new purchases the managers must sell some of their holdings. Occasionally, in strong markets the shares command a premium because the underlying stocks are deemed to be undervalued.

When you buy shares at a discount, your returns will be advantageous in that the dividends/interest are paid on a lower cost basis; i.e., closed-end fund shares have a NAV of $10 and pay an 8% annual dividend (80¢ per share). When they sell at a 20% discount ($8), that's a 10% yield.

Important Changes

Historically, mutual funds had one of three objectives: income, growth, or balance. Income funds invested in bonds, preferred stocks, and convertibles; growth funds concentrated on common stocks; and balance funds mixed their holding. Later, there were special funds that concentrated on securities in special groups: chemicals, electronics, natural resources, etc. In most cases, their performance was so poor that these limitations were abandoned.

In recent years there has been a revolution in the industry.

Taking a cue from magazine publishers, food processors, drug manufacturers, and automobile makers, investment companies started to package their funds to fit almost every type of investment objective, type of security, or stock market tactic.

This has shifted the emphasis of Wall Street from investing to marketing. Instead of offering funds for financial goals, the professionals decide what the investors want (or think they want) and then create funds and services that can be promoted. You name it and some fund has it! All too often, these new packages are speculations, not investments.

Variety of Funds

In recent years, funds have become so popular that the promoters have come up with special packages: for social goals, income plus growth, growth plus income, health care companies, and so on. You name it and it's available or will be soon. The most heavily promoted new funds are clones. When a major fund becomes so popular that its assets reach around a billion dollars, management shuts its door to new investors and starts a clone, usually with the same or a similar name and investment goal. So far, most of these duplicates have not turned out to be overly rewarding.

In general terms, almost all funds offer these benefits:

Modest investments: initially $1,000 with additions in smaller sums. By comparison, direct purchases of similar securities would require $25,000 or more.

Income reinvested for compounding. This is most valuable with fixed income funds. With personal portfolios, the semiannual interest of a debt security will be too small (say, $400 on a $10,000 investment) to buy more bonds so will probably end up in a low-yielding savings account or be spent. That's no way to build wealth.

Liquidity: the opportunity to withdraw money at any time by selling shares.

Regular checks: monthly, quarterly, semiannually by: (1) a fixed sum available from income and the sale of some shares; (2) dividends from several funds with different payout dates.

Thus, if you retire with $100,000, you can arrange for a monthly check of $1,000. With a good growth fund, your assets will continue to appreciate (except in down markets); with an income fund, you will probably have to cash in shares periodically. But with a 10% average yield, that $12,000 "annuity" will continue for eighteen years.

Beneficiary designation that uses a trust to permit you to name the recipient of the assets after your death. This can avoid probate, save costs, and speed transfer of funds.

Life insurance: term life without a medical exam when the investor is under age fifty-five and the shares are worth more than $18,000. This will assure full payment of an uncompleted contractual investment plan.

Personal loans. Some funds permit you to use your shares as collateral for loans at interest rates that can be lower than those charged by a bank. Typically, the minimum is $5,000 with a 50% margin ($5,000 loan for each $10,000 assets). There are seldom mandatory repayments, and you can arrange for the interest to be paid from the fund's income or appreciation.

Complete records of all transactions so that when you sell some shares, you can identify those that provide the best tax breaks. This is not so important under the new law, where all income and gains are taxed at the same rate but can be helpful to your accountant in preparing your tax return.

Switching between funds directed by the same firm. This involves a small fee but can make it easier for you to manage your portfolios: out of equities into debt when interest rates soar or vice versa when they fall.

To my mind, this is one of the major benefits of mutual funds. Here's a real-life example of how a neighbor used this service:

In 1981, when interest rates were 14%, Dr. Joe invested about 75% of his pension assets in bonds and preferred stocks, and 25% in growth shares. In 1982, when yields dropped to 10.5%, he shifted one-third of his fixed income holdings to a balanced fund. In 1983–84, he sold more bond shares and bought growth shares so that his portfolio was 40% fixed income, 20% balanced, and 20% growth. In early 1985, as the stock market roared up, he shifted again to 20% fixed income, 20% balance, and 60% growth.

This doesn't mean that you should go fund-hopping: selling fund A with a mediocre performance and buying fund B that is in a hot streak.This may make sense for aggressive investors at some periods. When money market funds were yielding over 14%, some "smart" operators jumped each month to the fund that had reported the best performance in the past month. They did pick up an extra 1%, but that small gain was seldom worthwhile when they counted the costs of telephone, postage, record-keeping, and, in some funds, the fees for entry or for exit.

Comment: Don't waste your money on switching services—reports that purport to tell what the market is going to do next so you can shift within a family of funds. Most editors use a moving average of a series of fund prices and when the current price of one is higher than the current thirty-nine-week MA, recommend switching into shares of another companion fund: from growth to income, etc. When the shares of your fund are below that MA, switch out. The process, at a slightly higher subscription cost, is available immediately from the Scooper-Dooper Telephone Switch Service.

Granted that with many fund families a switch is not expensive, there will be extra costs and usually you will lose some income and the full benefits of compounding.

There are times when it is wise to switch, but these are viable primarily when your goals or needs change and when the alternative clearly provides greater returns. But you don't have to pay for such advice. All the information you need is in the financial press, and the decision should be made on personal factors, not in an attempt to squeeze out a couple of extra bucks.

Information and service. With 800 numbers, you can make toll-free calls to check prices, minimum investments, charges, etc. Most funds provide forms for setting up pension programs and will keep you current on new regulations.

These personal benefits are supplementary to the basic advantages of all pooled investments:

Diversification. With stocks, diversification is by types of industries and within those categories, by products/services, with bonds, it is by types, location of issuer, and maturities. Unless you have $50,000, it's difficult to have a properly balanced portfolio, probably fewer than ten stocks when you buy in 100-share lots. For $1,000 in a mutual fund, you can own a portion of 100 companies.

Professional management. This is subject to interpretation, but most funds are under the direction of experienced Wall Streeters who utilize what they feel are meaningful research and fact-based judgments. They have access to detailed statistical information to compare quality and value and to computers that can be used to make projections and to facilitate timing of purchases and sales. When they stick to their standards, they usually can beat the averages and reach the stated goals.

Economic/market background. This is another area of information that is difficult for amateurs to obtain and maintain: *overall,* money supply, foreign exchange, relevant commodity prices, new government regulations, etc.; *in the stock market,* reports on insider trading, new financing, sources of major transactions and recommendations; and *within the management firm,* historical data that can be used for comparisons, to spot trends, and to improve decisions. Some professionals do not always use these tools wisely, but the good ones learn from their mistakes and the inept managers go back to being brokers.

Choosing Mutual Funds

No matter how attractive the name, package, or sales pitch, always check these points before you invest any money in any type of pooled funds. Despite the promotional claims of circulars, there is no magic formula for successful money management. Each fund manager relies on the same statistics as are available to his/her peers. The individual's skill, or luck, is the result primarily of selection and timing: picking stocks that roar up to target prices in a few months rather than in the anticipated year or two.

The keys to long-term successful money management are quality and value, with timing a tertiary, and usually temporary, factor. For investing, choose funds as you would stocks: do your homework, make logical projections, and be patient. If the gains come quickly, rejoice but do not cry "Eureka!" nor believe that the fund managers have found the secret of making lots of money. With every fund, consider: (1) objectives and (2) investment philosophy.

OBJECTIVES

These are the stated goals of the prospectus—income, growth, balance, or speculation. You want to be sure that you are getting what you pay for and that the money managers try to achieve specific goals. This sound puerile but it's surprising how often, especially in the euphoria of a bull market, standards are modified or revised.

INVESTMENT PHILOSOPHY

Investment philosophy refers to the criteria used by the managers in selecting and selling securities. A conservative fund will concentrate on stocks listed on the NYSE; an aggressive fund will include shares of stocks listed on the AMEX and OTC; and a speculative fund will emphasize new issues, shares of hi-tech companies, and swinging situations such as junk bonds and takeover candidates, where the profits can be quick and high but the losses can be alarming.

Be cautious with specialty funds that state they will speculate by selling short, buying options, or using margin. All of these techniques involve leverage that can bring extra gains in strong markets but can be disastrous when prices fall.

It's also important to discover how the managers plan to operate. Some professionals pick stocks from the top down, starting with the broad political and economic projections affecting the market and specific industries and then zeroing in on individual companies. They look for trends first and then select stocks that they feel will benefit the most. Other managers work from the bottom up, looking first for individual companies that appear undervalued and have prospects of improved earnings and popularity. Both methods can be successful, so choose the style that fits your personal philosophy and sleep-well level.

Once you have determined what the managers plan to do, check the portfolios for the last couple of years to see the types of securities held and how effectively they meet the stated criteria. In other words, if Super-Stable Fund owns a big block of Whiz-Bang Electronics, watch out!

Similarly, they keep buying Slow and Steady, Inc., for several years even though the stock has barely moved and failed to raise its dividend. This is a sure indication that management is either lazy or smug.

Don't be suckered in by the headlines of reports. If the stated goal is income, check the quality of the debt issues and utilities. A fund with bonds rated B or lower may show a high yield but it's not worth the risks.

Further Checkpoints

Before you make any commitment, get copies of the annual reports of the funds for the past five years and look for information on these subjects:

TIMING

How long have large blocks of stocks of major corporations been held? Were thousands of shares of IBM bought at around 60 in 1981 or at 150 in 1985? Does the fund still hold Avon Products from 1974, when its price was over 100, or were those shares acquired in 1982 at 20?

BIG WINNERS/LOSERS

Such lists are often shown in quarterly statements. Find out when these stocks were bought: way back when, last year, or last month? Were the losers sold soon after a downturn or held on in hope for months? This doesn't mean that the manager should sell a quality holding just because its price is temporarily depressed, but it does mean that there should be clearly defined parameters.

LEVERAGE

Beware of all funds that use leverage: borrowing to trade, to sell short, or to speculate. This is especially risky when interest rates are high. When margin money costs over 10%, the fund managers must score extraordinary profits to have money left to distribute to shareholders.

DIVERSIFICATION

There should be no more than 10% of holdings in any one company nor more than 20% in any one industry—with the possible exception of A-rated bonds or utility stocks—and a maximum of 20% in any one economic segment, such as financial institutions, energy companies, electronics, etc.

TURNOVER

Turnover should be under 50% in two, and preferably, three years. Higher activity indicates the fund managers either made a lot of mistakes or were more interested in trading than investing. Most funds show this figure in their annual report. If it's not available, call the management.

Frequent selling and buying is expensive. With round-trip commissions of 0.5%, that's a 1% haircut, so the fund must outperform the market just to stay even. Over a couple of years, in a booming period, a high turnover may be profitable but over a long time span there is no correlation between high turnover and performance.

High turnovers are especially dangerous with speculative funds that deal in OTC stocks traded on a bid and asked basis where there's no way to check the spreads. Too often, the fund manager may "cooperate" with friendly brokers.

Still, some managers can't resist the chance to boast. One highly promoted fund reported an annual turnover rate of 233% on every $100 of net assets. The per unit commissions were $1.34 plus expenses of 99¢. Even a stupid speculator would never permit such costs with his own money!

SIZE AND LONGEVITY

Avoid any fund that has assets of less than $50 million for any period of time. The performance must have been so poor that new shares could not be sold. Be wary of funds with assets of over $1 billion. At this size, the managers must limit their holdings to a relatively small number of major corporations that have millions of shares outstanding. This eliminates Junior Blue Chips, which usually grow rapidly.

MANAGEMENT

No significant changes should have occurred in top executives (except by death or retirement) or in control during the last three years. Investing is a long-term commitment that requires uniform policies, experience, and patience. None of these is likely with frequent shifts in personnel.

The management companies that sponsor mutual funds are business enterprises organized and operated for profit. The policies are spelled out in the prospectus, but that language can be obtuse and its interpretation misleading and, sometimes, self-serving. It's the old story of integrity. You may pay more for jewelry bought at Tiffany's than at a chain store, but you can be confident that you are getting quality merchandise.

Just as dangerous are speculative techniques whose risks are obscured in the "explanatory" language, i.e., with **plus** funds that enhance income by selling options. In a normal market, the yields may be temporarily higher because the income includes the premiums received for the calls, but in a rising period, when the price of the stock on which the option is written soars, the fund loses the extra gain.

Example: Freddie Fundmanager buys 1,000 shares of ZYX at 42 and sells ten six-month calls with a striking price of 45 at 2 ($2,000 minus commission). This does reduce the risk of a downturn below 40, but if the value of ZYX soars to 48, Freddie loses three-point profit ($3,000).

INTEGRITY

This is a bit hard to define but applies primarily to promotional claims. The headline of the advertisement boasts of returns of 10.1% to 12.8% so that investors assume that's what they can get with their savings. But in a volatile market, current yields can drop: for Treasuries, to 8.5%; to 11% for Ginnie Maes. After deduction of fees, there's no way the fund can fulfill what appears to be its promises (unless the reader checks the fine print).

Equally questionable are bragging statements in the press and on radio/TV. When any fund manager begins to be widely quoted, watch out. He/she can make the fatal mistake of believing the publicity and, to catch the headlines, will make strong statements and positive projections.

Older readers will remember the late 1960s when the "sure" way to financial success was to buy and hold one-decision stocks: Avon, Polaroid, etc. By 1982, almost all of these favorites had bombed!

The same caveat applies to overoptimism with bond funds. In the 1977–78 bear market, the Dow Jones Corporate Bond Index was 93.43 and the "experts" assured their trusting public that these were rock-solid investments. Baloney! In the 1981 bear market, the composite price of debt issues was down to 55.68!

Other areas of promotional zeal involve calculating yields. Fund A starts with interest for a seven-day period, then adds the capital gains for the quarter and projects these totals for the full year. Fund B projects the current interest rate for twelve months and adds the anticipated capital appreciation based on past performance with a dollop of enthusiasm. In a period of lower yields, the original rate of return will decline so that the net yield is sure to be lower than advertised unless the gains are above estimates. Fund C bases its return on anticipated dividends and gains, with no provision for probable failures to reach such goals. Fund D projects the current yield for all reinvestments for the next year.

And don't believe all of those claims of the Magic of Compounding by reinvestment of income. This is a valid benefit but is not always as profitable as you are led to believe because:

- Since this is a form of dollar-cost averaging, the maximum reinvestments are made when the stock market is high. Thus, those savings buy fewer shares of the fund than when the stock values are depressed. If you feel the market is vastly overpriced, take the cash and wait for the value of the shares to decline. Then, reinvest at a lower cost!
- The claims of the benefits of long-term compounding are unrealistic and do not take into account the time frame of your investments. Most funds start with a $1,000 purchase made many years ago and assume regular reinvestment in good times and bad. Because the stock market has always advanced, the gains appear to be substantial. But there is

no revision for the results of the investor who started his/her program when the market was at a temporary peak.

With tax-exempt unit trusts (which are a mystery to most folks anyway), there's another caveat: an advertised higher-than-competition yield, say, 8% when most municipals pay 7.25%. These managers use "current return" to gloss over the standard measures of "yield to first call" or "yield to maturity." The fallacy (for the investor) is that the "estimated current return" does not take into account the amortization of bonds trading at premiums.

Example: Bedroom Authority 10s are trading at 110 so the current yield is 9.1%. Since the bonds are callable in five years at 100, there's a loss of $100 per bond. The real return is 7.56%.

Another trick with bond funds is for the managers to buy a lot of zero-coupon tax-exempts to keep the per share offering price close to $1,000. Their gains are appreciation.

PERFORMANCE

This is, of course, the clincher. Gloss over the short-term results, for six months or one year, and concentrate on the long-term record, five and preferably ten years. When you get serious about a choice, check the published reports which usually compare the fund returns with those of the S&P 500. Pay special attention to whether the superior performances was across the board or erratic: from two or three stocks such as those of companies involved in mergers. Such "performance" is due more to luck than to skill, as, for example, with General Foods, whose stock doubled with the takeover by Philip Morris. Those superprofits are welcome, but they should be accompanied by better-than-average gains from other holdings.

One of the best guides to consistently superior performance is the annual rating of mutual funds in the August issue of *Forbes* magazine. This categorizes major funds by their total returns in both **up** and **down** markets over three cycles covering nine and three-quarters years. In 1986, the twenty-three honor-role funds delivered +20% (or better) compound annual rates of return.

The "winners" were the funds that were slow on the draw. Their managers bought slower, sold slower, and held longer than those of the group. That's the same approach that has made a few professional money managers successful, e.g., Wright Investors' Service.

In commenting on the ratings, the *Forbes* editors emphasize (year after year) many of the same points made in this book:

> Last year's results are a poor predictor of this year's. . . . If the market was up strongly in the previous year and is now headed down, then you can bet that last year's winners will be this year's losers.
>
> Forget about the hot performer list. Look for consistency: B or better in up markets; B or better in down markets.
>
> After a painful bear market, too many investors cling to the most conservative fund at the wrong time.
>
> It's a matter of arithmetic: a fair weather fund is +50% in a bull market and loses -35% when the market falters . . . a $10,000 investment would drop to $9,750. A steady performer is +25% in a bull market, -10% in the decline. That $10,000 is worth $11,250.

SPECIFIC CHECKPOINTS

Cash held in various types of stock markets. If the liquid assets stay high after the start of a bull market, the managers are overly cautious and will miss some of the best gains. If cash is low after the onset of a bear market, you're sure to lose money.

Big-name stocks. (Exxon, GM, IBM, Merck, Xerox). It's OK for any fund to hold sizable blocks of such shares, but when the big Blue Chips account for more than 40% of total assets, the managers are buying security and reputation, not profitable growth. There are, of course, exceptions when one or more of these major stocks are clearly undervalued: IBM in 1982 and

1984, Merck in 1983 and 1984, etc. You don't have to hire experts to make such selections.

Small companies whose shares are traded on the AMEX or OTC. Most of these firms are better speculations than investments. Their quality is marginal, their records limited, and their projections difficult.

Again, it's a matter of the number and size of such holdings, with a reasonable limit of 20% of the number of securities and 15% of total assets. You might buy shares of a speculative fund with a portion of your personal savings but never with pension assets.

Holdings at end of quarter. One of the tricks of the trade is to paper the quarterly results: to buy, a week or two before March 31, June 30, etc., a large number of shares of stocks that have appreciated sharply in the last month or two. Since there's no need for the managers to show when these winners were acquired, the unsuspecting investor assumes they were bought before the recent price rise!

Bond Funds

So far, we've discussed more or less standard stock funds. There are, of course, many other varieties including bond funds. With both taxable and tax-exempt bond funds, there are two broad types: unit trusts and managed funds.

UNIT TRUSTS

These invest in a fixed portfolio, diversified by type, geography, and maturity. There are no changes until the bonds are called, redeemed, or, occasionally, defaulted. These trusts are sold with a load of about 4.5% and pay a fixed yield based on the interest rate at the time of issue, so that the market values of the shares fluctuate with the cost of money. Most trusts run for twenty-five years, but their shares can be sold back to the sponsor with the price depending on market conditions.

These funds are best for conservative investors who plan to hold their shares for ten years or more. For extra safety, but a lower yield of about twenty-five basis points (one quarter of 1%), there are insured funds that guarantee payment of interest and principal.

With tax-exempts, the income is tax-free when: (1) the firm is operated as a trust, not as an investment company; (2) the sponsor holds the portfolio to maturity.

The manager makes an initial purchase according to his/her preset criteria: (1) only A-rated bonds, (2) bonds to mature at a specific date, (3) hospital bonds, (4) debt issued within one state where there's an income tax.

Typically, a unit trust has about $50 million in assets. New trusts are packaged frequently. The initial investment, for the buyer, is $5,000 with smaller additions permitted later.

In making a choice, check these points:

- The quality of the bonds, preferably AA
- The performance of other unit trusts under the same management
- The commissions/fees charged
- The stated maturity and whether the fund will be disbanded when the assets fall below a certain percentage of the original assets, typically 20%
- The method of calculating the redemption price: the dollars to be received if the shares are cashed in early
- The timing of interest payments and whether the income can be reinvested for compounding
- The policy of redemption, since such a sale will incur a capital gain or loss for the shareholder

These strive for extra profits by trading in anticipation of shifts in interest rates. They are available as loads and no-loads. Generally, their yields are higher than those of unit trusts (that's what you pay for), but there can be substantial losses if the managers guess wrong. Or, when the projections are correct, there can be welcome capital gains.

Special Funds

These pool the money from the sale of shares and are available for almost every conceivable investment and speculation. They range from limited partnerships in oil/gas deals, real estate and venture capital packages to market sector "investments" in specific areas such as gold and precious metals, health care enterprises, commodities and on and on. Despite their promotional promises that these are "investments in the future," most are little more than repackaging of old, speculative concepts that carry hefty commissions and off-the-top expenses. They lack diversification and, because there may be so few firms in any one sector, the companies whose shares are held will compete with each other. The best that can be said for most of these "opportunities" is that you are buying an average of returns in one area. You will do better by buying stocks of the leading, and most profitable, corporations. In past years, many of these were structured for tax benefits but under the new law these are minimal and the risks are just as great.

On the theory that if you can't beat 'em, join 'em, some management companies sponsor "index" funds which by definition assure market average returns. The fund assets are invested in stocks of the S&P 500 Stock Composite. On paper, that average return is true, but the income/gains are reduced by a load of 8.5% and a maintenance fee of $6 per quarter. The administration costs are low because there's no research, few commissions because of the low turnover, and a modest management fee: 1/5 of 1% of share value.

Bank Sponsored Funds

For the small investor, funds offered by thrift institutions and small banks can be excellent deals. Typically, he/she has a choice of five pools with different objectives: total return, current income, growth of income, tax-deferred growth, and fixed income. Investments start as low as $500 with additions of $100 or more. When assets total more than $1,000, you can switch for a small fee.

The institution handles all details, provides monthly reports, arranges for withdrawals, in lump sum, or, after retirement, in periodic payments. You can even schedule regular purchases from your checking or savings accounts.

All activities are controlled by trustees independent of the institution with the actual money management by a professional firm. You get the convenience of a local business, deal with people whom you know (and who know you), have experienced direction, and receive detailed financial reports for your tax return, pension plan, or trust. Good deal.

Real Estate Investment Trusts (REITs)

These are first cousins to mutual funds. They sell shares whose proceeds are used to buy, finance, or manage real estate. Their income/gains are exempt from federal taxation when 95% of net earnings are distributed to shareholders. Since they get depreciation deductions, their taxes are limited and returns can be 8% or more. But they cannot pass along losses so, hopefully, these will be more than offset by profitable appreciation.

REITs can be classified into three categories:

1. *Equity trusts* which own income-producing properties, usually in a specific field such as hotels, shopping centers, etc.

2. *Mortgage funds* which invest in all types of real estate financing, with profits primarily from the interest. These do well in growth periods but can be devastated during recessions.

3. *Hybrid trusts* which combine ownership and lending, usually short-term financing and long-term investing. Many of these funds are associated with insurance companies.

Within these groups are two variations:

1. *Standard funds,* which have an infinite life. Every time a property is sold, another is purchased so that shareholders benefit when there's appreciation.

2. *New packages* with a finite life, usually seven to fifteen years, when the trust will be liquidated. Each time a property is sold or refinanced, the shareholder gets a return on investment.

Shares of most REITs sell at a discount from net asset value because there's no specific timetable for selling assets and making distributions. A $1 million fund with 100,000 shares (NAV of $10) typically would trade at 7. They are defensive holdings in that if the values of stocks fall, REIT shares will be buoyed by the values of the real estate. They also benefit from inflation in that this boosts the worth of both the properties and the rents.

Shares of a few funds are listed on exchanges but most are traded over the counter, where their prices are more or less controlled by the sponsors.

Checkpoints

As with all investments, quality—of the properties and management—is the key. This can be judged by the long-term record: few losses and steady, fairly consistent increases in income and capital gains. Buy REITs for income and hope for growth.

Types and locations of properties. The best performing funds concentrate geographically and specialize in similar properties where management has expertise.

Since all holdings are listed in the prospectus or financial reports, look for buildings near where you live and see whether they are well located, well managed, and profitable (according to your friendly broker). *Watch out for name/fame over value.* One trust boasted about "a prestigious commercial property in downtown West Palm Beach, center of the fastest growing area in the country." They failed to mention that this was only half rented, faced strong competition, and would be plagued by redevelopment digging/building for several years.

Leverage. If the properties are fully financed, there's not much upside potential. Try to find REITs with debt less than 50% of current value of equity or that have the ability to refinance—especially significant with lower interest rates.

Value. At best, this will be imprecise so there can be wide spreads between worth based on cost, reproduction, and/or income.

Liquidity. Concentrate on REITs that are widely traded or sponsored by a well-known firm. Most funds have thin markets so share prices can swing quickly.

Avoid blind pools where the properties are not specified. In an effort to lend at high interest rates, management may finance a developer whose properties are coming into an overbuilt market.

Transaction Techniques

For maximum returns and lowest net costs, schedule buying and selling of shares of all types of pooled funds to take advantage of tax breaks, fund practices, and market peculiarities. Check the date of distributions (dividends, interest, and capital gains): **buy** after; **sell** before.

Example: Dan buys 1,000 shares of Sooper Fund at 16—$16,000 with a no-load. A week later, there's a distribution of $3 per share: $1 income and $2 capital gains: $3,000, so his net cost is $13,000. Under the new tax law (starting in 1987), the tax will be $840 (a 28% rate). This raises Dan's base to $13,840.

If Dan had waited until after the distribution, he would have paid $13,000 for the shares (value reduced by the payout) and have had no taxes to pay until he sold them or until the next distribution.

Fund distributions are almost all taxable except when the fund has losses or the assets are in tax-exempt securities. To retain its tax-exemption status, the fund must pay out 97% of ordinary income and 90% of net realized capital gains by the end of each year. Shareholders are taxed in the same year that the income is earned. Most funds provide guidelines to help you calculate the taxes.

N.B. With shares of tax-exempt funds, double-check the annual report. When the income is reinvested, you buy new shares at a cost equal to the reported gains/losses from the sale subject to regular capital gains rules. If you sell at a loss within thirty-one days after receiving the payout, the loss will be disallowed as a wash sale.

To redeem shares, you must have your signature guaranteed by a commercial bank or stock brokerage firm. If you deal with a thrift institution, arrange for a code number for prompt identification and have the S&L manager send a guarantee to the fund management.

Using Printed Guides

One way to make the selection of mutual funds easier is to check one of the guides published by private advisers or financial magazines. Typically, these show returns and costs for the most recent reporting period: one year, three years, five years, and occasionally ten years. They usually include special data on:

- *Type:* growth, income, growth income, balance
- *Risk:* based on performance more than on current portfolios
- *Sales charge:* most significant with income funds where a lower fee can boost yields
- *Gains (losses)*: usually on a total return basis
- *Current yield:* best for income funds but useful with growth because everyone likes to be paid for the use of his/her money.

Summary

In choosing mutual funds, the final decision should be based on your objectives, your current and anticipated tax rate, your resources, and your comfort level.

For a young person paying low taxes: 60% to 70% for growth, 20% for income, and the rest for balance.

For a middle-aged individual who is or expects to be in the highest tax bracket: 25% for growth, 25% for income, and 50% in tax-exempts.

For the older person readying for retirement: 40% for growth and 60% for income, with tax-exempts only for those in the highest tax bracket.

Repeat: in choosing mutual funds, use the same standards of quality and value as you do with stocks and bonds. Look for consistent performance in both bull and bear markets. Review the securities held and ask yourself if these are the types you would buy yourself. If you, or your spouse, have any doubts, look elsewhere.

Dollarwise, your best bet will be no-loads, but if you are not willing to handle details, pay the broker. Still, if you follow the counsel in this guide, do your homework, and use common sense, you can do better on your own.

Chapter 9

HOW PROFESSIONALS ANALYZE COMPANIES

This chapter is both a summary and a checklist: a summary of the financial information developed on some 3,000 major corporations, American and foreign; a checklist of the key factors used by professional investment managers to analyze the corporation to determine whether its stock should be bought, held, or sold. The collation was prepared by Wright Investors' Service using its own data for companies whose stocks are traded on American exchanges plus statistics collected by the Center for International Financial Analysis and Research.

To present comparable information, the figures for foreign firms have been presented in unified format based on studies of U.S. companies. The data for these overseas corporations may not always be as accurate or as complete as those for U.S. firms subject to tough SEC and NYSE reporting, but there is a relatively uniform basis for comparison. The statistics, under the trademarked name of *WORLDSCOPE,* are published in both printed and electronic form and marketed by Wright.

Table 9-1 shows the data for Emerson Electric Co. (EMR), a top-quality corporation with a long record of strong, profitable growth. Most of the categories are self-explanatory, but, to help you learn how the experts do it, here are answers to some questions asked by a friend of mine who wants to know how to be a successful investor for: (1) personal funds, about $100,000; (2) the pension plan of a small corporation of which he is a director, $900,000; (3) a trust fund for two grandchildren, $75,000; and (4) a charitable trust for a community agency that has established a pooled income plan for generous benefactors, $1.2 million.

Financial Statement Data

INCOME STATEMENT

In the six years between 1980 and 1985, EMR has grown by almost 33% to revenues of $4,649 million from $3,067 million. Note that interest expense was low until the last year. Usually, this is a key item. The increase may be OK if used constructively—for acquisitions, expansion, etc.—but always find out why the extra borrowings were needed.

BALANCE SHEET—ASSETS

Read these figures in relation to net receivables. Here, there were no problems. The liquid assets (cash and short-term instruments) were up in years of high interest rates and down in 1985 when the cost of money declined.

Inventories rose in line with net sales, and *net property* rose indicating ever-higher investments in new plants and equipment so that *total assets* in 1985 were 69% greater than in 1980. EMR was investing for the future.

TABLE 9-1 Data for Emerson Electric Co. (EMR)

Financial Statement Data	1985	1984	1983	1982	1981	1980
	(Millions of U.S. dollars)					
Income Statement						
Net Sales	4,649	4,179	3,476	3,502	3,429	3,067
Depreciation, Deple. & Amort.	148	123	104	102	92	82
Operating Income	740	649	533	547	523	453
Interest Expense	37	28	16	20	28	29
Pretax Income	694	618	538	535	491	430
Net Income	401	349	303	300	273	238
Balance Sheet - Assets						
Cash & Short Term Investments	89	102	256	164	126	48
Receivables - Net	723	662	533	514	523	489
Inventories	1,156	1,080	916	895	871	777
Total Current Assets	2,085	1,921	1,737	1,638	1,586	1,370
Net Property,Plant & Equipment	844	753	661	595	555	496
Total Assets	3,257	2,980	2,493	2,320	2,202	1,929
Balance Sheet - Liabilities						
Total Current Liabilities	778	885	645	622	651	520
Long Term Debt	115	130	146	139	164	180
Preferred Stock	0	0	0	0	0	0
Common Equity	2,222	1,869	1,702	1,559	1,386	1,230
Liabilities & Equity	3,257	2,980	2,493	2,320	2,202	1,929
Sources & Uses of Funds						
From Operations	557	473	407	402	365	319
External Financing - Net	-22	-25	-9	-35	-12	-15
Dividends	190	158	144	137	112	99
Capital Expenditures	207	167	128	139	139	121
Change in Working Capital	57	424	121	23	86	88
International Business						
Foreign Assets	609	425	259	347	377	383
Foreign Sales	698	527	330	480	515	509
Foreign Income	90	58	40	41	32	30
Supplementary Data						
Employees	61,900	57,800	50,000	52,700	55,200	53,800
R & D Expense	140	116	93	90	NOM	
Common Shares (millions)	74	69	69	69	64	64

General Information

Chairman & CEO
C.F. KNIGHT
President & COO
E.L. KEYES, JR.
Chief Financial Officer
W.C. BOUSQUETTE
Treasurer
R.M. COX, JR.
Secretary
C. HANSEN
Address:
8000 WEST FLORISSANT AVENUE
ST. LOUIS, MO 63136
UNITED STATES
Telephone: (314) 553-2000

Exchange: NYSE BSE CIN MSE
Business:
MANUFACTURES COMMERCIAL & INDUSTRIAL PRODUCTS (63% OF FISCAL 1985 SALES); CONSUMER PRODUCTS (25%) & DEFENSE PRODUCTS (12%)

Fiscal Year End: September 30

Selected Data
U.S. Currency ($Mil)
Fiscal Year 1985

Market Capitalization	6,003
Common Equity	
Total Assets	3,257
Sales	4,649
Net Income	401

Profitability						
Operating Margin	15.9%	15.5%	15.3%	15.6%	15.2%	14.8%
Effective Tax Rate	42.2%	43.5%	43.7%	43.9%	44.4%	44.7%
Net Margin	8.6%	8.4%	8.7%	8.6%	8.0%	7.8%
Return on Assets	13.5%	14.0%	13.1%	13.6%	14.2%	14.0%
Return on Equity	21.5%	20.5%	19.4%	21.6%	22.2%	22.7%
Cash Flow/Sales	12.0%	11.3%	11.7%	11.5%	10.6%	10.4%
Sales Per Employee (000)	75	72	70	66	62	57
Asset Utilization						
Total Assets Turnover	1.4%	1.4%	1.4%	1.5%	1.6%	1.6%
Assets per Employee (000)	53	52	50	44	40	36
Capital Exp./Fixed Assets	13.1%	12.2%	10.6%	12.8%	14.1%	13.8%
Accum. Dep./Fixed Assets	46.4%	45.0%	45.5%	45.3%	43.8%	43.4%
Liquidity						
Current Ratio	2.7x	2.2x	2.7x	2.6x	2.4x	2.6x
Quick Ratio	1.0x	0.9x	1.2x	1.1x	1.0x	1.0x
Leverage						
Common Equity/Assets	68.2%	62.7%	68.3%	67.2%	63.0%	63.7%
Total Debt/Total Capital	4.9%	6.5%	7.9%	8.2%	10.6%	12.7%
EBIT/Fixed Charges	19.9x	23.4x	33.8x	27.6x	18.7x	15.8x
Oper. Cash/Fixed Charges	15.1x	17.2x	24.8x	20.0x	13.1x	11.0x
Growth						
Net Sales	11.3%	20.2%	-0.8%	2.1%	11.8%	17.3%
Operating Income	13.9%	21.7%	-2.5%	4.6%	15.4%	14.1%
Earnings per Share	4.0%	15.6%	3.4%	2.1%	14.7%	5.0%
Dividends per Share	11.2%	10.5%	6.2%	11.3%	10.3%	11.5%
Book Value per Share	8.0%	9.9%	9.2%	7.2%	9.6%	10.7%
Total Assets	9.3%	19.5%	7.5%	5.4%	14.1%	13.7%

Per Share Data and Investment Ratios (Calendar year basis)

Earnings per Share	EG5.46	EG5.25	EG4.54	EG4.39	BE4.30	B3.75
Dividends per Share	2.64	2.37	2.15	2.02	1.82	1.65
Book Value per Share	30.10	27.88	25.37	23.24	21.68	19.78
Market Price	81.25	69.50	66.50	60.50	45.37	36.50
Total Return	20.7%	8.1%	13.5%	37.8%	29.3%	8.6%
Price/Earnings Ratio	14.9x	13.2x	14.6x	13.8x	10.6x	9.7x
Price/Book Value Ratio	2.7x	2.5x	2.6x	2.6x	2.1x	1.8x
Dividend Yield	3.2%	3.4%	3.2%	3.3%	4.0%	4.5%
Dividend Payout	48%	45%	47%	46%	42%	44%

Notes: (A): NOT APPLICABLE OR NOT AVAILABLE; (B): BASED ON COMMON AND COMMON EQUIVALENT SHARES; (C): NOT APPLICABLE OR NOT AVAILABLE; (D): INCLUDES THE EFFECTS OF AN ACCOUNTING CHANGE; - ADOPTED FASB 52 TO ACCOUNT FOR FOREIGN CURRENCY TRANS IN 81. EARNINGS IMPACT IMMATERIAL (E): INCLUDES FOREIGN CURRENCY TRANSLATION GAINS/LOSSES; , ($.01) IN FIS 82 , $.01 IN FIS 83 , $.02 IN FIS 84 , INCLS FOREIGN CURRENCY TRANS GAIN/(LOSS) EQUAL TO $.03 IN FIS 85 (F): NOT APPLICABLE OR NOT AVAILABLE; (G): BASED ON AVERAGE SHARES OUTSTANDING;

Growth Rates

Net Sales	+8.7%
Net Income	+11.0%
Total Assets	+11.0%
Employees	+2.8%
Earnings per Share	+7.8%
Dividends per Share	+9.9%
Book Value per Share	+8.8%

Financial Ratios 5 Year Average

Operating Margin	15.5%
Net Margin - After Tax	8.4%
Return on Assets - After Tax	13.7%
Return on Equity	21.1%
Reinvestment Rate	11.0%
Price/Earnings Ratio	13.2x
Price/Book Value Ratio	2.5x
Dividend Yield	3.4%
Dividend Payout	46.0%

Accounting Practices

Acct. Standards: US STANDARDS(GAAP)
Acct. for Goodwill: AMORTIZED
Consol. Practices: FINL SVC, EQUITY; OTHER, CONSOL
Contingent Liab.: OTHER GUAR & BILLS DISC BY CO
Deferred Taxes: YES
Deprec. Method: ACCELERATED DEPRECIATION
Discret. Reserves: NOT ALLOWED
EPS Numerator: N I AFTER PREFERRED DIVIDENDS
Fin. Stat. Cost Basis: HISTORICAL COST ENTIRELY
Foreign Curr. Gain/Loss: TAKEN TO SHRHOLDERS EQUITY
Funds Definition: MODIFIED CASH
Inventory Cost Method: FIFO
Marketable Securities: LOWER OF COST OR MARKET
Minority Interest: BEF REPORTED N/I, EXCLUDED D/E
Treas. Stock Gain/Loss: TAKEN TO SHRHOLDERS' EQUITY

Source: Wright Investors' Service

BALANCE SHEET—LIABILITIES

Current liabilities rose slowly to a peak in 1984 and then dipped; *long-term debt* was $65 million lower in 1985 than in 1980, and *common equity* (the value of the assets owned by common stockholders) continued to increase. *Liabilities and equity* (the sum of liabilities—short and long—plus equity capital, including retained earnings and capital surplus) continued to rise steadily.

SOURCES AND USE OF FUNDS

This is a prime category as it shows where the money came from and how it was allocated by management. The dollars from *operations* rose regularly (with only a small gain in difficult 1982 and 1983). *Dividends* were raised every year so that the dollar payout was almost double that of the first year. *Capital expenditures* were up every year except 1983 but increased sharply in 1984 and 1985 with higher revenues and profits. *Change in working capital* shows the sources and use of working capital between two dates; it lists the factors which contributed to the increase and those which resulted in a decrease.

INTERNATIONAL BUSINESS

Here again, there was continued expansion as the company moved into more foreign markets. By and large, the income from these overseas operations kept pace with sales but in 1985 was a lower percentage, indicating that this was an area to be watched in the future.

Financial Ratios and Growth Rates

These summarize the "bottom line." *Operating Margin* stayed at about 15% (good compared to most companies). *Net Margin* edged up in 1985 with a slightly lower tax rate. *Return on assets* (after taxes at the beginning of the period): a superior rate of about 13% and a favorable *return on equity* of close to and above 20%: down in 1983 but moving up since. Management probably made significant changes to reduce costs—also indicated by the ever-higher sales per employee, +32% in the six years. *Leverage* is a measurement of the ratio between common equity (common stock) and debt. With EMR, this was low and declining, from 12.7% to 4.9%. No problem in *financial strength.*

EBIT (EARNINGS BEFORE INTEREST AND TAXES)

These earnings are reflected as a percentage of fixed charges (interest expenses plus preferred dividends, if any). After rising sharply in the first four years, they started dropping, an indication that management had a policy of reducing debt when feasible but still did not hesitate to borrow for expansion.

GROWTH

This is one of the indicators of able management but has to be related to other factors; e.g., some industries, such as cyclicals, almost always have up and down earnings. With EMR, *net sales* rose rapidly in 1980 and 1981, fell in 1983, came back strong (+20%) in 1984, and began to level out (+11%) in 1985. This is a point to recheck in 1986. *Operating income* more or less parallels the net sales and, except for down 1983, was good. *Earnings per share* is related to operating income in most years but in 1985 fell or did not grow at its normal rate. Find out why and review for 1986. *Dividends per share* increases well except in 1983 when this was +6% versus a five-year annual +10%. *Book value per share* shows the dollar assets, at historic cost, back of each share of common stock. Its growth included both earnings and dividend payouts. Note how steadily this grew: an annual average gain of +9%. Watch out: 1985 was down to +8%, possibly a warning for the future.

Per Share Data and Investment Ratios

Earnings and *dividends* were consistently higher and since the payout averaged about 46%, a little more than half of the profits were reinvested. Result: *book value per share* moved up strongly to become more than 50% higher over the six years. *Price/earnings ratio:* generally higher in recognition of the continued profitability of EMR but still in line with that of the overall stock market. That recent multiple (end of 1985) of 14.9 versus 13.2 five-year average is historically high so could decline with a dip in stock prices.

Checkpoints

For your personal analysis with companies whose stocks you own or are considering buying, the most important and easiest-to-use data is in the two boxes in the right-hand column: *5-Year Annual Growth Rates* and *Financial Ratios*. They show why EMR is a superior corporation. Its growth has been well above that of most companies: net income +11%; earnings per share +7.8%; dividends +9.9%; and book value per share +8.8%. These are annual gains, so, in broad terms, everything doubled every eight years but of course not necessarily at the same rate each year.

The same success is shown by the return on assets and equity. EMR is a quality company. Whether you should buy the stock is another related decision as explained in Chapters 2 and 3.

Comparison of Quality and Nonquality Corporations

This selection might also be titled "How to Pick Winners and Avoid Losers." Many of the criteria are discussed elsewhere but are presented here to dramatize the contrast between a quality and nonquality investment. Too often, a company is considered separately and there is no point of reference. Comparisons highlight the important differences. As shown here, the apparent pluses can be temporarily influential in the marketplace and the real minuses are not immediately recognized. Over time, however, quality will win!

The quality company (Q Co.) is rated ABA20 by Wright Investors' Service: A for outstanding investment acceptance; B for excellent financial strength; A for outstanding profitability; 20 for excellent growth. The nonquality company (NQ Co.) is not rated. See Table 9-2.

Average annual rate of earnings growth over 10 years: direct and adjusted for items that were temporary: nonrecurring or not avoidable by management. This analysis may not be stated in the same form in corporate reports and explanations but can usually be found in the footnotes or financial summaries. With Q Co., the reduction in per share rate of earnings growth was adjusted from +19.1% to +13.9% due to a strike, an acquisition, and write-offs. With NQ Co., there was no growth.

Equity growth: the average annual growth of equity (the assets owned by common shareholders): for Q Co., a good +13.3%; for NQ, a tiny +.05%.

Earned equity growth: net earnings retained after dividend payout, expressed as a percentage of shareholders' capital at the beginning of the year: for Q Co., a hefty +16.9%; for NQ, a miniscule +.05%.

Dividend growth (again at an annual rate per share). This is a column to be checked by investors who want their income to increase. Note that: (1) Q Co. boosted its payout at an average annual rate of over 20%. This was in keeping with its ever-higher profits. (2) NQ Co., despite a very low return on equity and, in the last year, deficit, kept paying dividends and since these were

TABLE 9-2

Comparison of Quality and Nonquality Corporations

Company	Growth Rating	Earnings Growth 10 Years		Equity Annual Total	Growth Rate Earned	Dividend Growth Annual Rate Per Share	Sales/Revenue Growth	Quality Rating
		Annual	Adjusted*					
Q Co.	16	+19.8%	+13.9%	+13.3%	+16.9%	+20.1%	+12.6%	ABA20
NQ Co.	N	D	+ 0.02	+ 0.5	D	+ 8.2	D	. . . .

COMPARATIVE INVESTMENT ANALYSIS

Q CO.

Years	Market price			Ratio of Price/Earnings	Dividend Yield	Equity Capital Profit Rate	Book Value Begin Year	Dividends % Earnings	Institutional Investors
	High	Low	Last						
5 Years	22	11	13	21–14	2.8%	30.7%	$ 1.05	46%	27
Year 1	12	7	10	21–12	2.9	38.8	1.47	47	
Year 2	15	10	14	20–13	2.6	38.5	1.95	44	
Year 3	17	10	16	23–16	3.0	31.0	2.71	48	
Year 4	22	15	19	22–14	2.5	31.5	3.05	44	
Year 5	21	13	16	16–10	2.8	23.4	4.01	51	
Year 6 (half)	16	10	13	13	4.1	21.9	4.53	53	

NQ CO.

Years	Market price			Ratio of Price/Earnings	Dividend Yield	Equity Capital Profit Rate	Book Value Begin Year	Dividends % Earnings	Institutional Investors
	High	Low	Last						
5 Years	39	31	15	32–21	4.7	3.8	26.25	. . .	11
Year 1	39	27	36	21–15	4.8	7.4	25.12	86	
Year 2	36	25	27	18–13	4.1	7.7	25.67	66	
Year 3	29	22	27	13–10	5.1	8.1	26.47	60	
Year 4	33	18	21	28–16	5.1	4.3	27.16	P**	
Year 5	22	15	16	D	4.1	D	26.90	P**	
Year 6 (half)	19	8	15	D	Nil	D	24.76	0	

* Adjusted for trends, cyclical variations, strikes and nonrecurring charges/credits

** Paid more than earned

Source: Wright Investors' Service

a very high percentage of profits (last column), there was little money left for reinvestment. It is little wonder its rating was blank.

Sales/Revenue Growth: for Q Co., this was a strong 12.6% so total revenues doubled every six years. NQ Co. struggled with flat and, eventually, diminishing volume. At this pace, NQ will have to sell out or file for bankruptcy.

Comparative Investment Analysis

This is the type of research that provides the basis for investment decisions. Analysts do look for other criteria but these are sufficient for most amateurs to select a winner over a loser.

The data are for five years and half of the sixth. Ten-year figures would be better but, with so many new companies, takeovers, etc., five years is easier to find and generally just as useful. See Table 9-2.

MARKET PRICES

These ranges provide a frame of reference for the popularity of the stock and how it has performed in the past: whether it has stayed within a narrow range for some time, spurted up or down, and how the current value compares with historical levels.

Note how Q Co. shares have not been too well received by Wall Street. In the past several years, prices have moved between 22 and 10 and, even though the profit rate of the company has been high, there's been little investor enthusiasm. Furthermore, when profitability declined, the stock came close to a six-year low. Investors were worried about the future and not anxious to buy. The quality was there but not the value.

NQ stock shows how easy it is to be misled by the whims of Wall Street. Despite the company's low profitability, the stock was in favor, rising to a high of 39 and holding in that area until earnings, as shown by the profit rate, dropped sharply and soon turned into a deficit. Apparently, the attraction was the relatively high yield. Even that benefit disappeared when dividends were omitted.

PRICE/EARNINGS RATIO

This ratio represents the dollars per share that investors were willing to pay for each dollar of profits. For Q Co., the multiple was high, over twenty times earnings as long as the return on equity was above average but plummeted to the 13–10 range when the company ran into trouble. Now the question is how soon Q Co. can come back.

For NQ Co., the P/E ratio started very high and kept falling as profits slowed. That multiple of 28 in year 5 was not a sign of investor enthusiasm but a delayed action when corporate earnings fell faster than the price of the stock.

DIVIDEND YIELD

For Q Co., the dividend yield stayed at a low level until profits rose sharply in year 5. Management was confident of the future and willing to distribute a higher percentage of earnings.

NQ Co. always paid out a very high percentage of profits—a low of 60% and a high of 86%. But, with deficits, management cut out all dividends. This removed the major attraction of this stock. Just why eleven institutional investors held shares is a puzzle.

PROFIT RATE
(RETURN ON EQUITY CAPITAL)

The profit rate shows the earnings as a percentage of invested capital. For Q Co., for the first four years, over 30%. Even when profits sagged, this ROE was a healthy 23.4% to 21.9%. Clearly, management was not doing so well and the stock should probably have been sold at around 16. Still, the company should be kept on a "future" list as its other characteristics were excellent. Wait until earnings start up again.

BOOK VALUE

This is a key base in analysis. It shows the dollars per share entrusted to management at the first of each year. The profit rate is calculated at the end of the year by dividing the book value by the earnings per share. By reinvesting about half of its profits, Q Co. kept raising its book value so that, at some point, this progress would be noticed and investors would bid up the price of the stock. So far, this has not happened because of the dip in profitability.

NQ Co. had so few extra assets that its book value per share stayed almost the same. The company was treading water.

DIVIDENDS AS A PERCENTAGE OF EARNINGS

This shows management policy: Q Co. keeps a balance, about half each to shareholders and to reinvestment. With NQ Co., the stockholders get the benefits and the company suffers because there is so little money left to build for the future.

CONCLUSION

Q Co. stock **may** be a bargain if the company is able to regain its previous profit rate and spark investor interest. To consider buying, wait for two successive quarters of higher earnings and get projections for the next year from your broker. With NQ, forget it. Unless you are willing to speculate by selling shares short, this stock is not worth bothering with. Nor will it be until there is new corporate management.

Part 5

INVESTMENT INFORMATION AND ADVICE

This section of the book is personal in that it deals with areas over which the investor has control. How this information/advice is used depends on the individual: his/her resources, goals, temperament, willingness to spend time in research analysis and calculations, and to seek and follow wise counsel. These chapters:

- Point out that information, not hearsay or enthusiasm, is the basis for successful investing. In essence, they show why you should never buy any security until you fully understand the risks and rewards, have a good idea of the ability of corporate management, and can look forward to total annual rates of return of over 10% with debt holdings and over 15% with equities.
- Review the most frequent investment mistakes.
- Show how to calculate the true impact (or lack thereof) of taxes.
- Outline sources of information.
- Provide guidelines for choosing people who can help you make more money with your savings.

Chapter 10

INVESTMENT MISTAKES AND HOW TO AVOID REPEATING THEM

What to Avoid

A complete list of investment mistakes would take a long chapter, so for a quick check here are: (1) the mistakes most frequently made by amateurs, and (2) guidelines to avoid them at the start and to minimize their repetition. After every loss, write down the reasons that you feel led to this unhappy result.

Failure to set goals: income, growth, or total returns. If you don't know where you are going, success will be due to luck, not wisdom or skill. Too many people save and invest because it's the thing to do. They accumulate securities without clear objectives so that their portfolios become a messy collection, not the base for a rewarding investment program.

Greed: trying to get rich quick. Other than as the result of an inheritance from a wealthy relative, sudden wealth can be gained only with speculation. If profits come fast and easy, so will the losses. Even experienced traders consider themselves smart if half of their deals prove profitable.

The primary purpose of investing is to preserve capital, then to achieve income and/or growth. Success takes time. If you want to double your money overnight, go to Las Vegas. You may lose your stake, but you'll have more fun than you can by gambling on Wall Street.

Overcaution. This can be almost as unproductive as being too aggressive. You preserve dollars but not purchasing power. Typically, this means: (1) investing solely for income and thus losing the opportunity for capital appreciation, which is the mark of successful investing, (2) delaying purchases too long so that ultimate gains are reduced, (3) refusing to diversify to take advantage of changing trends and conditions.

Committing more money than you can afford to lose. This applies primarily to speculations but can also involve investments bought on margin. Even quality stocks do not always move up as anticipated. If their prices decline temporarily, you will have to come up with more collateral or be sold out. That's not only a mistake; it's stupid!

Buying reputation, not results. For years, Wall Street was awed by the managerial acumen of Harold Geneen, who built ITT from a foreign telephone company into a vast conglomerate that included Sheraton Hotels, electronic companies, and textile manufacturers. The master financier operated by the numbers, focused on the bottom line, showed no mercy when profits lagged, and preached the gospel of maximizing returns on assets. Yet, the company never achieved a quality status nor financial success. Between 1975 and the early 1980s, the price of ITT stock rose from 24 to only about 46—total returns less than could have been attained with CDs.

In the same period, two quality companies, Hilton Hotels and Hewlett-Packard, stuck to their areas of expertise. The values of their shares soared from 7 to 50 and from 9 to over 40 respectively.

Lack of patience: (1) failing to recognize that most significant price gains take twenty-four to thirty months except in strong markets, (2) selling winners and holding losers. *The result:* modest gains, steady losses, and ever-smaller assets.

Acting on the basis of technical analysis alone. To a degree, this means following the leaders blindly: buying when price and volume rise; selling when there's a downturn with extra activity. Charts and technical indicators should be supplements for fundamental analysis, not the other way around.

Averaging down: buying more shares when the price of the stock declines sharply. You feel that since the stock was a good buy at 50, it must be a better buy at 40. Once in a while this will be true, but remember that to offset that 20% loss you have to score a 25% gain and a 50% rise to make a reasonable profit. That's not easy unless the stock is a superior value with logical prospects of a comeback soon.

Failure to sell "too soon," when the stock becomes overvalued by basic criteria. This occurs:

- *With income stocks,* when the yield drops 33% below the prime rate, i.e., for a utility, a dividend of 4% compared with the 6% interest paid on T-bills. This is the time to switch to debt issues.
- *With growth stocks,* when the price-earnings ratio soars far above the average multiple for the overall stock market and that at which the stock has sold in the past; i.e., when Dazzling, Inc. trades at thirty times the last twelve-month profits compared to an average of seventeen for the S&P 500 and the stock's high ratio of eighteen over the past decade. At this point, the risks of retention are greater than the rewards of selling.

Hanging on in hope of breaking even after a stock has declined from your cost. You bought Superwhiz at 40, and, after edging up to 44, it starts to drop because management projects flat earnings for the next several quarters. Soon, SW is below 40 and, after the announcement is confirmed, falls to 36.

Instead of recognizing that this loss was justified, too many amateurs refuse to admit a mistake and hold on to break even. For the short-term, do not argue with Wall Street. Take the loss and put the proceeds in an upmoving situation.

For the long-term, however, it will probably be wise to hold the stock *if* you are convinced, by your own research, that the troubles are temporary and that fairly soon there will be higher earnings and thus a comeback for the stock. This applies only to quality companies; e.g., in 1986, IBM rose from 145 to 160, fell back to 145, rose erratically to 162, plummeted to 130, and by early fall was up to 145 again.

At that time, capital gains were taxed at the lowest rate, so the wealthy individual would be reluctant to sell at a profit. But now that there is no tax time factor, that person might act differently and trade: selling at a modest profit (or selling short) and buying back at a lower price, etc. Still, the true investor would hold IBM because it's a quality company that will continue to make more money over the years.

Buying/selling for your own ego: acquiring shares of stock in the news even though it is already overvalued; refusing to sell a bummer because you don't want to admit a mistake. Forget about your pride. The goal of investing is to make money, not to salve your ego.

Not learning from your mistakes: failing to analyze every loss to understand what went wrong and setting guidelines to make certain that such errors are not repeated.

Leaving decisions to someone else: a relative, adviser, broker, etc. Even when you turn your portfolio over to a professional, who usually will insist on full authority, review the decisions frequently and ask for explanations.

This applies especially to your broker. He/she may be

knowledgeable but relies on commissions for income and, with some firms, may be under pressure to meet quotas, especially with issues sponsored by the firm. Listen to his/her suggestions but, before you spend your money, do your own research and make your own decisions.

Dealing with "special opportunities" such as options, futures, indexes directly or through pooled funds. All of these are basically speculations. In most cases, their attraction is leverage (except for writing covered options). With a rise of a couple of points, you can make a bundle fast. But if you err, you will have to come up with extra collateral every night and can lose everything. All of these areas are dominated by professionals who have more skill, knowledge, and money than you have. Do you really think you can beat Jack Nicklaus without a handicap?

Not understanding what you are getting into. If you cannot explain the rewards and risks of the security/package to your spouse, do not buy it. There should be no problems with most stocks and bonds, but are you sure you can unravel that new tax shelter?

Falling for low-priced stocks. Too many people prefer to own 1,000 shares at $1 rather than ten shares at $100. Generally, a stock selling below $10 is a speculation. It should be triple-checked before purchase and then bought only with funds half of which you can afford to lose.

Neglecting to update projections. In a bull market, the first gains reflect undervaluation and investor enthusiasm. Once there's been a strong rise, the future progress of your stock will depend on better earnings. If these are not likely soon, there's no logical reason to expect a higher price. Keep updating your projections.

Not doing your own research against clearly defined criteria. In no area of business/finance is there more information than with publicly owned corporations, especially those listed on the New York Stock Exchange. To be a successful investor, you must keep the odds in your favor. That means gathering as much data as you can, comparing these with those of other companies in the same industry and concentrating on quality companies.

What to Do

To minimize or, hopefully, avoid mistakes, follow these guidelines to develop successful strategies and to implement effective tactics.

Investigate before you invest. Make all investments according to your specific plan, preferably one that shows buying and selling zones and allocates funds according to your goals of income and/or growth.

Write down the information you have and when there are gaps, get help from your broker's research department or library.

Be realistic. Returns of 15% to 20% annually are 66% to 100% better than the stock market (averaging +9% over sixty years). It is almost impossible to get a good, long-term rate of return if you suffer serious negative numbers. A single year of −30% means that you have to get 30% per year positive returns for the next four years. If you get +20% for four years and then lose 30%, your five-year annual average return is only 7%. Keep these goals at the top of your checklist.

To put it another way, be conservative, not conventional. Why follow fads that will lead to disaster? Why try to double your money in a year with high risk when an achievable long-term return will make you rich without unnecessary risks?

Be comfortable. Avoid all securities that make you and/or your spouse nervous. If you wince when a stock drops two points, start with bonds and utility stocks. Then, as confidence grows with their higher values, some of your fears should be eased and you can start making real money.

Set up a cash reserve fund of interest-bearing bank deposits, CDs, money market funds, or government securities: $1,000 to $5,000 depending on available assets. Increase these holdings with proceeds from profitable sales when the stock market rises above reasonable levels. Reinvest in stocks when you find bargains, especially when there is a substantial correction.

Look for fertile fields: areas/industries that appear likely to grow steadily in the years ahead. Then, narrow the list to quality companies: those that earn 15% on stockholders' equity and continue to report higher profits and dividends. By definition, these will be largely companies listed on the NYSE with a few on the AMEX or traded over the counter.

Buy only when you can anticipate a 25% to 50% rise in the value of the stock in the next eighteen to twenty-four months.

Think in percentages, not points. Your goal should be to achieve average annual total returns of 15% or more. To do this, some stocks will have to move up rapidly because on the average a realistic rise will be about +15%. Hopefully, the dividends will offset the commissions.

Diversify to spread the risk: with debt issues, by type (U.S. Treasuries, corporate bonds, and pass-throughs); with stocks, no more than 10% in any one issue and 20% in any one industry with a limit of ten stocks for every $100,000 investment.

But do not diversify too widely. The biggest profits will come from a few stocks. As you become more skillful and knowledgeable, you can concentrate on what your experience indicates will be the biggest winners.

Review regularly—at least every quarter to determine if every holding is now, or soon will be, able to fulfill your objectives. Consider selling your weakest securities. As a rule of thumb, plan to change 20% of your portfolio every year. This will strengthen your portfolio and also minimize mistakes.

Subscribe to at least one well-known financial publication, read it carefully, and clip out articles about companies whose securities you own or plan to buy.

Know when to switch: from debt to equity when interest rates are dropping and stocks beginning to move up; from equity to debt when stocks reach a peak and economic prospects are becoming unfavorable. In strong markets, keep 90% or more of your assets in common stocks; in uncertain periods, move 25% or more into debt. Vary these percentages according to the type of portfolio (personal or fiduciary) and your own sleep-well level.

Chapter

11

TAXES SHOULD NEVER (WELL, HARDLY EVER) BE A FACTOR IN INVESTMENT DECISIONS

Taxes are seldom a major consideration in profitable money management. They can be significant for those in high income brackets in the selection of the types of securities—tax-exempt versus taxable securities to avoid an AMT (alternative minimum tax)—but for most investors they are seldom important in determining when and whether to sell.

Under the Tax Reform Act, all taxable income—whether from interest, dividends, or capital gains—is taxed at the same rate, and all losses, whether short or long-term, can be used to offset income/profits up to an annual $3,000. Now, the AMT applies to those in the highest tax bracket (33% in 1988) and seeks to make certain that almost everyone pays at least 21% despite deductions for incentive stock options, oil drilling investments, accelerated depreciation, or tax-shelter deals. It's a tax on tax deductions.

The revisions:

- Do not affect retirement funds where taxes on income/gains are deferred until withdrawal unless there are excess accumulations that provide annual benefits of over $112,500 or a lump-sum payment of $562,500—both indexed for future inflation.
- Do affect new trust funds for children, as their income, until the beneficiary reaches age fourteen, are taxed at the same rate as the donor.

Investment Impact

There's no sure way to predict how tax reform will influence investor decisions, but to varying degrees they are likely to favor new approaches in the types of securities selected and the timing of transactions. Some folks will opt for income over appreciation, traders will take profits more quickly, and smart investors will pay less attention to the tax consequences. Once in a while, it may be wise to take a small loss to offset income, but this benefit is now minimal and most decisions will be based on the unfavorable outlook for the company.

Read this chapter with caution, and when any substantial sums are involved, call your tax adviser. The broad outlines of tax reform are summarized in Table 11-1, but many of the details will not be determined for months. Shrewd lawyers will question interpretations and the IRS, or tax courts, will set different rules. Besides, as has happened in the past, Wall Street deal-makers will find ways to circumvent some provisions.

The projections of the impact of the new legislation on returns from various investments show: +45% for long-term bonds where there's high yield and no growth; +18% for a high-yield stock (5% dividend, 3% growth); +3% for a typical stock (3.5% dividend plus 7% growth); and negative results for growth stocks with low yields and good-to-excellent appreciation.

TABLE 11-1

How Tax Reform Impacts on Relative Returns*

	1986 Return			1987 Return			% Change in After-Tax Return
	Yield Taxed at 50%	Growth Taxed at 20%	After-Tax Return	Yield Taxed at 28%	Growth Taxed at 28%	After-Tax Return	
Long-term gov't bond: 7.7% yield 0% growth	3.8%	. . .	3.8%	5.5%	. . .	5.5%	+45%
High-yield stock: 5% yield; 3% growth	2.5	2.4%	4.9	3.6	2.2%	5.8	+18
Typical stock: (S&P 500) 3.5% yield; 7% growth	1.7	5.6	7.3	2.5	5.0	7.5	+ 3
Growth stock: 2% yield; 11% growth	1.0	8.8	9.8	1.4	7.9	9.3	− 4
Fast-growth stock: 1% yield; 15% growth	0.5	12.0	12.5	0.7	10.8	11.5	− 8

* For one-year investment period

Source: T. Rowe Price

Whether these assumptions are correct or not, they will affect the stock market for a while if only because they provide material for impressive pontifications by Wall Street pundits. One significant omission: that 75% of all stock transactions on the NYSE are by institutional investors whose pension and trust funds are only partially subject to taxes.

Furthermore, over time, most corporations faced with higher taxes will find ways to restore their after-tax returns by price increases, economies, and redesigned products/services. Successful investors will still make their decisions on the fundamentals of quality and value on a company-by-company basis.

There will be shifts in favored groups because:

- The corporate tax rate drops from 46% to 34%, thus benefiting corporations paying taxes at high rates.
- Some industries, such as utilities, oil companies, and financial institutions, will pay comparatively higher dividends.
- Some companies that pay no or small dividends—Dow Jones, Teledyne, Wal-Mart Stores—may start or raise payouts.
- Corporations with large deferred taxes—oil firms and utilities—will report high, one-shot gains.
- Long-term, high-yielding bonds will be more popular.
- Tax-exempt securities will be less attractive because the interest will be less beneficial: at the old 50% maximum tax rate, a municipal bond paying 6% was equal to 12% taxable income. At the 28% rate, this compares to a 8.33% yield.

Caveat: check state and local income taxes which follow the federal format. Instead of taxing 40% of long-term capital gains, these levies will apply to 100% of profits. There will be some savings since these taxes are deductible, but the total tax liability will be greater: in New York City, the couple with a $100,000 income will pay 11.6% versus 3.9% before—unless the law is changed.

Tax Losses are Better for Brokers than Investors

Tax-loss selling is usually foolish, is always expensive, seldom provides worthwhile savings, and is more beneficial to the broker than to the investor. As with so many glib Wall Street savings, people neglect to do their homework and find out the real consequences.

With the highest tax bracket (for most people) at 28%, it rarely pays to establish a tax loss of less than 20%. At best, all you have done is to postpone the ultimate tax; at worst, your capital is depleted. When you sell any security at a loss and use that as a credit against tax payments, that's the end of the tax benefit.

When the proceeds of the sale are used to make a new investment, you will have less money, so your new tax base, on the acquired securities, will be lower than that of the old property. When a profit is realized, the tax will be greater.

Do your research and get answers to questions like these:

- Will the tax loss reduce taxes substantially after the costs of selling and buying a replacement? What starts out as a 20% loss will be reduced by out-of-pocket expenses: round-trip commissions/fees of 5% so that the true tax benefits will be minimal.
- Can the proceeds of the sale buy new securities where the profit potential is great enough to offset the loss and still show worthwhile total returns? With that 20% loss, the new holding must assure a 30% gain to break even.

Examples: in 1987, Bill Bustle, in the 33% tax bracket, buys 100 shares of PDQ at $60 each. A few months later, the stock is down to $50. At the urging of his broker, Bill sells for a $1,000 loss. With a $100 commission, his total investment is $6,100. He bails out at $4,910: $5,000 sales price minus $90 commission for a loss of $1,190. He writes this off against income so he "saved" $357 in taxes. That's 5.8% of his original investment, not exactly enough to boast about.

If PDQ stock fell to 45, the loss would be $1,600: 26% of his capital and a tax benefit of $528, welcome but still only marginally worthwhile because of the erosion of capital.

The real test is whether PDQ will be profitable enough soon enough to move its stock prices up. When the maximum tax rate is 28%, tax consequences are not as important as the future prospects for the company.

Here's an example of the type of tax-loss decision recommended for some brokers who often skip over the investment factor.

Daphne has 100 shares of each of two companies: company A, bought at 40 and now at 61 with splendid long-term prospects; company B, a loser, down from 40 to 20¾. Original investment: $8,000; current value: $8,175. Her eager broker urges: "Sell both because the loss of B will offset the profit on A and in two months, if prospects are good, you can buy back A."

(That sixty-one-day hiatus is necessary to avoid a wash sale: the sale and purchase of the same or substantially identical securities within thirty days before or after the loss sale. Such losses are not tax-deductible.)

If she does this, with A, the $6,100 gross sale price is cut to $6,000 by the commission, so the profit is $2,000. With B, the loss is $1,925 plus $75 commission for a total of $2,000.

Since the profit is offset by the loss, there is no tax to pay. Daphne has $8,000 for reinvestment, but her money stood still and she has used up a good share of the $3,000 annual deduction on her federal income tax return.

The broker will also point out that she "saved" $560: the taxes she would have had to pay on the $2,000 profit.

Such offsetting sales make sense when the winning stock should be sold because of its fair or overvaluation but not if there are good prospects for a continued price rise. In sixty days, A could be up to 70 so that the extra cost of repurchase—higher price and two commissions—would cancel all or most of the tax savings. The big winner is the broker.

Folly of Tax-Loss Selling

In early 1982, the stock of Merck & Co., Inc. (MRK), the pharmaceutical firm, was around 80, down from a high of 103. From available information, I felt that even though there might be a further temporary decline, the stock was within a buying range.

This decision was too early as Wall Street was not ready to accept the same conclusion. The price of MRK continued to drop, with heavy volume, to 64, a 20% loss by mid-1982. For some individuals, a sale might have been wise because at the time the top tax bracket was 50% and the capital loss could be used to offset other income.

But I was in a much lower tax bracket and was impressed by the fact that MRK management was optimistic and quarterly earnings were better than those of the year before . . . not much, but enough to indicate that the company was taking the steps necessary to control costs. Add hopes of several new products and there were logical reasons to anticipate that the stock could not only make up the 20% loss but might even break 100 for a 25% gain—as much as could be achieved with most quality stocks. Better yet, the tax base would be 80, not the 65 that would have to be used if MRK stock were sold and another security purchased.

I held and sold the shares at 103 because of a slump in earnings. I kept watching the company and, in early 1985, bought back, in the low 90s when profits started up and volume soared.

After a three-for-two stock split, I sold two-thirds of the shares at about 100 (equivalent to the old 150). *At no time* were taxes a major consideration except when I delayed the sale until after the shares had been held for six months to take advantage of the then-available lower long-term capital gains tax. Now even that tax factor is gone.

Failing to Sell Because of Taxes

One of the most frequent lamentations I hear at investment courses I teach for retirees is "I can't afford to sell because I will have to pay such a huge tax on the gains." This is stupid at any time and even more so when the individual needs income.

Example: in 1983, Uncle Al bought 500 shares of Centel Corporation, a telephone systems company, at 35, a $17,500 investment. At that time, CNT paid a dividend of $2.28 per share so the yield was 6.5% and the annual income was $1,140.

This proved to be a smart move because by mid-1986 the stock rose to 57 ($28,500) for a long-term gain of $11,000. The dividend did not keep pace and edged up only to $2.44 per share for a current yield of 4.3% and $1,220 annual income.

Al refused to sell. According to his calculations: (1) he was now getting a return of 6.9%, based on his original cost; (2) the tax on the $11,000 profit, at a 16% rate, would be $1,760, which he felt was exorbitant because it was more than the total dividends.

Al's conclusion may have been convoluted but it was typical of folks who do not want to make decisions. The truth was that the current yield was no longer competitive and, even after paying the tax, the proceeds of a sale could be reinvested to provide more income.

Illness forced Al to act. He needed more income so he sold Centel shares of $28,500 with net-after-tax proceeds of about $26,700, which he used to buy 1,100 shares of FPL Group (Florida Power & Light) at 25. With a $1.96 per share dividend, this yield was 7.8% for total income of $2,156 (versus $1,220) plus prospects of future increases, as the company had boosted payouts steadily. At long last, Al realized that his goal was extra income and that taxes were not important.

To Reduce Taxes Because of a Higher Tax Bracket

This is a switch from income to appreciation. Such a tactic can be effective for those who have received a substantial raise that moves them into the $70,000 range in 1988 when they will be paying at the 33% tax rate.

It means buying:

1. *Quality stocks that pay no dividends.* Without that income, they can stay at the 28% rate. They will pay taxes only when the stock is sold, in a year or two, at a higher price.

The following list provided by Wright Investors' Service shows some of these opportunities.

Quality Corporations That Pay No Dividends

Analog Devices	Lin Broadcasting
Computer Sciences	National Education
Crown Cork & Seal	Pic "n" Save Corp.
Digital Equipment	Tandy Corp.
Dynatech Corp.	Telex Corporation
Fluke (John) Mfg.	Toys "R" Us, Inc.

Here's how this might work: in late 1986, the stock of Crown Cork & Seal (CCK), a highly profitable, growing packaging/closure firm, was selling at 108: about fourteen times its earnings of $7.55 per share. Historically, CCK had raised its profits by better than 10% a year, so annual profits, per share could be projected to $8.31 in 1987 and to $9.14 in 1988.

At the same multiples, the stock price would be 128—all tax-free gains until sold. But watch such Scroogy companies. They may start paying dividends in an attempt to attract investors.

2. *Tax-exempt bonds in your state of residence or those of Puerto Rico.* The yields will be between 6% and 7%, the

income will not be counted in tax returns (except for those of affluent retirees), and there will be appreciation if interest rates drop.

In investing in municipal bonds, the number 1 factor is *quality:* the assurance of prompt payment of interest and, at maturity, principal. Buy only bonds with an A in their rating. Lower quality tax-exempts will yield more, but the risks are not worthwhile.

If you are in a position to make substantial commitments ($50,000 or more), ask yourself these questions first. (As will be explained later, smaller investments should be made in tax-exempt bond funds.)

- What do you anticipate ten years from now? Will your tax rate be higher, lower, or the same? Will there be added federal, state, or local levies?
- Is the spread between tax-exempts and taxable bonds significant now and what can it be expected to be in the future?
- What maturity dates are best for personal and family needs?
- What are the call provisions? (1) *Optional call* gives the issuer the right to retire bonds, usually after ten years, for any reason. (2) *Extraordinary call* enables, or requires, the issuer to retire the debt if the proceeds cannot be put to use. (3) *Sinking fund call,* typically found with long-term issues, mandates retirement of a portion of the outstanding bonds each year, usually fifteen to twenty years after issue. These terms are most important with high coupon issues when interest rates decline and new borrowing can be at a lower rate of interest. Be sure your broker keeps abreast of such developments. As a rule, there must be thirty days notice. If you miss the announcement, you may have trouble in righting the situation and will lose income.
- How much liquidity and marketability do you want with these holdings?
- Do you plan to sell or swap these bonds?

- Are these bonds being offered at a higher or lower yield than similarly rated debt issues?
- Will the broker/dealer buy them back, and if so, at how much of a spread?

Be Cautious with Swaps of Tax-Exempts

A favorite gimmick of brokers is the year-end swap of municipal bonds. This may, but does not have to, involve a tax loss. *The sales pitch:* sell your present low-yielding municipals and buy new holdings at a discount. This was a wise move under the old, high tax rates but may not be so rewarding today. Still, it can be profitable when repeated and carefully analyzed.

Example: Dr. Phiz owns $50,000 of tax-exempt bonds paying a tax-free 5.5%: $2,750 a year for the next decade. At maturity, the total returns will be $77,500 nontaxable.

His broker recommends selling the bonds at par and buying a package of discounted issues with a current yield of 4.9% and a yield to maturity of 6.75%. Dr. Phiz would receive $2,450 a year interest for a ten-year total of $24,500, and at redemption the bonds would be worth $70,000. After paying a 28% tax on the $20,000 appreciation ($5,600), he would net $64,400 which, plus the interest ($24,500), would total $88,900: $11,400 more than he will have if he stands pat with his present portfolio.

This sounds tempting but: (1) the broker should have advised buying discount bonds in the first place; (2) the prices of the bonds may not be the same as the glib quotations. *Remember:* the broker is in business to make a profit. With small lots of bonds, he sets his own prices: selling at a higher quotation than that at which he buys. There's no way an individual can beat the broker at his own game. To Dr. Phiz, the price spreads may seem small, but they can reduce the projected benefits; if he needs money in the next few years, he may have to sell at even lower prices than he pays, if interest rates should rise.

TABLE 11-2
Yields: Municipals Versus Taxables

To Equal Tax-Exempt Paying Taxable bond, in This Bracket	5%	6%	7%	8%
	1987			
38.5%	8.13%	9.76%	11.38%	13.01%
35	7.69	9.23	10.77	12.31
28	6.94	8.33	9.72	11.11
15	5.88	7.06	8.23	9.41
11	5.62	6.74	7.87	8.99
	1988			
33%	7.46	8.96	10.45	11.94
28	6.94	8.33	9.72	11.11
15	5.88	7.06	8.23	9.41

Source: Internal Revenue Service

Tax-Exempt Funds

Just as with taxable bonds, there are two types of mutual funds that invest in tax-exempt securities:

Unit trusts. In these: (1) the fund is operated as a trust, not as an investment company; (2) portfolios are held to maturity or to a time when most of the bonds have been called or redeemed.

Initially, the managers purchase fifteen to twenty different issues according to their criteria such as: (1) only A-rated bonds, (2) bonds to mature at a specific date; (3) hospital bonds, (4) bonds issued within one state that has an income tax. Typically, assets total about $50 million and the minimum investment is $5,000 with smaller additions permitted.

Municipal bond funds. These are open-end funds where the managers can sell and buy bonds according to their forecasts of interest rates. If they guess right, your investment rises in value; if they are wrong (as they often are), your assets will be worth less.

There are management fees of about 0.7% of the total money invested so total costs, over the years, will be greater than if you had bought individual bonds. But you can arrange to have the interest reinvested for compounding or to draw regular checks.

Before making a choice of type of specific trust/fund, check these points:

- The performance of other unit trusts under the same management.
- The stated yield at the outset. This will be the return for the life of the trust.
- The commission/fees charged. Over fifteen to twenty years, these can mount up.
- The stated maturity and whether and when the fund will be disbanded. Usually, this will take place when the assets are down to 20% of the original investment.
- The credit criteria with a double-check on the lowest-rated issues.
- The type and scope of diversification: by geographic area, by categories of bonds, etc.
- The method of calculating the redemption price: the dollars to be received when the shares are cashed in early. There can be wide variations.
- The timing of interest payments and whether the income can be reinvested.
- The policy for redemption since a sale will incur a capital gain or loss for the shareholder.

Bond funds are not just higher-yielding money market funds. Like equity funds, they present price risks because of the shifts in interest rates.

Forget about special funds that hedge with futures contracts, sell calls, etc. When interest rates fluctuate, you may be whipsawed. Very few of such tactics have been successful over a period of time. These money managers are guessing, not investing.

Tax-Exempt Zeros

Among the most recent Wall Street instruments are zero-coupon tax-exempt bonds. They are noncallable municipal debt sold at deep discounts, pay no interest, and are redeemed at par at some future date. They are part of stripped tax-free bonds that the sponsoring brokers separate into two parts: the bond's semiannual interest coupons (representing the fixed dollar amounts to be paid) and the corpus which stays as an investment entity. Each part is sold: the coupons as a series of interest chits with six-month maturities; the other as a zero-coupon bond to be redeemed for $1,000.

Example: a thirty-year 7.5% municipal bond with a redemption value of $1,000 will cost about $110. In effect, the income is reinvested semiannually at 7.5% to build a compound annual rate of return of 7.64%. All appreciation is free of federal taxes and, when issued in the state of residence, of state levies.

These may be worthwhile investments but at this time have not been around long enough to permit a proper evaluation.

Insured Municipals

For super safety, buy bonds (or shares of funds) that are insured against default by a consortium of insurance companies. The issuing government/agency pays a premium of $10 to $20 per bond but saves money because this protection raises the rating of the issue to AAA and thus lowers the interest rate. With funds, the sponsor pays the premium and uses this guarantee as a sales tool.

Chapter 12

GETTING AND USING STOCK MARKET INFORMATION

No area of American business provides more complete information than Wall Street. Much of the data is required by law or by the rules of the stock exchanges. Corporations seeking new funds, making acquisitions, or planning major structural changes must file a prospectus with the Securities and Exchange Commission and must submit more-detailed information in a Form 10-K report. You can get the prospectus from your broker and the 10-K from the corporation secretary.

Unfortunately, not enough investors, including many so-called professionals, take the time to read these revealing documents. With the eternal hope of quick profits, too many people act on misinformation: hot tips, rumors, and half-baked recommendations based on emotions and hopes, not facts. The best investment advice is still: *investigate* before you invest, while you hold securities, and, to avoid making the same mistake again, after you have sold.

For background, ask the reference director at your local library for names of investment-oriented books—old as well as new. For general information, ask your broker for copies of monthly stock and bond guides published by Standard & Poor's and Moody's Investors Service.

For specific information, check Standard & Poor's financial publications and research reports and Value Line, which provides a summary of the essential corporate data, often rates the company and its prospects, and periodically makes recommendations for purchase or sale. At first glance, this one-page review may appear formidable, but, with a little study and help from your broker, you will soon master the figures and be able to draw your own conclusions.

To keep current, subscribe to *The Wall Street Journal* and one or two financial publications such as *Forbes, Barrons, Investor's Daily,* or *Financial World.* You may also find it worthwhile to watch *Wall Street Week* on your local public television station. But beware of pontificators on cable TV, especially when they pay for the time!

Watch for articles on industries and companies whose shares you own or plan to buy. Keep abreast of trends that may be helpful in your investment timing, and when you pick up something of interest (positive or negative), check with your broker's research department for more information.

Where to Get Data

Here are the primary sources for corporate information:

1. *The company whose shares you own:* the annual and quarterly reports, special news releases, and letters to stockholders and proxy forms (more on these later).
2. *Your brokerage firm,* especially for companies followed by the research analysts. These reports will vary from ten-line summaries to forty-page tomes designed to impress institutional clients. Keep in mind, however, that while the data may be correct, the interpretations are likely to be optimistic because the primary role of such

services is to encourage buying shares of that company. Only rarely will there be recommendations to sell.

3. *Statistical services/reports* as noted and, for mutual funds, such publications as *Lipper Analytical Services, The Mutual Fund Almanac* and *Wiesenberger's Investment Companies Services.*
4. *Subscription reports/services* from investment advisory firms, priced from $100 to $5,000 a year (see Chapter 13). For an example of one of the most complete summaries, see *Worldscope,* Table 9-1.

How to Get the Most Out of Annual Reports

The single most important, most useful source of financial information is the annual report of the corporations whose shares you own or plan to buy. The colorful pictures of products, research activities, new buildings, and employees at work may be interesting, the remarks of the president may be encouraging, and the charts may be dramatic, but for the investor the figures are what count—not just the bottom line of earnings, but how these were achieved, whether they are likely to increase, and if they reflect a superior return on your investment. Before you make any major financial commitment, get a copy of the latest annual report from your broker, at the library, or from the secretary of the company.

Annual reports have become major public relations vehicles, not just financial summaries of the past year's results. Consumer goods companies show products in use in an effort to build stockholder interest. Industrial firms use superb color photos to dramatize the intricacies of production and skills of employees. Presidents discuss governmental policies (usually critically) and guest authors write about social or political problems. All of these presentations are designed to build a stronger bond between the company and its stockholders, impress the reader with the character and concern of management, and present an image of success. But none of these efforts should obscure the basic financial facts of corporate performance. As one who has invested or is about to commit hard-earned dollars, you want to know:

- Is this company in sound financial condition?
- Does its record show it is likely to grow and prosper?
- Is management able, effective, and profit-minded?
- Will this investment help you to reach your financial goals?

The annual report has the answers to these and other questions *if* you know where to look. In fifteen minutes, you can get a good idea as to whether this is the kind of company whose shares you want to own; in thirty minutes, you can catch trends of the business and be able to decide whether to investigate further; in an hour, you should have almost all the data needed to make an intelligent investment decision. With experience, you can cut these time frames and still be able to explain to your spouse why you reached these conclusions.

Here's how to get the most from a corporate annual report:

Read in reverse: start at the back with the auditor's notes and watch for hedging phrases such as "except for" or "subject to." These can signal present or future problems: difficulty in getting accurate information; forecast of write-offs, unexpected liabilities, or costly lawsuits.

Then, turn to the footnotes that reveal unusual costs or areas of concern: heavy markdowns of obsolete inventory; rollovers of loans, hard-to-collect accounts due, or inadequate reserves.

Study the president's report and compare the financial figures with those in the tabular data. If the CEO boasts of higher earnings, find out whether these are the result of operations or of bookkeeping: change in accounting methods, lower depreciation, or cash from overfunded pension assets. The best profits reflect management's skill, not manipulation.

Check the debt. For quality corporations, the long-term debt should be moderate: as a percentage of total capital, no more than 40% for industrial/service companies, 60% for utilities, 70% for financial firms.

Pay special heed to significant changes in the current loans. If they drop sharply, find out how they were paid: by extra cash from earnings (good); from sales of assets (maybe); from defeasance (bad). See Chapter 4.

Concentrate on return on equity (ROE). This measures management's ability to make money with the dollars entrusted by shareholders. With most companies, this ROE should be close to 15% year after year; with utilities, whose profits are regulated, it can be 11%.

Find out the quality of the earnings. With equity accounting, for example, full profits can be included when the reporting corporation owns more than 20% of another firm. These are not real returns because there are no cash dividends that can be used for expansion or payments to shareholders. With conglomerates, such inclusive savings can be difficult to identify.

With LIFO (last in, first out) accounting, the sales are related to the most recent costs so earnings can rise sharply as older, less expensive-to-make items are moved out. When oil prices soared, some firms used LIFO to report superhigh profits and set up financial reserves. With FIFO (first in, first out) accounting, the situation is reversed and extra profits can be shown when prices fall. Either way, a change in accounting usually enhances profits temporarily.

Cash flow. This is determined by taking the company's after-tax earnings, adding the annual depreciation for fixed assets, and subtracting the preferred stock dividends. Usually, this is related to earning power and, with quality corporations, will increase over the years. Some analysts regard cash flow as *the* key to performance, but most recognize that the reports can be "interpreted" so that its importance is limited and should be considered as a supplementary checkpoint.

Total dollar earnings, not the reported per share profits. If the company bought back a million shares, the per share earnings should be much higher even though the net dollars are about the same.

Intangible assets: the amount set aside for goodwill in excess of the fair value of an acquisition. This creates an obligation against future earnings so should not be burdensome and should be reduced regularly. Problems can occur when aggressive management makes frequent acquisitions above book value.

Pension obligations. The larger these commitments, the greater the future charges against earnings. Pay special attention to the assumed rate of return as set by actuaries. When interest rates soared, many companies boosted their projected yields and thus were able to lower their annual contributions. But now that interest rates are down, these assumptions may be too generous so may have to be recalculated at the expense of future profits. On the other hand, if pension fund assets rise while the number of employees declines, the company may withdraw substantial cash for corporate operations.

Foreign business. Are earnings affected by foreign exchange fluctuations? Is there substantial exposure in politically volatile countries? And, most important, what is management doing or planning to do to correct or hedge these problems?

Labor contracts. Are there major agreements coming up soon? Have relations been favorable, or is a long, costly strike possible?

Management: have there been major changes of top management? If so, were the new people brought in, or were there promotions from within? Is there a reasonably clear line of succession? Too many outsiders can be disruptive and an indication that there are major problems.

Review the balance sheet: Did cash/liquid assets increase or decrease? If so, why? Is the debt higher or lower than in the year before? If higher, was this the result of borrowing from banks or floating bonds? If lower, was high-interest debt paid off with cash or refinanced at more favorable rates?

Study the financial summary in comparison to the previous year and five years back. This provides a quick review of financial progress (or lack thereof).

Remember: with most major companies, change comes slowly. Significant improvements occur over several years and real problems seldom develop overnight. The quality corporation continues its profitable growth so that its future can be projected with reasonable accuracy. Similarly, problems are forecast: dwindling cash, higher inventories, larger liabilities, and flat revenues. It's all in the annual report if you spend time for analysis.

Watch the trends in total revenues, return on equity, debt, and earnings. Even the best-managed firms run into trouble now and then, but the mark of able management is the ability to take constructive steps early.

In sum, **use** annual reports. Go beyond the subjects discussed by the officers, dig into the financial data, be skeptical and make 'em prove superior performance. You wouldn't buy a house after driving around the block, so why make a major investment without a detailed appraisal? The bottom line (earnings per share) is only the starting point. It's impossible to reduce all of the business activities of a large corporation to a single common denominator, as so many brokers advisers tell you.

Computers: Better for Fun than Profit

According to some advertisements, computers and related software are the *only* tools needed for stock market success. To say the least, this is an exaggeration. These electronic systems do speed information and provide a certain amount of convenience, but they can be repetitive, plethoric, and expensive for investors. They are best for fun and for personal finances, records, budgets, and recreation.

True, information is the base on which stock market profits can be built, but the important data—financial strength, earnings, dividends, return on equity, etc.—are the same whether obtained electronically or via verbal or printed reports. Fast facts can be essential for traders, but for long-term investors there's no rush. All the investor needs to know can be found through Value Line, Standard & Poor's, and similar statistical services.

The benefits of computers are:

1. *Speed.* You enter your query, press the switch, and almost instantly the data is flashed on the screen. To get the same material, you must have a research-minded broker, access to statistical reports, and time to gather news articles, financial statements, and so forth. Many of these will have comments not available in software services.

2. *Convenience.* Historical data, comparisons, and projections can be presented in visual formats designed to answer specific questions. The most dramatic displays are charts but, as explained in Chapter 3, these must be properly interpreted—no easy task for most amateurs. Computers make available instant summaries of news and, if you so desire, retrieval of previous stories on the same subjects. Most investors, with limited resources and twice-a-month trading, get a lot more information than they can understand or use. It can be fascinating to compare the dividend growth rates of sixteen companies over the past decade, but what you really want to know is which of three stocks has the best prospects of raising dividends soon.

3. *The ability to have your orders executed without human contact.* With that computer, you can enter your electronic order ticket, which is transmitted by phone to the brokerage

firm's computers and then to its trading desk. After the trade, the confirmation flashes on your screen. The order will be completed promptly or, if placed after hours, at the next morning's opening. But, honestly now, how does this improve investment performance?

4. *Noninvestment uses:* to structure and monitor budgets, prepare tax returns, etc. For my money, this should be the primary function of a personal computer.

5. *For fun,* as described by Neighbor Ned, who has a roomful of electronic equipment: "When a new broker calls to tout 'a greeeeeat opportunity,' I go on-line with one of my computer software firms and puncture the sales pitch by citing information from the screen. I say, 'If you think this stock is so good, how come it is trading at a six-month high, its earnings are expected to be down 10% this year, and its P/E ratio is far above that of other companies in the same business?' "

Checkpoints for Computers and Software Programs

In investing, the real value of computers and programs is in aiding professionals to prepare and present information on thousands of publicly owned corporations. Without computers, the vast financial markets could not exist. For amateurs who want to emulate these experts—to a very small degree—here are some guidelines for purchase and use of computers.

Shop and compare before you buy any equipment or program. This is a new business and so has attracted promoters whose integrity is questionable and whose promises are more enthusiastic than realistic. Deal with established firms, understand what you are buying, and check out capacity and programs to be sure they meet your current and future needs.

Ask for a demonstration so that you can run through a basic program to find out whether it is understandable and realistic. There can be a big difference between software that works well for a $1 million pension fund and one that is designed for a $100,000 personal portfolio.

Beware of claims of success: "In two hours over a weekend, you can spot ten bargains." Maybe so, but finding these undervalued situations is only the start.

Add up total costs: (1) the equipment, from $2,500 depending on type, capacity, etc; (2) half as much for software; (3) operating fees per minute from about $1.70 in prime time (8 A.M. to 6 P.M.) and 60¢ off-peak and weekends. The charges start when you go on-line. If you fumble with the code, you can spend $5 before you get moving, another $5 to get simple information, and twice as much for other data only part of which will be relevant to your decision. Overall, says Neighbor Ned, "With the elimination of the investment tax credit (10% of the initial cost), the amateur must outperform the market, or his own non-computer-aided returns, by 2%."

Be cautious with packaged deals, i.e., any that show stocks selling below book value. It's more important to know why these stocks are trading at such discounts.

Recognize your own limitations in money, time, and experience. Too many amateurs become intrigued with the mechanics and flow of information. Yet, if they cannot utilize these data, they can end up with losses plus the bill for the service.

Chapter 13

HOW TO JUDGE AND CHOOSE INVESTMENT ADVISERS

In the financial world, almost everyone offers "investment advice," sometimes free, more often for a fee. Whether printed or personal, the right kind of counsel can help you attain your financial goals, keep you from making some mistakes, and in time teach you how to be your own money manager. As with most things, you usually get what you pay for.

With modest assets, the key is information from financial magazines, brokers' reports, statistical services, and market letters. With holdings of $200,000 or more (less with busy individuals responsible for management of fiduciary funds, such as physicians), an investment adviser can be worthwhile. With wise selection and sensible implementation, the costs of such services will be returned many times over, in dollars and in peace of mind—your own and your spouse's.

The choice of a broker can also be important, but usually this is more a matter of personal convenience than a means to improve investment results.

Advisers Versus Planners

Before we get into details, let's separate financial planners from investment advisers. Both can be important, but each has a specific role even though they may be combined.

The planner reviews your assets, discusses your goals, outlines budgets, and prepares programs to be implemented while you live and after you die. Some charge a flat fee, but most make their money by commissions from the sale of shares of mutual funds and/or limited partnerships.

Investment advisers focus on money management. The best are financial physicians who help to heal ailing investments, prescribe a regimen to nurture your wealth, and enhance your fiscal fitness via periodic checkups and profitable money management.

Broadly, there are two types: (1) those who charge for information, directly or through printed media, and make recommendations that you can accept, reject, or modify; (2) those who manage your money for a fee based on the value of your assets. As professionals, they offer:

- A systematic approach to investing through standards and formalized procedures based on experience, knowledge, rules, and discipline.
- Tough-minded, unemotional, fact-based management of your assets. They do their research, balance rewards versus risks, diversify and invest to meet your goals.
- Administration: maintaining accurate records, preparing data for tax reports, and, with pension plans, keeping participants informed.
- Comments to explain their reasoning and their decisions.

Checkpoints

In looking for and choosing any type of investment adviser, keep in mind that you hope this will be a long-term relationship that will involve personalities as well as performance. There will be high returns in bull markets and possible losses in bear markets. To handle such situations, there must be respect and trust. This explains the order of these checkpoints. For many investors, peace of mind can be more important than profits.

1. COMFORT

Select someone with whom you feel at ease, whose advice you are willing to follow or, with discretionary accounts, accept—someone who operates in a professional manner with integrity, intelligence, and prudence. These are the factors that will ease your doubts and your spouse's fears.

These criteria require compatibility; an investment philosophy to match your resources, objectives, and risk levels; a management style that you understand and approve of.

If you are conservative, stay away from swingers who tout new issues, trade frequently, and denigrate the value of income from interest and dividends. If you are aggressive, look for someone who keeps up on growth opportunities and is smart enough to recognize that no one should always be fully invested in equities and recommends bonds, convertibles, or liquid assets when stock market prospects are unfavorable.

2. REPUTATION

This is indicated by the longevity of the adviser's organization, the experience of top executives, and the opinions of clients whom you know or respect.

That reputation should be professional, not personal. Do not be impressed with individuals who project the image of success via cultured accents, Bond Street suits, and Gucci shoes. As *Forbes* columnist David Dreman notes, "Clothes may make the man or woman but they don't do much for your investment results."

3. SUPERIOR PERFORMANCE

You should look for superior performance over at least ten years to cover bear and bull markets. Anyone can be lucky with a few securities for a few years. The true test of a successful money manager is the annual average rate of total returns: income plus appreciation or minus depreciation. The records should have outperformed the Standard & Poor's averages: for stocks, the 500 Stock Composite; for bonds, the AA Bond Average.

Beating these norms sounds easy, but the sad fact is that 80% of professionals have long-term records that are worse than those of the overall market. Only by including the superprofits of the recent bull market can most money managers boast of their success.

A worthwhile investment adviser should be able to report total returns of 2% to 5% above those of the market average in bull markets and no lower in bear periods. With every $100,000, this will mean an extra $2,000 to $5,000 a year, more when compounded.

Caveat: to be fair, consider the types of clients. When most are pension funds, which mandate ample liquid assets to meet withdrawals, the results will tend to be more stable than those of portfolios of individuals.

To double-check, ask these questions: Were the holdings quality securities with a few big winners, a majority of steady gainers, and only a handful of losers? Were the securities the type that you would select? Were there results diversified by bonds and stocks?

4. MARKET TIMING

This refers to timing as shown by switches from stocks to bonds (or vice versa) with changes in the cost of money. Ask for typical portfolios to see whether stocks that reached peaks a few years ago are still held and whether the recent purchases were made at highs or lows. Pay special attention to long-term holdings. Was

Xerox bought at 100, 28 or 70? And how heavy were the commitments?

5. CLIENTS

Do present customers have assets and goals similar to yours? If you are a physician, does the adviser manage portfolios of pension plans? If you're a widow, is the adviser familiar with income-producing securities? Every money manager works from a limited list so you want to be sure that the choices are suitable for your goals.

6. SERVICES AND SERVICE

Find out exactly how your account will be handled and who will be responsible: a senior executive or a young assistant? What reports will you receive? Can you arrange for regular or periodic additions and withdrawals?

From friends and clients, find out the efficiency of their service. Is extra cash moved quickly into money market funds? Are orders executed promptly and correctly? Are dividends posted promptly? Are questions answered fully and quickly?

If your savings are small, will they be placed in pooled funds? At what point will your assets be individually managed? Can you get your money out in less than two weeks?

7. STRATEGY/TACTICS

Where does the adviser get his ideas? From in-house research? From one brokerage firm? From a variety of sources?

What are the stock-picking criteria? Out-of-favor stocks with low price/earnings ratios? Small company growth stocks? Larger corporations whose shares are undervalued on the basis of predictable earnings expectations? And how many of the typical holdings meet quality standards?

If you are conservative or dealing with fiduciary funds, check the annual turnover rate. This should not be over 20% in normal markets nor over 30% in high-volume periods. Those commissions can cut your profits, and such activity probably reflects speculating more than investing.

8. FEES

These should be competitive and related to your total assets. Typically, these range from 0.5% to 3% depending on the amount of managed funds. Check the brokerage commissions because these are extra. They should be less than 1%. A higher percentage means that the adviser trades frequently and could be churning your account.

Market Letters

These are weekly or semimonthly publications that are supposed to keep you informed about the stock market and specific securities. Some are rambling pontifications, others provide statistical data in convenient form, and most make recommendations to buy or sell. They cost from $75 to $5,000 a year, tax-deductible.

The best publications are those that have been around a while, analyze the market, explain their recommendations, and provide statistics and projections that you can interpret. The worst market letters trumpet their successes, recommend specific stocks (usually of little-known companies traded over the counter), or make predictions of the price of gold or silver.

You can get trial subscriptions to twenty letters for $11.95 from Select Information Exchange, 2095 Broadway, New York, NY 10023 or to twenty-five services for $25 from The Hirsch Organization, 6 Deer Trail, Old Tappan, NJ 07675.

For most investors, one market letter should be sufficient as you can check others at your local library. Keep in mind that if you subscribe to any letter and follow its "advice," you are, in effect, turning the management of your money over to that publisher/adviser.

Do not fall for the sales pitch that, because the publication is expensive, it's got to be good. A thoughtful investor can get a lot more advice from *Standard & Poor's Outlook* ($145 a year) than from *Professor Marvel's Super-Profit-Maker* ($2,000 a year).

Before subscribing to any market letter, check these points:

- Does it provide information to help you meet your investment goals? Does it cover both fixed income and equity securities? If the emphasis is on "hot" stocks (as most of those you receive in the mail are), forget it.
- What is the publisher's investment philosophy: preservation of capital, growth, income, or speculation?
- Is the thrust on fundamental analysis as in *Babson's Reports, United Business Service,* and *Value Line?* Or on technical analysis as in *Indicator Digest?*
- What is the circulation? If the report goes to 50,000 or more, its recommendations must emphasize widely traded stocks. If it's limited, its text will be specialized and probably not suited to your types of holdings.
- Is the letter clear and easy to understand? It's difficult enough to invest successfully when you understand the advice. Be wary of obfuscations and pontifications.
- Is the advice too positive? There are few certainties in the stock market. The wise market letter does not offer blanket assurance. Rather, it reports factual information, predicts probable results, and explains how it reaches its conclusions.
- Watch for useless generalities such as "Buy on weakness," "Sell on strength," or "Businessman's risk." You want specific target prices and logical reasons why certain actions should be taken. You are investing, not

trading. If the comments are flip or obscure, cancel your subscription.

- How many recommendations are made? If too few, you won't have a broad choice; if too many, you still won't know what to do. Look for model portfolios against which you can plot your investment strategy.
- How good is the adviser's record? If the predictions and recommendations are right 60% of the time, that's a good average. One or two big successes are the result of luck as much as skill.
- How honorable is the publishing firm? If it's had any brush with the law or Securities and Exchange Commission, forget it.

Recommendation: Pick out a market letter that you enjoy reading, that creates a feeling of confidence, that discusses the types of securities you want, and, most important, that makes sense.

Institutional Advisers

Mindful of the profit opportunities and anxious to make broader use of the research for their own portfolios, many institutions are moving into the investment advisory field, especially in connection with retirement plans.

BANKS

These have seldom achieved superior results. Most bank officers are accustomed to thinking in terms of preservation of capital rather than long-term growth. They tend to follow the crowd, buy at peaks, sell at bottoms, keep their costs low, and avoid controversy by buying stocks on the basis of name and fame, rather than current/future value.

Bank holding companies and competition are improving the situation. More financial institutions offer specialized investment services and are reporting better results. Get the annual reports of bank common trust funds and watch for those that show better-than-average rates of return.

INSURANCE COMPANIES

In an effort to broaden their services, many insurance firms train their agents to be "investment advisers." They can be convenient and comfortable because they are familiar with your needs, but their knowledge is limited, most have to rely on home-office expertise, and all are oriented toward insurance products. Your savings will probably be invested in a combination of life insurance and pooled funds for fixed income (mortgages and bonds) or variable returns (equities and debt). The sales pitch: you can buy protection plus the right to an annuity. You receive a stated rate of return until retirement when you can take the cash or roll it over into lifetime payments. The income accumulates tax-free, but there are sizable penalties for early withdrawals.

BROKERAGE FIRMS

Almost all major stock exchange members provide what they call advice on investment policy, i.e., on whether or not to buy or sell, on how the economy is going to move and, therefore, the direction of the stock market, and on what stocks to buy, hold, or sell. Many firms, especially at their branch offices, invite customers to periodic meetings at which a speaker with a reputation for something or other pontificates or prognosticates. There are seldom valid reasons to believe that such "information" reflects their knowledge or enhances your judgment. With few exceptions, all such activity is a sales pitch that is usually more interesting than useful. *Repeat:* **all brokers are salespeople, not investment advisers.**

Once in a great while, some of these registered representatives can provide valuable information/advice, but in most cases the goal is to create commissions. Still, it may pay you to attend these meetings if only to get background for discussion with your regular investment adviser.

Choosing a Broker

This section is only indirectly related to the subject of investment adviser, but it's part of the overall selection of people to be involved with your investments.

By definition, a broker is a salesperson and executor of orders. Preferably, he/she should be with a firm that is a member of the New York Stock Exchange and thus must meet rigid financial standards and operate under strict codes of ethics and responsibility. Their salespersons are required to have extensive training, be of good character, and conduct themselves honorably and honestly (although recent revelations show that there can be exceptions).

A good broker can, and should, expand routine services. He/she should alert you to new laws and regulations affecting investments; keep you advised of stock splits, bond calls, and expiration dates; interpret takeover proposals; and execute your orders at the lowest cost and highest profits. Your broker should be able to provide pertinent data, ask and answer questions, discuss your ideas intelligently, and make suggestions based on personal or firm experience. But, except under unusual circumstances such as your prolonged absence, the broker should *never* make investment decisions. It's your money!

In selecting a broker, you can choose a friend or relative, but it's better to approach this choice in a businesslike manner. Personal empathy is not as important as capability.

Here's how to proceed:

1. Make a list of brokers in your area. Get them from ads in the newspaper, the Yellow Pages, and recommendations from friends and business associates. Be cautious of suggestions by your banker, lawyer, or insurance agent. The banker is in competition with the broker because of your savings. The lawyer, trained as a trustee, is probably more interested in security than in total investment returns. And the insurance agent will tend to favor his/her clients.

2. Get copies of the firm's research reports. These can give you an idea of the approach to investing, the types of securities they recommend, and the scope of services offered. Long, detailed industry studies are geared to institutional investors; short, newsy reports come from trading houses. Look for research that concentrates on Blue Chips, gives specific recommendations, and explains how these conclusions are reached. The analyst may not always be right but he should be able to justify, to your satisfaction, his counsel. Avoid all firms that tout new issues and small companies whose shares are traded over the counter. You are an investor, not a speculator.

3. Visit the top three choices, meet the office manager, talk with several registered representatives, and discuss your investment goals. At that time, ask for copies of reports issued a year or two ago. Then, compare the performance of the recommended stocks with the overall market. You may find that these stocks do not fit your criteria or that one or two stocks scored high gains but the majority of the selections were not rewarding.

4. Ask friends with similar assets and lifestyles about their experience with the firm: were orders executed promptly? Are monthly statements sent on time? Are errors caught and corrected without hassle? Does the customer feel comfortable with the firm and any specific broker?

When you are offered a choice of individuals to handle your account, look for someone with these characteristics:

1. *A minimum of five years' experience.* Don't let a young broker learn the trade by experimenting on your account. Inexperienced representatives seldom take the long view so essential to a long-term investment program. They tend to become excited about stocks in the news and usually have to rely on the judgment of the firm's packaged recommendations. In Wall Street, there is no substitute for knowledge and discipline.

2. *Earnings of at least $40,000 a year.* No matter how small your initial assets, do business only with a successful broker. The commissions will be the same whether you deal with a low-producing novice making $15,000 a year or a proven producer who earns three times that amount. The new broker will be more interested in making a buck personally than in increasing your capital. The more trades, the higher his/her income. A successful broker does not have to churn for a living.

3. *Understanding of technical analysis.* The broker should recognize the importance of fundamentals but should also heed technical indicators in timing. He/she should have access to charts, know how to interpret their signals, and be able to relate them to your decisions.

4. *Knowledge of the profession.* There is no sure way to determine how well the broker knows the retail brokerage business. One approach is to ask for an explanation of some of the subjects discussed in this book. Another is to write down your questions and, every couple of months, spend an hour to get answers.

5. *A workable rapport with you.* The broker should not try to force an opinion on any customer. If he/she doesn't know, has

"bad feelings," or is not sure and wants to ask the firm's research department, great. The integrity of an able broker shows in willingness to admit incomplete knowledge. A bad broker will give an opinion based on a desire to make commissions even though he/she may believe the trade would be unprofitable or unwise.

Discount Brokers

It's always pleasant to save money in buying/selling securities through a discount broker. But the wise investor should keep things in perspective and relate savings at one end with the total services at the other. Commissions should be only one factor in choosing and using a broker.

Dollarwise, there are wide gaps between costs of full-service firms and discounters: on 300 shares of a stock at 15, the full-service broker charges about $115 versus $61 for a regular discounter and $40 for a super discounter. On 1,000 shares of a stock at 60, the figures are $630, $180, and $105 respectively.

These savings may be worthwhile when you are dealing with a Blue Chip stock which you have researched fully. But if you need information on a little-known firm in an unfamiliar field, such savings may not be wise and, at all times, a skilled broker can execute orders more profitably.

The discounter arranges for your order to be carried out at a preset or market price. He/she does not check to time the deal for the best price. The skilled broker works more carefully and teams with the firm's representative on the floor of the exchange. Instead of taking the first offer, the skilled broker will look for a better deal on a regional exchange, wait for a better price after a block transaction or blanket in the morning (when an order is placed at the opening, it will go to whatever price is paid on the first transaction).

This situation applies primarily to large orders but the concept is valid for all transactions. A skilled broker may cost more but he will make more money for clients.

This extra care is especially valuable in erratic markets where prices shift rapidly and with special securities which are not widely traded: bonds, preferreds, and convertibles.

Rules for Using a Discount Broker

Using a discount broker makes sense when:

- You have a portfolio of $100,000 or more.
- You trade at least twice a month in units of 300 shares or more.
- You have a clear understanding of where you're going and have solid experience in the stock market.
- You do not need advice on taxes, technical analysis, or research.
- You feel so confident about what you're doing that you don't want anyone to question your trading orders.
- You keep close tabs on financial news such as stock splits, dividends, ex-dividend dates, etc.
- You are not involved with convertibles, warrants, or options, where accurate information is hard to dig out.

Part 6

PROFITABLE PORTFOLIOS

Here comes the payoff: how to build profitable investment portfolios and an example of moneymaking Blue Chips. There's no specific reference to planning, but, as with all types of personal/business involvement, no one plans to fail but too many people fail to plan.

Even if you are persuaded that you are smart enough to make a million dollars with investments, read Chapter 14 carefully, heed the counsel, and note the results.

Once you grasp the techniques, you can vary the application but:

1. Stick to fundamentals that have proven successful over the years by buying Blue Chips.
2. Recognize that these suggested securities are good investments at this time but that conditions can change rapidly. Companies that deserve quality ratings today may become mediocre performers tomorrow. It's a tough, competitive world out there.

3. Manage your investments: review every holding quarterly and the entire portfolio annually to be certain that every security is meeting—or will soon achieve—your goal.
4. Have fun. If you feel that all the research, evaluation, and decisions are boring or irritating, turn your money over to someone else: buy shares of mutual funds or when you have ample assets, retain a professional money manager.

Blue Chip investing should be enjoyable as well as profitable. It can be, as shown by a real-life portfolio.

Chapter 14

BUILDING PORTFOLIOS FOR INVESTMENT GOALS

As an amateur with limited resources and information, you cannot manage your money in quite the same way as do professionals, but you should understand their approach, and, in broad terms, follow their methods. You may not score as high returns in some periods, but, over the years of a true investment program, you will beat the averages and, with compounding, double your assets every five years. The rules and techniques have been explained throughout this book and are summarized here to help you build profitable portfolios.

The first thing to recognize is that successful investing is a battle and, as such, involves strategy and policy. They are not interchangeable.

Strategy is the distribution of available funds between types of securities: equities and long-term fixed income holdings and short-term debt such as T-bills, CDs, and money market funds. Usually, strategy is expressed in a two-part percentage ratio: 75% equities, 25% fixed income, etc. The allocation should be determined by whether or not the investor is: (1) likely to need to withdraw significant sums soon (up to three years), (2) prepared to sustain the fluctuations in the current market values of the portfolio, inevitable with equities, and probable, to a lesser degree, with bonds.

In practice, strategy is always the responsibility of the investor, though he/she may rely on the advisory assistance of a professional money manager. You always have to know where you are, what you have, the goals you seek, and, in general terms, the steps to take to attain your objectives.

Policy is based on the investor's view of the outlook for the economy, the securities market, future values of assets, and the application of these conclusions to the management of the portfolio. At some point, policy translates into investment timing of the purchase and sale of securities and the concurrent accumulation or reduction of reserves in the form of cash equivalents.

Investment timing is not the same as market timing. Both market timers and stock technicians make their decisions largely on judgments of what they think other investors are going to do. Very few market timers are successful over a period of time. They may catch trends for a few years, but the records show they are more successful as speculators than investors.

Investment timers, on the other hand, are consistently successful over the long term because they buy quality securities when they are undervalued and sell them when they become fully priced. They take the long view.

Building Portfolios

The composition of all investment portfolios should be related to your objectives, available resources, and risk tolerance. Table 14-1 shows the what and why of typical holdings for various times of your life, for both personal and pension savings. These percentages are for reference only: to start your financial programs and, later, to keep a balance. *Repeat:* it is always more important to be comfortable than to reach for maximum returns.

Here's what the percentage allocations mean:

TABLE 14-1
Portfolio Diversification: Personal and Pension

Age	25–35		36–50		151–65	
Investments	Personal	Pension	Personal	Pension	Personal	Pension
Money market	5%	5%	5%	5%	5%	5%
Bonds: straight	. . .	. . .	5	10	10	20
Bonds: zeros	. . .	20	. . .	20	. . .	10
Bonds: tax-exempts	5	. . .	10	. . .	20	. . .
Stocks: Income	20	30	20	20	25	30
Stocks: growth	55	45	50	45	35	35
Speculations	15	. . .	10	. . .	5	. . .

The same percentages apply to mutual funds.

MONEY MARKET FUND

These are reserves waiting for investment opportunities. Usually, this portion should be tied in with your brokerage account so that all income can be swept into the fund quickly and keep earning interest. If you prefer to hold these assets separately, choose an established management firm and stay put unless there are signs of overreaching, i.e., overly high yields because of the purchase of foreign debt or low-rated commercial paper.

For all age groups, 5% in these liquid assets is adequate. Most individuals have credit cards for emergency expenses; cash equivalents are not needed with IRAs but may be wise with Keogh and Professional Corporation trusts to pay withdrawals at termination or retirement of a participant.

STRAIGHT BONDS

Except in periods of high interest rates, these are better for pension portfolios than for personal savings. In small lots, their

TABLE 14-2
Typical Fixed Income Securities

Straight Bonds	S&P Rating	Security Price	Yield
AT&T 8⅝, '26	AA	96	9.0%
Com.Edison 7⅝, '03	A	86⅜	8.8
GTE 9⅜, '99	A	100	9.3
Pacific G&E 9⅛, '06	A+	100	9.1
Pacific TT 9, '18	A+	97⅝	9.2
So. Bell 8¾, '24	Aa-1	97	9.02
U.S.Treas. 7⅝, '02	AAA	98.26	7.69
U.S.Treas. 7¼, '16	AAA	96.10	7.56
Zero Coupon Bonds			
Allied Corp. '09	A	12⅞	10.0*
CATS '03	AAA	3½	10.0*
Preferred Stocks			
American Brands $2.75	A	33¼	8.3%
Common.Edison $8.38	AA	91	9.2
Consol.Edison $5.00	AA	60	8.3
Mellon Bank $2.80	A+	31½	8.9

* Approximate

Source: New York Stock Exchange; *Wall Street Journal*

purchase involves hefty commissions, and, unless bought at substantial discounts, the total returns are seldom better than those of utility stocks.

Most young folks do not have sufficient money to warrant such holdings; middle-agers may add a few for balance; older folks who can afford to invest $10,000 or more should consider allocating up to 10% for personal portfolios and up to 20% for fiduciary funds.

For all holdings, U.S. Treasuries are the safest but not the most rewarding (Table 14-2): governments due in the year 2016 yield 7.56% versus 9.2% for Pacific Telephone 9s, 2018.

ZERO COUPON BONDS

These are not suitable for personal holdings because the imputed interest (annual appreciation) is subject to federal income tax; they are excellent for pension funds where all taxes are deferred until withdrawal. On the table the differences reflect current prices. The yields of Allied Corp. debt and CATS (certificates of accrual on Treasury securities) are about the same, but the governments cost less and mature earlier.

With all bonds, work backwards: select the year in which you will need money and find issues that mature at that time.

BONDS: TAX-EXEMPTS

These are for well-to-dos: for young folks, about 5% of assets rising to 20% for ready-to-retires who presumably are paying at the highest tax rate (33% in 1988). Make sure that the yields are competitive with those of taxable debts: a tax-free coupon of 6.5% equals a 7.64% to 9.02% taxable return, depending on tax bracket.

For most savings, the best choice is a mutual fund. You buy diversification, compounding, and the privilege of withdrawing small sums. If you live in an income tax state, choose funds that invest only in debt of that state.

STOCKS

As stressed throughout this book, these are the best long-term holdings since the values of shares of Blue Chip corporations will grow and grow and grow.

For income: Table 14-3 lists companies that pay high dividends. Most of these are utilities, so future gains will be slow. Still, quality gas and electric and telephone companies keep raising their payouts so your returns on your original investment will keep growing; e.g., TECO Energy paid a dividend of $1.00 per share in 1975, $2.48 in 1986, and projects $3.25 for 1991. The price of the stock moved—and will move—with the higher income so the investor gets a double whammy: more dollars plus a capital gain.

For both types of portfolios, 20% in income stocks is a reasonable allocation until nearing retirement, when this can be upped to assure ample income when paychecks stop.

Note that the price/earnings ratios of these stocks are about the same except for Southwestern Public Service, whose earnings slowed recently (but will be back), and for Exxon, whose profits fell in 1986 so there was no increase in the dividend.

Here again, a good way to make the final choice is to work backwards: once you have decided how much you can invest, look for those stocks that you can buy in units of 100 shares; i.e., if you have about $3,500, Central & Southwest at 30 or Northern States Power at 35. Buying in round lots will reduce commissions.

For growth: for personal holdings, from 55% for youngsters down to 35% for oldsters; for pension plans, from 45% to 35% respectively. Table 14-4.

All of these stocks are interchangeable in that, based on past performance and future prospects, they will be worth more soon.

These are suggestions for the types of securities to be included in investment portfolios. Their quality and value should be checked before making any commitment because conditions can change.

Note that Wright, from long experience, sets broad ranges for the target prices five years hence. Estimates for the next two years can be reasonably accurate, but those for 1991 cannot factor in economic and industry shifts or unexpected corporate problems. In some cases, the goals could be too low.

These growth stocks are all quality companies and, with the exception of J&J and Motorola (both coming back from troubled years) are selling at modest P/E ratios.

Young investors who opt for appreciation should consider no/low dividend payers such as Tandy and Zayre; middle-agers, with greater savings and more concerned with income to pay for

TABLE 14-3
Some Quality Stocks with High Yields

Company	P/E Ratio		Return Equity		Earnings		Yield	Recent	Target Prices	
	1976–85	1986	1976–85	1986	1976–85	1987*	1986	Price	1988	1991
Am.Info.Tech	7.6–6.1	12	12.6%	15.4%	+ 8%	+ 7%	6.0%	136	163	175–155
Bell Atlantic	8.2–6.7	12	12.2	15.0	+ 7	+ 5	5.9	69	84	90–63
Central & SW	7.7–5.7	8.6	15.3	15.9	+ 8	+ 9	7.4	31	39	45–41
Cons.Edison	6.5–4.9	11	13.3	13.0	+ 9	+ 9	6.7	44	53	56–34
Duke Power	8.0–6.1	12	13.2	14.0	+ 7	+ 9	6.8	45	50	55–48
Exxon Corp.	7.2–5.5	7.5	18.6	16.3	+10	− 9	6.4	60	71	88–77
FPL Group	8.1–6.3	11	13.1	14.7	+ 6	+ 1	6.5	32	38	41–36
No. States Pwr	8.1–6.2	11	14.8	15.5	+ 7	+10	6.2	35	39	43–38
Nynex Corp.	7.3–5.8	12	12.2	14.5	+ 8	+ 4	6.0	67	77	80–73
SW Bell	8.7–6.9	11	12.1	13.5	+10	+ 9	6.7	109	127	145–130
S.W. Pub. Serv.	9.1–6.6	13	19.3	19.6	+ 7	+11	7.0	32	40	43–39
TECO Energy	8.7–6.9	13	14.5	14.8	+ 6	+13	6.2	46	54	58–42
U.S. West	8.0–6.5	12	12.9	13.6	+ 8	+13	6.2	55	64	70–63
Wisconsin Elec.	8.5–6.5	12	14.7	14.8	+11	+10	6.6	49	58	55–50

* Estimated

Source: Based on data from Wright Investors' Service

TABLE 14-4
Some Quality Stocks for Future Appreciation

	P/E Ratio		Return Equity		Earnings		Yield	Recent	Target prices	
Company	1976–85	1986	1976–85	1986	1976–85	1987*	1986	Price	1988	1991
Alco Standard	10–6.8	19	17.5%	14.6%	+ 5%	+ 19%	3.1%	42	55	80–67
Carlisle Cos.	12–6.0	15	20.5	13.7	+26	+ 25	3.0	35	55	91–70
Diebold, Inc.**	16–10	18	17.5	10.9	+15	+ 37	2.6	39	64	118–95
E-Systems, Inc.**	18–10	24	21.6	20.8	+15	+ 19	3.1	35	55	84–67
Emerson Elec.**	14–11	16	20.7	19.4	+12	+ 10	3.1	87	106	138–122
Gr.Lakes Chem.	19–11	23	22.0	18.6	+15	+ 24	3.1	38	63	103–83
Harland (John)	17–10	23	26.0	26.4	+21	+ 16	1.5	44	68	110–83
J. & J.**	17–12	43	19.4	10.7	+12	+114	2.2	72	91	125–106
Motorola, Inc.**	19–11	63	13.5	8.1	+ 2	+ 39	1.4	40	64	84–68
Salomon, Inc.**	11–5.7	12	25.0	22.0	+17	+ 32	1.5	48	78	124–94
Southland Cp.**	11–6.7	22	16.5	8.3	+15	– 46	2.1	54	68	100–80
Tandy Corp.**	19–8.9	14	29.6	16.9	+29	+ 34	. . .	32	82	149–111
TRW, Inc.**	11–8	24	17.3	23.9	+ 2	+114	3.4	101	124	162–140
Tektronix, Inc.**	16–11	20	14.9	8.9	+ 8	+ 40	1.5	59	92	126–105
Zayre Corp.	12–6	16	15.1	13.3	+24	+36	1.0	25	54	68–51

* Estimated
** Options traded
Based on data from Wright Investors' Service

college costs, might choose Alco Standard, Emerson Electric, or TRW, Inc.; older people who have built stronger portfolios may want to look for companies in industries not now represented in their portfolios.

SPECULATIONS

These are not recommendations but an attempt to recognize reality. Young people who have many years to recoup losses can take risks with junk bonds, shares of low-rated companies, or new issues. Even after several successes, the total holdings should be limited to 15% of assets. This percentage should be reduced in middle age (unless you inherit a bundle) and cut to 5% when you near retirement. There should never be speculative holdings in any pension plan.

Unfortunately, the opposite usually happens. Young people, with limited assets, prefer safety while middle-agers tend to be more reckless and older investors hang on to their losers. Keep in mind that my definition of speculations is broader than that of most brokers and include securities of marginal firms, even though they may be temporary market favorites.

These suggested percentage allocations can vary according to the outlook for the economy, the trend of interest rates, and your own tax bracket. By and large, the same divisions apply to mutual funds.

Operational Techniques

Within these portfolio management parameters, you should:

Diversify: Spread the risk with at least ten securities but no more than can be properly analyzed and continually reviewed. As a rule of thumb, use these breakdowns:

- Under $100,000, ten issues, preferably in five groups.
- $100,000 to $1,000,000, not more than twenty issues, say, three debt securities and seventeen equities, with no one holding representing more than 10% of total funds at cost or 15% at market value.

No matter how high the quality or the value of the securities, all will not move at the same pace. Even the best of stocks become unpopular now and then, and when interest rates rise, the prices of bonds will fall. By diversifying, you may limit the potential appreciation but you will also lessen the risks of decline. Diversify, but not too much. The highest profits come from a few big winners.

Never be in a hurry to spend your money. The enemies of successful investing are ego, impatience, and greed. If you cannot find satisfactory vehicles or have serious reservations regarding the future of the economy or the stock market, go slow and hold part of your funds in short-term, nonfluctuating fixed income securities.

And if you do not feel comfortable about equities, don't buy 'em. That does not mean that you should always look for safety, but it does mean that you should never reach for profits.

Be patient. Wait until your projections are confirmed, the overall market is moving up, and specific stocks are attracting institutional interest. Usually, a stock has to flex its muscles—up a little, down a little—before taking off. Such patience is not easy when the downswing comes soon after you make a commitment. If the fundamentals are right, hang in there until after the next quarterly earnings report.

Review periodically to avoid excess concentration in various industry groups or stocks which have common investment characteristics, such as: (1) high sensitivity to interest rates or cyclical economic changes, (2) large or small capitalization, high or low yields, etc.

What happens is that, when you pick one winner, you add

to your holdings with other stocks in this group. They keep going up but suddenly these holdings represent 30% to 40% of your portfolio. Even if you feel that profits can still be made, start unloading. When the inevitable plateau or reversal comes, you will have to sell too many securities too quickly. Try to keep close to your original balance.

Trust your own judgment. It's OK to check your conclusions with others but, if you have done your homework, chances are that you will make the correct decisions. Competent professionals can be valuable when you can afford to pay for their counsel but too many self-styled experts are wrong as often as they are right. The able advisers operate under clearly defined rules and discipline and trust their own experience. Go thou and do likewise. Just be sure your facts are correct and up-to-date.

Stick to Blue Chips as measured by quality and value. The risks are small; the profits sure. You are buying shares in growing, profitable corporations that provide the sinews and success of the American economy, which is still the most powerful on earth.

Formula Plans for Convenience

If you're the type who agonizes over the timing of decisions, formula-plan investing can be useful. This is action by rote in that the portfolio mix is determined by a ratio or investments are made with fixed sums at fixed intervals. Success requires discipline and patience and, of course, wise selections. Here are the three most widely used formulas.

RATIO PLANS

Here, the same percentage mix of a portfolio is maintained. With a 50% formula, you keep half of your assets in fixed income securities and half in equities. You buy and sell in line with changes in the total value of your savings.

Example: Young Dr. Carson decides to use a formula for his Keogh Plan: 75% stocks and 25% fixed incomes, with new money to be added every three months. In January, he starts with $25,000 and buys $18,750 worth of quality stocks and $6,250 of Treasury notes. By April, the value of the stock portion is up to $21,000 and that of the notes to $6,700, for a total of $27,700. He adds $2,300 in new money: $1,500 in stocks to bring this portion to $22,500 and $800 in new debt holdings.

In July, as the result of a takeover, one of his stocks soars so the equity portion is now $28,000 and total assets are $36,000. To maintain his ratio, he sells $1,000 in stocks to drop that portion to $27,000 (75% of $36,000) and buys $1,000 Treasury notes to boost the fixed income holdings to $9,000 (25% of $36,000).

If the portfolio value declines, he reverses this process. This action is expensive and difficult with small sums as it requires dealing in odd lots which involve relatively high commissions.

PERCENTAGE CHANGE PLAN

With this, action is taken when the value of the portfolio increases, or decreases, by a set percentage. The change can be the same each way or varied; i.e., sell when the value of the portfolio goes up 25%, buy when it drops by 20%. For convenience, split the original holdings between equity and debt. When there's a gain of 25%, sell some stocks and buy more bonds. Or when the value dips 20%, sell bonds and buy equity to establish the original percentage. For best results, act every three months, preferably when new money is added.

A variation of this is the percentage shift. Make changes only when the value of the portfolio rises or falls by a set percentage, say 10%, regardless of the time frame. To provide a reference point, plot a moving average (MA) on a chart. Each week, add the worth of the portfolio based on closing prices. Then, set up a thirty-week MA by dividing the total by 30 to establish a base. At the end of the thirty-first week, add the value at that point and subtract that of the first week, again dividing by 30. When the chart line falls 10% or more below the MA, sell some losing stocks and put the proceeds in a money market fund. Conversely, when the last figure rises 10% above the MA, start buying more stocks.

This sounds better for trading than for investing but surprisingly it doesn't work out that way. If you stick to quality stocks, the price fluctuations will be relatively small and you'll discover that most trends continue longer than anticipated and that the 10% decline will not come as quickly nor as often as you may anticipate. Do not use this approach with volatile stocks where you can be whipsawed!

DOLLAR-COST AVERAGING (DCA)

Here, investments are made with fixed dollars and usually at fixed intervals. Since the same dollars buy more shares at low prices than at high, the average cost will always be lower than the average price during the accumulation period (Table 14-5). Again, to be successful, DCA must be maintained for several years.

DCA takes patience and courage. The lower the market value of the stock, the more shares you buy: with each $100, twenty shares when the stock is at 5, fifty shares when the price falls to 2, and ten shares when it rises to 10. For a total investment of $700, you acquire 150 shares with a per share average cost of $4.66 versus an average price of $6.00. Thus, when the stock goes up, your profits will be greater. But you must have faith in the ultimate value of your investments.

For best results, concentrate on quality stocks with these characteristics:

Volatility (but not too much). Preferably, the ten-year high should be at least two and a half times the low: with Coca-Cola, it's about a 4:1 ratio. You must be ready to accept price declines and take losses on already-held shares but when the upswing

TABLE 14-5
Dollar Cost Averaging

Price per Share	$100 will buy
$10	10 shares
8	12.5
5	20
4	25
2	50
5	20
8	12.5
Total shares	150
Total investment	$700
Average cost per share	$4.66
Average price per share	$6.00

comes, you are sure to do well if your original judgments were sound. *Remember:* the shares of quality corporations will always be worth more over the years.

High profitability. An average return on equity of 15%. Such profitability will assure that the true value of the corporation will double in about five years and eventually boost the price of your investment.

Long-term growth. Look for companies that can be expected to raise earnings steadily for the next three or more years. Such performance should attract investor support and, soon, higher values. If the stock fails to outperform the market (high gains in bull markets and lower declines in bear periods), you will lose the main advantage of DCA.

Steady, ample dividends. Such income, by itself, has little to do with formula plans but rising payouts can help to provide the regular sums needed for periodic investments and, over the long term, may be enough to eliminate the need for new savings.

DCA is an excellent way to buy shares of mutual funds. These provide diversification, automatic reinvestment of all income for compounding and, with proper selections, will outperform the stock market averages.

Index